COLLECTED WORKS OF
HENRY VAN DYKE

CONTENTS

THE LOST WORD

A Christmas Legend of Long Ago

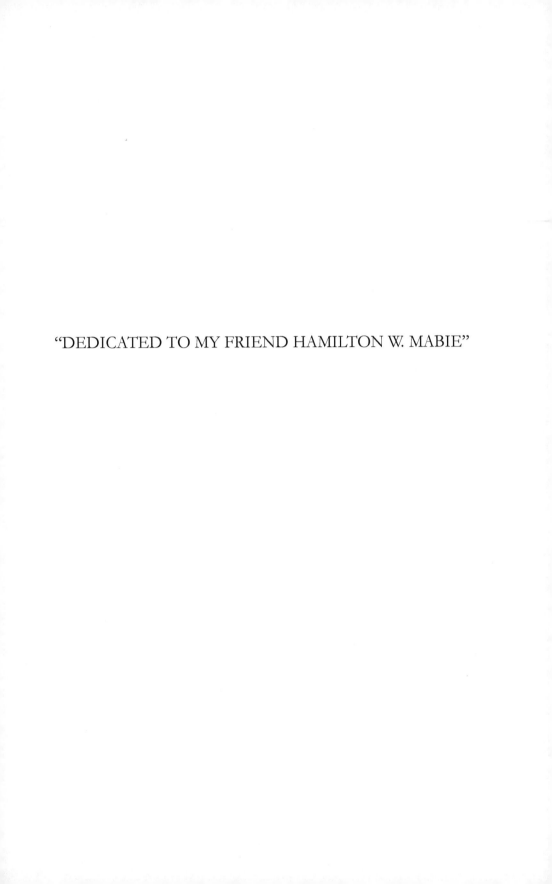

"DEDICATED TO MY FRIEND HAMILTON W. MABIE"

I.

THE POVERTY OF HERMAS

"COME down, Hermas, come down! The night is past. It is time to be stirring. Christ is born to-day. Peace be with you in His name. Make haste and come down!"

A little group of young men were standing in a street of Antioch, in the dusk of early morning, fifteen hundred years ago. It was a class of candidates who had nearly finished their two years of training for the Christian church. They had come to call their fellow-student Hermas from his lodging.

Their voices rang out cheerily through the cool air. They were full of that glad sense of life which the young feel when they awake and come to rouse one who is still sleeping. There was a note of friendly triumph in their call, as if they were exulting unconsciously in having begun the adventure of the new day before their comrade.

But Hermas was not asleep. He had been waking for hours, and the dark walls of his narrow lodging had been a prison to his restless heart. A nameless sorrow and discontent had fallen upon him, and he could find no escape from the heaviness of his own thoughts.

There is a sadness of youth into which the old cannot enter. It seems to them unreal and causeless. But it is even more bitter and burdensome than the sadness of age. There is a sting of resentment in it, a fever of angry surprise that the world should so soon be a disappointment, and life so early take on the look of a failure. It has little reason in it, perhaps, but it has all the more weariness and gloom, because the man who is oppressed by it feels dimly that it is an unnatural and an unreasonable thing, that he should be separated from the joy of his companions, and tired of living before he has fairly begun to live.

Hermas had fallen into the very depths of this strange self-pity. He was out of tune with everything around him. He had been thinking, through the dead, still night, of all that he had given up when he left the house of his father, the wealthy pagan Demetrius, to join the company of the Christians. Only two years ago he had been one of the richest young men in Antioch. Now he was one of the poorest. And the worst of it was that, though he had made the choice willingly and accepted the sacrifice with a kind of enthusiasm, he was already dissatisfied with it.

The new life was no happier than the old. He was weary of vigils and fasts, weary of studies and penances, weary of prayers and sermons. He felt like a slave in a treadmill. He knew that he must go on. His honour, his conscience, his sense of duty, bound him. He could not go back to the old careless pagan life again; for something had happened within him which made a return impossible. Doubtless he had found the true religion, but he had found it only as a task and a burden; its joy and peace had slipped away from him.

He felt disillusioned and robbed. He sat beside his hard little couch, waiting without expectancy for the gray dawn of another empty day, and hardly lifting his head at the shouts of his friends.

"Come down, Hermas, you sluggard! Come down! It is Christmas morn. Awake and be glad with us!"

"I am coming," he answered listlessly; "only have patience a moment. I have been awake since midnight, and waiting for the day."

"You hear him!" said his friends one to another. "How he puts us all to shame! He is more watchful, more eager, than any of us. Our master, John the Presbyter, does well to be proud of him. He is the best man in our class. When he is baptized the church will get a strong member."

While they were talking the door opened and Hermas stepped out. He was a figure to be remarked in any company—tall, broad-shouldered, straight-hipped, with a head proudly poised on the firm column of the neck, and short brown curls clustering over the square forehead. It was the perpetual type of vigourous and intelligent young manhood, such as may be found in every century among the throngs of ordinary men, as if to show what the flower of the race should be. But the light in his dark blue eyes was clouded and uncertain; his smooth cheeks were leaner than they should have been at twenty; and there were downward lines about his mouth which spoke of desires unsatisfied and ambitions repressed. He joined his companions with brief greetings,—a nod to one, a word to another,—and they passed together down the steep street.

Overhead the mystery of daybreak was silently transfiguring the sky. The curtain of darkness had lifted softly upward along the edge of the horizon. The ragged crests of Mount Silpius were outlined with pale rosy light. In the central vault of heaven a few large stars twinkled drowsily. The great city, still chiefly pagan, lay more than half asleep. But multitudes of the Christians, dressed in white and carrying lighted torches in their hands, were hurrying toward the Basilica of Constantine to keep the latest holy day of the church, the new festival of the birthday of their Master.

The vast, bare building was soon crowded, and the younger converts, who were not yet permitted to stand among the baptized, found it difficult to come to their appointed place between the first two pillars of the house, just within the threshold. There was some good-humoured pressing and jostling about the door; but the candidates pushed steadily forward.

"By your leave, friends, our station is beyond you. Will you let us pass? Many thanks."

A touch here, a courteous nod there, a little patience, a little persistence, and at last they stood in their place. Hermas was taller than his companions; he could look easily over their heads and survey the white sea of people stretching away through the columns, under the shadows of the high roof, as the tide spreads on a calm day into the pillared cavern of Staffa, quiet as if the ocean hardly dared to breathe. The light of many flambeaux fell, in flickering, uncertain rays, over the assembly. At the end of the vista there was a circle of clearer, steadier radiance. Hermas could see the bishop in his great chair, surrounded by the presbyters, the lofty desks on either side for the readers of the Scripture, the communion-table and the table of offerings in the middle of the church.

The call to prayer sounded down the long aisle. Thousands of hands were joyously lifted in the air, as if the sea had blossomed into waving lilies, and the "Amen" was like the murmur of countless ripples in an echoing place.

Then the singing began, led by the choir of a hundred trained voices which the Bishop Paul had founded in Antioch. Timidly, at first, the music felt its way, as the people joined with a broken and uncertain cadence, the mingling of many little waves not yet gathered into rhythm and harmony. Soon the longer, stronger billows of song rolled in, sweeping from side to side as the men and the women answered in the clear antiphony.

Hermas had often been carried on those "Tides of music's golden sea Setting toward eternity." But to-day his heart was a rock that stood motionless. The flood passed by and left him unmoved.

Looking out from his place at the foot of the pillar, he saw a man standing far off in the lofty bema. Short and slender, wasted by sickness, gray before his time, with pale cheeks and wrinkled brow, he seemed at first like a person of no significance—a reed shaken in the wind. But there was a look in his deep-set, poignant eyes, as he gathered all the glances of the multitude to himself, that belied his mean appearance and prophesied power. Hermas knew very well who it was: the man who had drawn him from his father's house, the teacher who was instructing him as a son in the Christian faith, the guide and trainer of his soul—John of Antioch, whose fame filled the city and began to overflow Asia, and who was called already Chrysostom, the golden-mouthed preacher.

16

Hermas had felt the magic of his eloquence many a time; and to-day, as the tense voice vibrated through the stillness, and the sentences moved onward, growing fuller and stronger, bearing argosies of costly rhetoric and treasures of homely speech in their bosom, and drawing the hearts of men with a resistless magic, Hermas knew that the preacher had never been more potent, more inspired.

He played on that immense congregation as a master on an instrument. He rebuked their sins, and they trembled. He touched their sorrows, and they wept. He spoke of the conflicts, the triumphs, the glories of their faith, and they broke out in thunders of applause. He hushed them into reverent silence, and led them tenderly, with the wise men of the East, to the lowly birthplace of Jesus.

"Do thou, therefore, likewise leave the Jewish people, the troubled city, the bloodthirsty tyrant, the pomp of the world, and hasten to Bethlehem, the sweet house of spiritual bread. For though thou be but a shepherd, and come hither, thou shalt behold the young Child in an inn. Though thou be a king, and come not hither, thy purple robe shall profit thee nothing. Though thou be one of the wise men, this shall be no hindrance to thee. Only let thy coming be to honour and adore, with trembling joy, the Son of God, to whose name be glory, on this His birthday, and forever and forever."

The soul of Hermas did not answer to the musician's touch. The strings of his heart were slack and soundless; there was no response within him. He was neither shepherd, nor king, nor wise man, only an unhappy, dissatisfied, questioning youth. He was out of sympathy with the eager preacher, the joyous hearers. In their harmony he had no part. Was it for this that he had forsaken his inheritance and narrowed his life to poverty and hardship? What was it all worth?

The gracious prayers with which the young converts were blessed and dismissed before the sacrament sounded hollow in his ears. Never had he felt so utterly lonely as in that praying throng. He went out with his companions like a man departing from a banquet where all but he had been fed.

"Farewell, Hermas," they cried, as he turned from them at the door. But he did not look back, nor wave his hand. He was alone already in his heart.

When he entered the broad Avenue of the Colonnades, the sun had already topped the eastern hills, and the ruddy light was streaming through the long double row of archways and over the pavements of crimson marble. But Hermas turned his back to the morning, and walked with his shadow before him.

The street began to swarm and whirl and quiver with the motley life of a huge city: beggars and jugglers, dancers and musicians, gilded youths in their chariots, and daughters of joy looking out from their windows, all intoxicated with the mere delight of living and the gladness of a new day. The pagan populace of Antioch—reckless, pleasure-loving, spendthrift— were preparing for the Saturnalia. But all this Hermas had renounced. He cleft his way through the crowd slowly, like a reluctant swimmer weary of breasting the tide.

At the corner of the street where the narrow, populous Lane of the Camel-drivers crossed the Colonnades, a story-teller had bewitched a circle of people around him. It was the same old tale of love and adventure that many generations have listened to; but the lively fancy of the hearers lent it new interest, and the wit of the improviser drew forth sighs of interest and shouts of laughter.

A yellow-haired girl on the edge of the throng turned, as Hermas passed, and smiled in his face. She put out her hand and caught him by the sleeve.

"Stay," she said, "and laugh a bit with us. I know who you are—the son of Demetrius. You must have bags of gold. Why do you look so black? Love is alive yet."

Hermas shook off her hand, but not ungently.

"I don't know what you mean," he said. "You are mistaken in me. I am poorer than you are."

But as he passed on, he felt the warm touch of her fingers through the cloth on his arm. It seemed as if she had plucked him by the heart.

He went out by the Western Gate, under the golden cherubim that the Emperor Titus had stolen from the ruined Temple of Jerusalem and fixed upon the arch of triumph. He turned to the left, and climbed the hill to the road that led to the Grove of Daphne.

In all the world there was no other highway as beautiful. It wound for five miles along the foot of the mountains, among gardens and villas, plantations of myrtles and mulberries, with wide outlooks over the valley of Orontes and the distant, shimmering sea.

The richest of all the dwellings was the House of the Golden Pillars, the mansion of Demetrius. He had won the favor of the apostate Emperor Julian, whose vain efforts to restore the worship of the heathen gods, some twenty years ago, had opened an easy way to wealth and power for all who would mock and oppose Christianity. Demetrius was not a sincere fanatic like his royal master; but he was bitter enough in his professed scorn of the new religion, to make him a favourite at the court where the old religion was in fashion. He had reaped a rich reward of his policy, and a strange sense of consistency made him more fiercely loyal to it than if it had been a real faith. He was proud of being called "the friend of Julian"; and when his son joined himself to the Christians, and acknowledged the unseen God, it seemed like an insult to his father's success. He drove the boy from his door and disinherited him.

The glittering portico of the serene, haughty house, the repose of the well-ordered garden, still blooming with belated flowers, seemed at once to deride and to invite the young outcast plodding along the dusty road. "This is your birthright," whispered the clambering rose-trees by the gate; and the closed portals of carven bronze said: "You have sold it for a thought—a dream."

II.

A CHRISTMAS LOSS

HERMAS found the Grove of Daphne quite deserted. There was no sound in the enchanted vale but the rustling of the light winds chasing each other through the laurel thickets, and the babble of innumerable streams. Memories of the days and nights of delicate pleasure that the grove had often seen still haunted the bewildered paths and broken fountains. At the foot of a rocky eminence, crowned with the ruins of Apollo's temple, which had been mysteriously destroyed by fire just after Julian had restored and reconsecrated it, Hermas sat down beside a gushing spring, and gave himself up to sadness.

"How beautiful the world would be, how joyful, how easy to live in, without religion. These questions about unseen things, perhaps about unreal things, these restraints and duties and sacrifices—if I were only free from them all, and could only forget them all, then I could live my life as I pleased, and be happy."

"Why not?" said a quiet voice at his back.

He turned, and saw an old man with a long beard and a threadbare cloak (the garb affected by the pagan philosophers) standing behind him and smiling curiously.

"How is it that you answer that which has not been spoken?" said Hermas; "and who are you that honour me with your company?"

"Forgive the intrusion," answered the stranger; "it is not ill meant. A friendly interest is as good as an introduction."

"But to what singular circumstance do I owe this interest?"

"To your face," said the old man, with a courteous inclination. "Perhaps also a little to the fact that I am the oldest inhabitant here, and feel as if all visitors were my guests, in a way."

"Are you, then, one of the keepers of the grove? And have you given up your work with the trees to take a holiday as a philosopher?"

"Not at all. The robe of philosophy is a mere affectation, I must confess. I think little of it. My profession is the care of altars. In fact, I am that solitary priest of Apollo whom the Emperor Julian found here when he came to revive the worship of the grove, some twenty years ago. You have heard of the incident?"

"Yes," said Hermas, beginning to be interested; "the whole city must have heard of it, for it is still talked of. But surely it was a strange sacrifice that you brought to celebrate the restoration of Apollo's temple?"

"You mean the goose? Well, perhaps it was not precisely what the emperor expected. But it was all that I had, and it seemed to me not inappropriate. You will agree to that if you are a Christian, as I guess from your dress."

"You speak lightly for a priest of Apollo."

"Oh, as for that, I am no bigot. The priesthood is a professional matter, and the name of Apollo is as good as any other. How many altars do you think there have been in this grove?"

"I do not know."

"Just four-and-twenty, including that of the martyr Babylas, whose ruined chapel you see just beyond us. I have had something to do with most of them in my time. They—are transitory. They give employment to care-takers for a while. But the thing that lasts, and the thing that interests me, is the human life that plays around them. The game has been going on for centuries. It still disports itself very pleasantly on summer evenings through these shady walks. Believe me, for I know. Daphne and Apollo were shadows. But the flying maidens and the pursuing lovers, the music and the dances, these are the realities. Life is the game, and the world keeps it up merrily. But you? You are of a sad countenance for one so young and so fair. Are you a loser in the game?"

The words and tone of the speaker fitted Hermas' mood as a key fits the lock. He opened his heart to the old man, and told him the story of his life: his luxurious boyhood in his father's house; the irresistible spell which compelled him to forsake it when he heard John's preaching of the new religion; his lonely year with the anchorites among the mountains; the strict discipline in his teacher's house at Antioch; his weariness of duty, his distaste for poverty, his discontent with worship.

"And to-day," said he, "I have been thinking that I am a fool. My life is swept as bare as a hermit's cell. There is nothing in it but a dream, a thought of God, which does not satisfy me."

The singular smile deepened on his companion's face. "You are ready, then," he suggested, "to renounce your new religion and go back to that of your father?"

"No; I renounce nothing, I accept nothing. I do not wish to think about it. I only wish to live."

"A very reasonable wish, and I think you are about to see its accomplishment. Indeed, I may even say that I can put you in the way of securing it. Do you believe in magic?"

"I have told you already that I do not know whether I believe in anything. This is not a day on which I care to make professions of faith. I believe in what I see. I want what will give me pleasure."

"Well," said the old man, soothingly, as he plucked a leaf from the laurel-tree above them and dipped it in the spring, "let us dismiss the riddles of belief. I like them as little as you do. You know this is a Castalian fountain. The Emperor Hadrian once read his fortune here from a leaf dipped in the water. Let us see what this leaf tells us. It is already turning yellow. How do you read that?"

"Wealth," said Hermas, laughing, as he looked at his mean garments.

"And here is a bud on the stem that seems to be swelling. What is that?"

"Pleasure," answered Hermas, bitterly.

"And here is a tracing of wreaths upon the surface. What do you make of that?"

"What you will," said Hermas, not even taking the trouble to look. "Suppose we say success and fame?"

"Yes," said the stranger; "it is all written here. I promise that you shall enjoy it all. But you do not need to believe in my promise. I am not in the habit of requiring faith of those whom I would serve. No such hard conditions for me! There is only one thing that I ask. This is the season that you Christians call the Christmas, and you have taken up the pagan custom of exchanging gifts. Well, if I give to you, you must give to me. It is a small thing, and really the thing you can best afford to part with: a single word—the name of Him you profess to worship. Let me take that word and all that belongs to it entirely out of your life, so that you shall never need to hear it or speak it again. You will be richer without it. I promise you everything, and this is all I ask in return. Do you consent?"

"Yes, I consent," said Hermas, mocking. "If you can take your price, a word, you can keep your promise, a dream."

The stranger laid the long, cool, wet leaf softly across the young man's eyes. An icicle of pain darted through them; every nerve in his body was drawn together there in a knot of agony.

Then all the tangle of pain seemed to be lifted out of him. A cool languor of delight flowed back through every vein, and he sank into a profound sleep.

III.

PARTING, BUT NO FAREWELL

THERE is a slumber so deep that it annihilates time. It is like a fragment of eternity. Beneath its enchantment of vacancy, a day seems like a thousand years, and a thousand years might well pass as one day.

It was such a sleep that fell upon Hermas in the Grove of Daphne. An immeasurable period, an interval of life so blank and empty that he could not tell whether it was long or short, had passed over him when his senses began to stir again. The setting sun was shooting arrows of gold under the glossy laurel-leaves. He rose and stretched his arms, grasping a smooth branch above him and shaking it, to make sure that he was alive. Then he hurried back toward Antioch, treading lightly as if on air.

The ground seemed to spring beneath his feet. Already his life had changed, he knew not how. Something that did not belong to him had dropped away; he had returned to a former state of being. He felt as if anything might happen to him, and he was ready for anything. He was a new man, yet curiously familiar to himself—as if he had done with playing a tiresome part and returned to his natural state. He was buoyant and free, without a care, a doubt, a fear.

As he drew near to his father's house he saw a confusion of servants in the porch, and the old steward ran down to meet him at the gate.

"Lord, we have been seeking you everywhere. The master is at the point of death, and has sent for you. Since the sixth hour he calls your name continually. Come to him quickly, lord, for I fear the time is short."

24

Hermas entered the house at once; nothing could amaze him to-day. His father lay on an ivory couch in the inmost chamber, with shrunken face and restless eyes, his lean fingers picking incessantly at the silken coverlet.

"My son!" he murmured; "Hermas, my son! It is good that you have come back to me. I have missed you. I was wrong to send you away. You shall never leave me again. You are my son, my heir. I have changed everything. Hermas, my son, come nearer—close beside me. Take my hand, my son!"

The young man obeyed, and, kneeling by the couch, gathered his father's cold, twitching fingers in his firm, warm grasp.

"Hermas, life is passing—long, rich, prosperous; the last sands, I—cannot stay them. My religion, a good policy—Julian was my friend. But now he is gone—where? My soul is empty—nothing beyond—very dark—I am afraid. But you know something better. You found something that made you willing to give up your life for it—it must have been almost like dying—yet you were happy. What was it you found? See, I am giving you everything. I have forgiven you. Now forgive me. Tell me, what is it? Your secret, your faith—give it to me before I go."

At the sound of this broken pleading a strange passion of pity and love took the young man by the throat. His voice shook a little as he answered eagerly:

"Father, there is nothing to forgive. I am your son; I will gladly tell, you all that I know. I will give you the secret of faith. Father, you must believe with all your heart, and soul, and strength in—"

Where was the word—the word that he had been used to utter night and morning, the word that had meant to him more than he had ever known? What had become of it?

He groped for it in the dark room of his mind. He had thought he could lay his hand upon it in a moment, but it was gone. Some one had taken it away. Everything else was most clear to him: the terror of death; the lonely soul appealing from his father's eyes; the instant need of comfort and help. But at the one point where he looked for help he could find nothing; only an empty space. The word of hope had vanished. He felt for it blindly and in desperate haste.

"Father, wait! I have forgotten something—it has slipped away from me. I shall find it in a moment. There is hope—I will tell you presently—oh, wait!"

The bony hand gripped his like a vice; the glazed eyes opened wider. "Tell me," whispered the old man; "tell me quickly, for I must go."

The voice sank into a dull rattle. The fingers closed once more, and relaxed. The light behind the eyes went out.

Hermas, the master of the House of the Golden Pillars, was keeping watch by the dead.

IV.

LOVE IN SEARCH OF A WORD

THE break with the old life was as clean as if it had been cut with a knife. Some faint image of a hermit's cell, a bare lodging in a back street of Antioch, a class-room full of earnest students, remained in Hermas' memory. Some dull echo of the voice of John the Presbyter, and the murmured sound of chanting, and the murmur of great congregations, still lingered in his ears; but it was like something that had happened to another person, something that he had read long ago, but of which he had lost the meaning.

His new life was full and smooth and rich—too rich for any sense of loss to make itself felt. There were a hundred affairs to busy him, and the days ran swiftly by as if they were shod with winged sandals.

Nothing needed to be considered, prepared for, begun. Everything was ready and waiting for him. All that he had to do was to go on with it. The estate of Demetrius was even greater than the world had supposed. There were fertile lands in Syria which the emperor had given him, marble-quarries in Phrygia, and forests of valuable timber in Cilicia; the vaults of the villa contained chests of gold and silver; the secret cabinets in the master's room were full of precious stones. The stewards were diligent and faithful. The servants of the magnificent household rejoiced at the young master's return. His table was spread; the rose-garland of pleasure was woven for his head, and his cup was already filled with the spicy wine of power.

The period of mourning for his father came at a fortunate moment, to seclude and safeguard him from the storm of political troubles and persecutions that fell upon Antioch after the insults offered by the mob to the imperial statues in the year 887. The friends of Demetrius, prudent and conservative persons, gathered around Hermas and made him welcome to their circle. Chief among them was Libanius, the sophist, his nearest neighbour, whose daughter Athenais had been the playmate of Hermas in the old days.

He had left her a child. He found her a beautiful woman. What transformation is so magical, so charming, as this? To see the uncertain lines of-youth rounded into firmness and symmetry, to discover the half-ripe, merry, changing face of the girl matured into perfect loveliness, and looking at you with calm, clear, serious eyes, not forgetting the past, but fully conscious of the changed present—this is to behold a miracle in the flesh.

"Where have you been, these two years?" said Athenais, as they walked together through the garden of lilies where they had so often played.

"In a land of tiresome dreams," answered Hermas; "but you have wakened me, and I am never going back again."

It was not to be supposed that the sudden disappearance of Hermas from among his former associates could long remain unnoticed. At first it was a mystery. There was a fear, for two or three days, that he might be lost. Some of his more intimate companions maintained that his devotion had led him out into the desert to join the anchorites. But the news of his return to the House of the Golden Pillars, and of his new life as its master, filtered quickly through the gossip of the city.

Then the church was filled with dismay and grief and reproach. Messengers and letters were sent to Hermas. They disturbed him a little, but they took no hold upon him. It seemed to him as if the messengers spoke in a strange language. As he read the letters there were words blotted out of the writing which made the full sense unintelligible.

His old companions came to reprove him for leaving them, to warn him of the peril of apostasy, to entreat him to return. It all sounded vague and futile. They spoke as if he had betrayed or offended some one; but when they came to name the object of his fear—the one whom he had displeased, and to whom he should return—he heard nothing; there was a blur of silence in their speech. The clock pointed to the hour, but the bell did not strike. At last Hermas refused to see them any more.

One day John the Presbyter stood in the atrium. Hermas was entertaining Libanius and Athenais in the banquet-hall. When the visit of the Presbyter was announced, the young master loosed a collar of gold and jewels from his neck, and gave it to his scribe.

"Take this to John of Antioch, and tell him it is a gift from his former pupil—as a token of remembrance, or to spend for the poor of the city. I will always send him what he wants, but it is idle for us to talk together any more. I do not understand what he says. I have not gone to the temple, nor offered sacrifice, nor denied his teaching. I have simply forgotten. I do not think about those things any longer. I am only living. A happy man wishes him all happiness and farewell."

But John let the golden collar fall on the marble floor. "Tell your master that we shall talk together again, after all," said he, as he passed sadly out of the hall.

The love of Athenais and Hermas was like a tiny rivulet that sinks out of sight in a cavern, but emerges again as a bright and brimming stream. The careless comradery of childhood was mysteriously changed into a complete companionship.

When Athenais entered the House of the Golden Pillars as a bride, all the music of life came with her. Hermas called the feast of her welcome "the banquet of the full chord." Day after day, night after night, week after week, month after month, the bliss of the home unfolded like a rose of a thousand leaves. When a child came to them, a strong, beautiful boy, worthy to be the heir of such a house, the heart of the rose was filled with overflowing fragrance. Happiness was heaped upon happiness.

Every wish brought its own accomplishment. Wealth, honour, beauty, peace, love—it was an abundance of felicity so great that the soul of Hermas could hardly contain it.

Strangely enough, it began to press upon him, to trouble him with the very excess of joy. He felt as if there were something yet needed to complete and secure it all. There was an urgency within him, a longing to find some outlet for his feelings, he knew not how—some expression and culmination of his happiness, he knew not what.

Under his joyous demeanour a secret fire of restlessness began to burn—an expectancy of something yet to come which should put the touch of perfection on his life, He spoke of it to Athenais, as they sat together, one summer evening, in a bower of jasmine, with their boy playing at their feet. There had been music in the garden; but now the singers and lute-players had withdrawn, leaving the master and mistress alone in the lingering twilight, tremulous with inarticulate melody of unseen birds. There was a secret voice in the hour seeking vainly for utterance—a word waiting to be spoken at the centre of the charm.

"How deep is our happiness, my beloved!" said Hermas; "deeper than the sea that slumbers yonder, below the city. And yet I feel it is not quite full and perfect. There is a depth of joy that we have not yet known—a repose of happiness that is still beyond us. What is it? I have no superstitious fears, like the king who cast his signet-ring into the sea because he dreaded that some secret vengeance would fall on his unbroken good fortune. That was an idle terror. But there is something that oppresses me like an invisible burden. There is something still undone, unspoken, unfelt—something that we need to complete everything. Have you not felt it, too? Can you not lead me to it?"

"Yes," she answered, lifting her eyes to his face; "I, too, have felt it, Hermas, this burden, this need, this unsatisfied longing. I think I know what it means. It is gratitude—the language of the heart, the music of happiness. There is no perfect joy without gratitude. But we have never learned it, and the want of it troubles us. It is like being dumb with a heart full of love. We must find the word for it, and say it together. Then we shall be perfectly joined in perfect joy. Come, my dear lord, let us take the boy with us, and give thanks."

Hermas lifted the child in his arms, and turned with Athenais into the depth of the garden. There was a dismantled shrine of some forgotten fashion of worship half hidden among the luxuriant flowers. A fallen image lay beside it, face downward in the grass. They stood there, hand in hand, the boy drowsily resting on his father's shoulder—a threefold harmony of strength and beauty and innocence.

Silently the roseate light caressed the tall spires of the cypress-trees; silently the shadows gathered at their feet; silently the crystal stars looked out from the deepening arch of heaven. The very breath of being paused. It was the hour of culmination, the supreme moment of felicity waiting for its crown. The tones of Hermas were clear and low as he began, half speaking and half chanting, in the rhythm of an ancient song:

"Fair is the world, the sea, the sky, the double kingdom of day and night, in the glow of morning, in the shadow of evening, and under the dripping light of stars.

"Fairer still is life in our breasts, with its manifold music and meaning, with its wonder of seeing and hearing and feeling and knowing and being.

"Fairer and still more fair is love, that draws us together, mingles our lives in its flow, and bears them along like a river, strong and clear and swift, rejecting the stars in its bosom.

"Wide is our world; we are rich; we have all things. Life is abundant within us—a measureless deep. Deepest of all is our love, and it longs to speak.

"Come, thou final word! Come, thou crown of speech! Come, thou charm of peace! Open the gates of our hearts. Lift the weight of our joy and bear it upward.

"For all good gifts, for all perfect gifts, for love, for life, for the world, we praise, we bless, we thank—"

As a soaring bird, struck by an arrow, falls headlong from the sky, so the song of Hermas fell. At the end of his flight of gratitude there was nothing—a blank, a hollow space.

He looked for a face, and saw a void. He sought for a hand, and clasped vacancy. His heart was throbbing and swelling with passion; the bell swung to and fro within him, beating from side to side as if it would burst; but not a single note came from it. All the fulness of his feeling, that had risen upward like a living fountain, fell back from the empty sky, as cold as snow, as hard as hail, frozen and dead. There was no meaning in his happiness. No one had sent it to him. There was no one to thank for it. His felicity was a closed circle, a wall of eternal ice.

"Let us go back," he said sadly to Athenais; "the child is heavy upon my shoulder. We will lay him to sleep, and go into the library. The air grows chilly. We were mistaken. The gratitude of life is only a dream. There is no one to thank."

And in the garden it was already night.

V.

RICHES WITHOUT REST

NO outward change came to the House of the Golden Pillars. Everything moved as smoothly, as delicately, as prosperously, as before. But inwardly there was a subtle, inexplicable transformation. A vague discontent—a final and inevitable sense of incompleteness, overshadowed existence from that night when Hermas realized that his joy could never go beyond itself.

The next morning the old man whom he had seen in the Grove of Daphne, but never since, appeared mysteriously at the door of the house, as if he had been sent for, and entered, to dwell there like an invited guest.

Hermas could not but make him welcome, and at first he tried to regard him with reverence and affection as the one through whom fortune had come. But it was impossible. There was a chill in the inscrutable smile of Marcion, as he called himself, that seemed to mock at reverence. He was in the house as one watching a strange experiment—tranquil, interested, ready to supply anything that might be needed for its completion, but thoroughly indifferent to the feelings of the subject; an anatomist of life, looking curiously to see how long it would continue, and how it would behave, after the heart had been removed.

In his presence Hermas was conscious of a certain irritation, a resentful anger against the calm, frigid scrutiny of the eyes that followed him everywhere, like a pair of spies, peering out over the smiling mouth and the long white beard.

"Why do you look at me so curiously?" asked Hermas, one morning, as they sat together in the library. "Do you see anything strange in me?"

"No," answered Marcion; "something familiar."

"And what is that?"

"A singular likeness to a discontented young man that I met some years ago in the Grove of Daphne."

"But why should that interest you? Surely it was to be expected."

"A thing that we expect often surprises us when we see it. Besides, my curiosity is piqued. I suspect you of keeping a secret from me."

"You are jesting with me. There is nothing in my life that you do not know. What is the secret?"

"Nothing more than the wish to have one. You are growing tired of your bargain. The game wearies you. That is foolish. Do you want to try a new part?"

The question was like a mirror upon which one comes suddenly in a half-lighted. room, A quick illumination falls on it, and the passer-by is startled by the look of his own face.

"You are right," said Hermas. "I am tired. We have been going on stupidly in this house, as if nothing were possible but what my father had done before me. There is nothing original in being rich, and well fed, and well dressed. Thousands of men have tried it, and have not been very well satisfied. Let us do something new. Let us make a mark in the world."

"It is well said," nodded the old man; "you are speaking again like a man after my own heart. There is no folly but the loss of an opportunity to enjoy a new sensation."

From that day Hermas seemed to be possessed with a perpetual haste, an uneasiness that left him no repose. The summit of life had been attained, the highest possible point of felicity. Henceforward the course could only be at a level—perhaps downward. It might be brief; at the

34

best it could not be very long. It was madness to lose a day, an hour. That would be the only fatal mistake: to forfeit anything of the bargain that he had made. He would have it, and hold it, and enjoy it all to the full. The world might have nothing better to give than it had already given; but surely it had many things that were new to bestow upon him, and Marcion should help him to find them.

Under his learned counsel the House of the Golden Pillars took on a new magnificence. Artists were brought from Corinth and Rome and Byzantium to adorn it with splendour. Its fame glittered around the world. Banquets of incredible luxury drew the most celebrated guests into its triclinium, and filled them with envious admiration. The bees swarmed and buzzed about the golden hive. The human insects, gorgeous moths of pleasure and greedy flies of appetite, parasites and flatterers and crowds of inquisitive idlers, danced and fluttered in the dazzling light that surrounded Hermas.

Everything that he touched prospered. He bought a tract of land in the Caucasus, and emeralds were discovered among the mountains. He sent a fleet of wheat-ships to Italy, and the price of grain doubled while it was on the way. He sought political favour with the emperor, and was rewarded with the governorship of the city. His name was a word to conjure with.

The beauty of Athenais lost nothing with the passing seasons, but grew more perfect, even under the inexplicable shade of dissatisfaction that sometimes veiled it as a translucent cloud that passes before the full moon. "Fair as the wife of Hermas" was a proverb in Antioch; and soon men began to add to it, "Beautiful as the son of Hermas"; for the child developed swiftly in that favouring clime. At nine years of age he was straight and strong, firm of limb and clear of eye. His brown head was on a level with his father's heart. He was the jewel of the House of the Golden Pillars; the pride of Hermas, the new Fortunatus.

That year another drop of success fell into his brimming cup. His black Numidian horses, which he had been training for three years for the world-renowned chariot-races of Antioch, won the victory over a score of rivals. Hermas received the prize carelessly from the judge's hands, and turned to drive once more around the circus, to show himself to the people. He lifted the eager boy into the chariot beside him to share his triumph.

Here, indeed, was the glory of his life—this matchless son, his brighter counterpart carved in breathing ivory, touching his arm, and balancing himself proudly on the swaying floor of the chariot. As the horses pranced around the ring, a great shout of applause filled the amphitheatre, and thousands of spectators wavd their salutations of praise: "Hail, fortunate Hermas, master of success! Hail, little Hermas, prince of good luck!"

The sudden tempest of acclamation, the swift fluttering of innumerable garments in the air, startled the horses. They dashed violently forward, and plunged upon the bits. The left rein broke. They swerved to the right, swinging the chariot sideways with a grating noise, and dashing it against the stone parapet of the arena. In an instant the wheel was shattered. The axle struck the ground, and the chariot was dragged onward, rocking and staggering.

By a strenuous effort Hermas kept his place on the frail platform, clinging to the unbroken rein. But the boy was tossed lightly from his side at the first shock. His head struck the wall. And when Hermas turned to look for him, he was lying like a broken flower on the sand.

VI.

GREAT FEAR AND RECOVERED JOY

THEY carried the boy in a litter to the House of the Golden Pillars, summoning the most skilful physician of Antioch to attend him. For hours the child was as quiet as death. Hermas watched the white eyelids, folded close like lily-buds at night, even as one watches for the morning. At last they opened; but the fire of fever was burning in the eyes, and the lips were moving in a wild delirium.

Hour after hour that sweet childish voice rang through the halls and chambers of the splendid, helpless house, now rising in shrill calls of distress and senseless laughter, now sinking in weariness and dull moaning. The stars waxed and waned; the sun rose and set; the roses bloomed and fell in the garden, the birds sang and slept among the jasmine-bowers. But in the heart of Hermas there was no song, no bloom, no light—only speechless anguish, and a certain fearful looking-for of desolation.

He was like a man in a nightmare. He saw the shapeless terror that was moving toward him, but he was impotent to stay or to escape it. He had done all that he could. There was nothing left but to wait.

He paced to and fro, now hurrying to the boy's bed as if he could not bear to be away from it, now turning back as if he could not endure to be near it. The people of the house, even Athenais, feared to speak to him, there was something so vacant and desperate in his face.

At nightfall, on the second of those eternal days, he shut himself in the library. The unfilled lamp had gone out, leaving a trail of smoke in the air. The sprigs of mignonette and rosemary, with which the room was sprinkled every day, were unrenewed, and scented the gloom with a close odor of decay. A costly manuscript of Theocritus was tumbled in disorder on the floor. Hermas sank into a chair like a man in whom the very spring of being is broken. Through the darkness some one drew near. He did not even lift his head. A hand touched him; a soft arm was laid over his shoulders. It was Athenais, kneeling beside him and speaking very low:

"Hermas—it is almost over—the child! His voice grows weaker hour by hour. He moans and calls for some one to help him; then he laughs. It breaks my heart. He has just fallen asleep. The moon is rising now. Unless a change comes he cannot last till sunrise. Is there nothing we can do? Is there no power that can save him? Is there no one to pity us and spare us? Let us call, let us beg for compassion and help; let us pray for his life!"

Yes; that was what he wanted—that was the only thing that could bring relief: to pray; to pour out his sorrow somewhere; to find a greater strength than his own, and cling to it and plead for mercy and help. To leave that undone was to be false to his manhood; it was to be no better than the dumb beasts when their young perish. How could he let his boy suffer and die, without an effort, a cry, a prayer?

He sank on his knees beside Athenais.

"Out of the depths—out of the depths we call for pity. The light of our eyes is fading—the child is dying. Oh, the child, the child! Spare the child's life, thou merciful—"

Not a word; only that deathly blank. The hands of Hermas, stretched out in supplication, touched the marble table. He felt the cool hardness of the polished stone beneath his fingers. A book, dislodged by his touch, fell rustling to the floor. Through the open door, faint and far off, came the footsteps of the servants, moving cautiously. The heart of Hermas was like a lump of ice in his bosom. He rose slowly to his feet, lifting Athenais with him.

"It is in vain," he said; "there is nothing for us to do. Long ago I knew something. I think it would have helped us. But I have forgotten it. It is all gone. But I would give all that I have, if I could bring it back again now, at this hour, in this time of our bitter trouble."

A slave entered the room while he was speaking, and approached hesitatingly.

"Master," he said, "John of Antioch, whom we were forbidden to admit to the house, has come again. He would take no denial. Even now he waits in the peristyle; and the old man Marcion is with him, seeking to turn him away."

"Come," said Hermas to his wife, "let us go to him; for I think I see the beginning of a way that may lead us out of this dreadful darkness."

In the central hall the two men were standing; Marcion, with disdainful eyes and sneering lips, taunting the unbidden guest to depart; John silent, quiet, patient, while the wondering slaves looked on in dismay. He lifted his searching gaze to the haggard face of Hermas.

"My son, I knew that I should see you again, even though you did not send for me. I have come to you because I have heard that you are in trouble."

"It is true," answered Hermas, passionately; "we are in trouble, desperate trouble, trouble accursed. Our child is dying. We are poor, we are destitute, we are afflicted. In all this house, in all the world, there is no one that can help us. I knew something long ago, when I was with you,—a word, a name,—in which we might have found hope. But I have lost it. I gave it to this man. He has taken it away from me forever."

He pointed to Marcion. The old man's lips curled scornfully. "A word, a name!" he sneered. "What is that, O most wise and holy Presbyter? A thing of air, an unreal thing that men make to describe their own dreams and fancies. Who would go about to rob any one of such a thing as that? It is a prize that only a fool would think of taking. Besides, the young man parted with it of his own free will. He bargained with me cleverly. I promised him wealth and pleasure and fame. What did he give in return? An empty name, which was a burden—"

"Servant of demons, be still!" The voice of John rang clear, like a trumpet, through the hall. "There is a name which none shall dare to take in vain. There is a name which none can lose without being lost. There is a name at which the devils tremble. Depart quickly, before I speak it!"

Marcion had shrunk into the shadow of one of the pillars. A bright lamp near him tottered on its pedestal and fell with a crash. In the confusion he vanished, as noiselessly as a shade.

John turned to Hermas, and his tone softened as he said: "My son, you have sinned deeper than you know. The word with which you parted so lightly is the key-word of all life and joy and peace. Without it the world has no meaning, and existence no rest, and death no refuge. It is the word that purifies love, and comforts grief, and keeps hope alive forever. It is the most precious thing that ever ear has heard, or mind has known, or heart has conceived. It is the name of Him who has given us life and breath and all things richly to enjoy; the name of Him who, though we may forget Him, never forgets us; the name of Him who pities us as you pity your suffering child; the name of Him who, though we wander far from Him, seeks us in the wilderness, and sent His Son, even as His Son has sent me this night, to breathe again that forgotten name in the heart that is perishing without it. Listen, my son, listen with all your soul to the blessed name of God our Father."

The cold agony in the breast of Hermas dissolved like a fragment of ice that melts in the summer sea. A sense of sweet release spread through him from head to foot. The lost was found. The dew of a divine peace fell on his parched soul, and the withering flower of human love lifted its head again. The light of a new hope shone on his face. He stood upright, and lifted his hands high toward heaven.

"Out of the depths have I cried unto Thee, O Lord! O my God, be merciful to me, for my soul trusteth in Thee. My God, Thou hast given;

40

take not Thy gift away from me, O my God! Spare the life of this my child, O Thou God, my Father, my Father!"

A deep hush followed the cry. "Listen!" whispered Athenais, breathlessly.

Was it an echo? It could not be, for it came again—the voice of the child, clear and low, waking from sleep, and calling: "My father, my father!"

THE HOUSE OF RIMMON

A DRAMA IN FOUR ACTS

"Behold the sacrifice! Bow down, bow down!"

DRAMATIS PERSONAE

BENHADAD: King of Damascus.

REZON: High Priest of the House of Rimmon.

SABALLIDIN: A Noble of Damascus.

HAZAEL
IZDUBHAR   }   Courtiers of Damascus.
RAKHAZ

SHUMAKIM: The King's Fool.

ELISHA: Prophet of Israel.

NAAMAN: Captain of the Armies of Damascus.

RUAHMAH: A Captive Maid of Israel.

TSARPI: Wife to Naaman.

KHAMMA
NUBTA   }   Attendants of Tsarpi.

Soldiers, Servants, Citizens, etc., etc.

SCENE: *Damascus and the Mountains of Samaria.*

TIME: *850 B. C.*

ACT I

SCENE I

Night, in the garden of NAAMAN at Damascus. At the left, on a slightly raised terrace, the palace, with softly gleaming lights and music coming from the open latticed windows. The garden is full of oleanders, roses, pomegranates, abundance of crimson flowers; the air is heavy with their fragrance: a fountain at the right is plashing gently: behind it is an arbour covered with vines. Near the centre of the garden stands a small, hideous image of the god Rimmon. Back of the arbour rises the lofty square tower of the House of Rimmon, which casts a shadow from the moon across the garden. The background is a wide, hilly landscape, with a high road passing over the mountains toward the snow-clad summits of Mount Hermon in the distance. Enter by the palace door, the lady TSARPI, robed in red and gold, and followed by her maids, KHAMMA and NUBTA. She remains on the terrace: they go down into the garden, looking about, and returning to her.

KHAMMA:

There's no one here; the garden is asleep.

NUBTA:

The flowers are nodding, all the birds abed,
And nothing wakes except the watchful stars!

KHAMMA:

    The stars are sentinels discreet and mute:
    How many things they know and never tell!

TSARPI: [Impatiently.]

    Unlike the stars, how many things you tell
    And do not know! When comes your master home?

NUBTA:

    Lady, his armour-bearer brought us word
    An hour ago, the master will be here
    At moonset, not before.

TSARPI:

    He haunts the camp
    And leaves me much alone; yet I can pass
    The time of absence not unhappily,
    If I but know the time of his return.
    An hour of moonlight yet! Khamma, my mirror!
    These curls are ill arranged, this veil too low,—
    So,—that is better, careless maids! Withdraw,—
    But warn me if your master should appear.

KHAMMA:

    Mistress, have no concern; for when we hear
    The clatter of his horse along the street,
    We'll run this way and lead your dancers down
    With song and laughter,—you shall know in time.

    [*Exeunt KHAMMA and NUBTA, laughing. TSARPI descends the steps.*]

TSARPI:

My guest is late; but he will surely come!
Hunger and thirst will bring him to my feet.
The man who burns to drain the cup of love,—
The priest whose greed of glory never fails,—
Both, both have need of me, and he will come.
And I,—what do I need? Why everything
That helps my beauty to a higher throne;
All that a priest can promise, all a man
Can give, and all a god bestow, I need:
This may a woman win, and this will I.

[Enter REZON quietly from the shadow of the trees. He stands behind TSARPI
and listens, smiling, to her last words. Then he drops his mantle of leopard-
skin, and lifts his high-priest's rod of bronze, shaped at one end like a star, at
the other like a thunderbolt.]

REZON:
Tsarpi!

TSARPI:

The mistress of the house of Naaman
Salutes the keeper of the House of Rimmon.

[She bows low before him.]

REZON:
Rimmon receives you with his star of peace;

[He lowers the star-point of the rod, which glows for a moment with rosy light
above her head.]

And I, his chosen minister, kneel down
Before your regal beauty, and implore
The welcome of the woman for the man.

TSARPI: [Giving him her hand, but holding off his embrace.]
Thus Tsarpi welcomes Rezon! Nay, no more!
Till I have heard what errand brings you here
By night, within the garden of the man
Who hates you most and fears you least in all Damascus.

REZON: [Rising, and speaking angrily.]
Trust me, I repay his scorn
With double hatred,—Naaman, the man
Whom the King honours and the people love,
Who stands against the nobles and the priests,
Against the oracles of Rimmon's House,
And cries, "We'll fight to keep Damascus free!"
This powerful fool, this impious devotee
Of liberty, who loves the city more
Than he reveres the city's ancient god:
This frigid husband who sets you below
His dream of duty to a horde of slaves:
This man I hate, and I will humble him.

TSARPI:
I think I hate him too. He stands apart
From me, ev'n while he holds me in his arms,
By something that I cannot understand,
Nor supple to my will, nor melt with tears,
Nor quite dissolve with blandishments, although
He swears he loves his wife next to his honour!
Next? That's too low! I will be first or nothing.

REZON:

    With me you are the first, the absolute!
    When you and I have triumphed you shall reign;
    And you and I will bring this hero down.

TSARPI:

    But how? For he is strong.

REZON:

    By these, the eyes
    Of Tsarpi; and by this, the rod of Rimmon.

TSARPI:

    Speak clearly; tell your plan.

REZON:

    You know the host
    Of the Assyrian king has broken forth
    Again to conquer us. Envoys have come
    From Shalmaneser to demand surrender.
    Our king Benhadad wavers, for he knows
    His weakness. All the nobles, all the rich,
    Would purchase peace that they may grow more rich:
    Only the people and the soldiers, led
    By Naaman, would fight for liberty.
    Blind fools! To-day the envoys came to pay
    Their worship to our god, whom they adore
    In Nineveh as Asshur's brother-god.
    They talked with me in secret. Promises,
    Great promises! For every noble house
    That urges peace, a noble recompense:
    The king, submissive, kept in royal state

And splendour: most of all, honour and wealth
Shall crown the House of Rimmon, and his priest,—
Yea, and his priestess. For we two will rise
Upon the city's fall. The common folk
Shall suffer; Naaman shall sink with them
In wreck; but I shall rise, and you shall rise
Above me! You shall climb, through incense-smoke,
And days of pomp, and nights of revelry,
Glorious rites and ecstasies of love,
Unto the topmost room in Rimmon's tower,
The secret, lofty room, the couch of bliss,
And the divine embraces of the god.

TSARPI: [Throwing out her arms in exultation.]
    All, all I wish! What must I do for this?

REZON:
    Turn Naaman away from thoughts of war;
    Or purchase him with love's delights to yield
    This point,—I care not how,—and afterwards
    The future shall be ours.

TSARPI:
    And if I fail?

REZON:
    I have another shaft. The last appeal,
    Before the king decides, is to the oracle
    Of Rimmon. You shall read the signs!
    A former priestess of his temple, you
    Shall be the interpreter of heaven, and speak

A word to melt this brazen soldier's heart
Within his breast.

TSARPI:

But if it flame instead?

REZON:

I know the way to quench that flame. The cup,
The parting cup your hand shall give to him!
What if the curse of Rimmon should infect
That wine with sacred venom, secretly
To work within his veins, week after week
Corrupting all the currents of his blood,
Dimming his eyes, wasting his flesh? What then?
Would he prevail in war? Would he come back
To glory, or to shame? What think you?

TSARPI:

I?
I do not think; I only do my part.
But can the gods bless this?

REZON:

The gods can bless
Whatever they decree; their will makes right;
And this is for the glory of the house
Of Rimmon,—and for thee, my queen. Come, come!
The night grows dark: we'll perfect our alliance.

[REZON *draws her with him, embracing her, through the shadows of the garden.*
RUAHMAH, who has been sleeping in the arbour, has been awakened
during the dialogue, and has been dimly visible in her white dress, behind the

vines. She parts them and comes out, pushing back her long, dark hair from her temples.]

RUAHMAH:

What have I heard? O God, what shame is this
Plotted beneath Thy pure and silent stars!
Was it for this that I was brought away
Captive from Israel's blessed hills to serve
A heathen mistress in a land of lies?
Ah, treacherous, shameful priest! Ah, shameless wife
Of one too noble to suspect thy guilt!
The very greatness of his generous heart
Betrays him to their hands. What can I do?
Nothing,—a slave,—hated and mocked by all
My fellow-slaves! O bitter prison-life!
I smother in this black, betraying air
Of lust and luxury; I faint beneath
The shadow of this House of Rimmon. God
Have mercy! Lead me out to Israel.
To Israel!

[*Music and laughter heard within the palace. The doors fly open and a flood of men and women, dancers, players, flushed with wine, dishevelled, pour down the steps, KHAMMA and NUBTA with them. They crown the image with roses and dance around it. RUAHMAH is discovered crouching beside the arbour. They drag her out before the image.*]

NUBTA:

Look! Here's the Hebrew maid,—
She's homesick; let us comfort her!

KHAMMA: [They put their arms around her.]
Yes, dancing is the cure for homesickness.
We'll make her dance.

RUAHMAH: [She slips away.]
I pray you, let me go!
I cannot dance, I do not know your measures.

KHAMMA:
Then sing for us,—a song of Israel!

RUAHMAH:
How can I sing the songs of Israel
In this strange country? O my heart would break
With grief in every note of that dear music.

A SERVANT:
A stubborn and unfriendly maid! We'll whip her.

[*They circle around her, striking her with rose-branches; she sinks to her knees, covering her face with her bare arms, which bleed.*]

NUBTA:
Look, look! She kneels to Rimmon, she is tamed.

RUAHMAH: [Springing up and lifting her arms.]
Nay, not to this dumb idol, but to Him
Who made Orion and the seven stars!

ALL:
She raves,—she mocks at Rimmon! Punish her!
The fountain! Wash her blasphemy away!

[They push her toward the fountain, laughing and shouting. In the open door of the palace NAAMAN appears, dressed in blue and silver, bareheaded and unarmed. He comes to the top of the steps and stands for a moment, astonished and angry.]

NAAMAN:

Silence! What drunken rout is this? Begone,
Ye barking dogs and mewing cats! Out, all!
Poor child, what have they done to thee?

[Exeunt all except RUAHMAH, who stands with her face covered by her hands. NAAMAN comes to her, laying his hand on her shoulder.]

RUAHMAH: [Looking up in his face.]
Nothing,
My lord and master! They have harmed me not.

NAAMAN: [Touching her arm.]
Dost call this nothing?

RUAHMAH:
Since my lord is come.

NAAMAN:
I do not know thy face,—who art thou, child?

RUAHMAH:
The handmaid of thy wife. These three years past
I have attended her.

NAAMAN:

    Whence comest thou?
    Thy voice is like thy mistress, but thy looks
    Have something foreign. Tell thy name, thy land.

RUAHMAH:

    Ruahmah is my name, a captive maid,
    The daughter of a prince in Israel,—
    Where once, in olden days, I saw my lord
    Ride through our highlands, when Samaria
    Was allied with Damascus to defeat
    Asshur, our common foe.

NAAMAN:

    O glorious days,
    Crowded with life! And thou rememberest them?

RUAHMAH:

    As clear as yesterday! Master, I saw
    Thee riding on a snow-white horse beside
    Our king; and all we joyful little maids
    Strewed boughs of palm along the victors' way;
    For you had driven out the enemy,
    Broken; and both our lands were friends and free.

NAAMAN: [Sadly.]

    Well, they are past, those noble days! The friends
    That fought for freedom stand apart, rivals
    For Asshur's favour, like two jealous dogs
    That snarl and bite each other, while they wait
    The master's whip, enforcing peace. The days
    When nations would imperil all to keep

Their liberties, are only memories now.
The common cause is lost,—and thou art brought,
The captive of some mercenary raid,
Some profitable, honourless foray,
To serve within my house. Dost thou fare well?

RUAHMAH:
Master, thou seest.

NAAMAN:
Yes, I see! My child,
Why do they hate thee so?

RUAHMAH:
I do not know,
Unless because I will not bow to Rimmon.

NAAMAN:
Thou needest not. I fear he is a god
Who pities not his people, will not save.
My heart is sick with doubt of him. But thou
Shalt hold thy faith,—I care not what it is,—
Worship thy god; but keep thy spirit free.
Here, take this chain and wear it with my seal,
None shall molest the maid who carries this.
Thou hast found favour in thy master's eyes;
Hast thou no other gift to ask of me?

RUAHMAH: [Earnestly.]
My lord, I do entreat thee not to go
To-morrow to the council. Seek the King

And speak with him in secret; but avoid
The audience-hall.

NAAMAN;
    Why, what is this? Thy wits
    Are wandering. Why dost thou ask this thing
    Impossible! My honour is engaged
    To speak for war, to lead in war against
    The Assyrian Bull and save Damascus.

RUAHMAH: [With confused earnestness.]
    Then, lord, if thou must go, I pray thee speak,—
    I know not how,—but so that all must hear.
    With magic of unanswerable words
    Persuade thy foes. Yet watch,—beware,—

NAAMAN:
    Of what?

RUAHMAH: [Turning aside.]
    I am entangled in my speech,—no light,—
    How shall I tell him? He will not believe.
    O my dear lord, thine enemies are they
    Of thine own house. I pray thee to beware,—
    Beware,—of Rimmon!

NAAMAN:
    Child, thy words are wild;
    Thy troubles have bewildered all thy brain.
    Go, now, and fret no more; but sleep, and dream
    Of Israel! For thou shall see thy home
    Among the hills again.

RUAHMAH:

> Master, good-night,
> And may thy slumber be as sweet and deep
> As if thou camped at snowy Hermon's foot,
> Amid the music of his waterfalls
> And watched by winged sentries of the sky.
> There friendly oak-trees bend their boughs above
> The weary head, pillowed on earth's kind breast,
> And unpolluted breezes lightly breathe
> A song of sleep among the murmuring leaves.
> There the big stars draw nearer, and the sun
> Looks forth serene, undimmed by city's mirk
> Or smoke of idol-temples, to behold
> The waking wonder of the wide-spread world,
> And life renews itself with every morn
> In purest joy of living. May the Lord
> Deliver thee, dear master, from the nets
> Laid for thy feet, and lead thee out, along
> The open path, beneath the open sky!
> Thou shall be followed always by the heart
> Of one poor captive maid who prays for thee.

[*Exit RUAHMAH: NAAMAN stands looking after her.*]

SCENE II.

TIME: *The following morning.*

The audience-hall in BENHADAD'S palace. The sides of the hall are lined with lofty columns: the back opens toward the city, with descending steps: the House of

Rimmon with its high tower is seen in the background. The throne is at the right in front: opposite is the royal door of entrance, guarded by four tall sentinels. Enter at the rear between the columns, RAKHAZ, SABALLIDIN, HAZAEL, IZDUBHAR.

IZDUBHAR: [An excited old man.]

The city is all in a turmoil. It boils like a pot of lentils. The people are foaming and bubbling round and round like beans in the pottage.

HAZAEL: [A lean, crafty man.]

Fear is a hot fire.

RAKHAZ: [A fat, pompous man.]

Well may they fear, for the Assyrians are not three days distant. They are blazing along like a waterspout to chop Damascus down like a pitcher of spilt milk.

SABALLIDIN: [Young and frank.]

Cannot Naaman drive them back?

RAKHAZ: [Puffing and blowing.]

Ho! Naaman? Where have you been living? Naaman is a broken reed whose claws have been cut. Build no hopes on that foundation, for it will upset in the midst of the sea and leave you hanging in the air.

SABALLIDIN:

He clatters like a windmill. What would he say, Hazael?

HAZAEL:

Naaman can do nothing without the command of the King; and the King fears to order the army to march without the approval of the gods. The High Priest is against it. The House of Rimmon is for peace with Asshur.

RAKHAZ:

Yes, and all the nobles are for peace. We are the men whose wisdom lights the rudder that upholds the chariot of state. Would we be rich if we were not wise? Do we not know better than the rabble what medicine will silence this fire that threatens to drown us?

IZDUBHAR:

But if the Assyrians come, we shall all perish; they will despoil us all.

HAZAEL:

Not us, my lord, only the common people. The envoys have offered favourable terms to the priests, and the nobles, and the King. No palace, no temple, shall be plundered. Only the shops, and the markets, and the houses of the multitude shall be given up to the Bull. He will eat his supper from the pot of lentils, not from our golden plate.

RAKHAZ:

Yes, and all who speak for peace in the council shall be enriched; our heads shall be crowned with seats of honour in the processions of the Assyrian king. He needs wise counsellors to help him guide the ship of empire onto the solid rock of prosperity. You must be with us, my lords Izdubhar and Saballidin, and let the stars of your wisdom roar loudly for peace.

IZDUBHAR:

He talks like a tablet read upside down,—a wild ass braying in the wilderness. Yet there is policy in his words.

SABALLIDIN:

I know not. Can a kingdom live without a people or an army? If we let the Bull in to sup on the lentils, will he not make his breakfast in our vineyards?

[*Enter other courtiers, following SHUMAKIM, a crooked little jester, in blue, green and red, a wreath of poppies around his neck and a flagon in his hand. He walks unsteadily, and stutters in his speech.*]

HAZAEL:

Here is Shumakim, the King's fool, with his legs full of last night's wine.

SHUMAKIM: [Balancing himself in front of them and chuckling.]

Wrong, my lords, very wrong! This is not last night's wine, but a draught the King's physician gave me this morning for a cure. It sobers me amazingly! I know you all, my lords: any fool would know you. You, master, are a statesman; and you are a politician; and you are a patriot.

RAKHAZ:

Am I a statesman? I felt something of the kind about me. But what is a statesman?

SHUMAKIM:

A politician that is stuffed with big words; a fat man in a mask; one that plays a solemn tune on a sackbut full o' wind.

HAZAEL:

And what is a politician?

SHUMAKIM:

A statesman that has dropped his mask and cracked his sackbut. Men trust him for what he is, and he never deceives them, because he always lies.

IZDUBHAR:

Why do you call me a patriot?

SHUMAKIM:

Because you know what is good for you; you love your country as you love your pelf. You feel for the common people,—as the wolf feels for the sheep.

SABALLIDIN:

And what am I?

SHUMAKIM:

A fool, master, just a plain fool; and there is hope of thee for that reason. Embrace me, brother, and taste this; but not too much,—it will intoxicate thee with sobriety.

[*The hall has been slowly filling with courtiers and soldiers: a crowd of people begin to come up the steps at the rear, where they are halted by a chain guarded by servants of the palace. A bell tolls; the royal door is thrown open; the aged King crosses the hall slowly and takes his seat on the throne with the four tall sentinels standing behind him. All bow down shading their eyes with their hands.*]

BENHADAD:

The hour of royal audience is come.
I'll hear the envoys of my brother king,
The Son of Asshur. Are my counsellors
At hand? Where are the priests of Rimmon's House?

[Gongs sound. REZON comes in from the rear, followed by a procession of priests in black and yellow. The courtiers bow; the King rises; REZON takes his stand on the steps of the throne at the left of the King.]

BENHADAD;
  Where is my faithful servant Naaman,
  The captain of my host?

[Trumpets sound from the city. The crowd on the steps divide; the chain is lowered; NAAMAN enters, followed by six soldiers. He is dressed in chain-mail, with a silver helmet and a cloak of blue. He uncovers, and kneels on the steps of the throne at the King's right.]

NAAMAN:
  My lord the King,
  The bearer of thy sword is here.

BENHADAD: [Giving NAAMAN his hand, and sitting down.]
  Welcome,
  My strong right arm that never failed me yet!
  I am in doubt,—but stay thou close to me
  While I decide this cause. Where are the envoys?
  Let them appear and give their message.

[Enter the Assyrian envoys; one in white and the other in red; both with the golden Bull's head embroidered oh their robes. They come from the right, rear, bow slightly before the throne, and take the centre of the hall.]

WHITE ENVOY: [Stepping forward.]
  Greeting from Shalmaneser, Asshur's son,
  The king who reigns at Nineveh
  And takes his tribute from a thousand cities,

Unto Benhadad, monarch in Damascus!
The conquering Bull has come out of the north;
The south has fallen before him, and the west
His feet have trodden; Hamath is laid waste;
He pauses at your gate, invincible,—
To offer peace. The princes of your court,
The priests of Rimmon's house, and you, the King,
If you pay homage to your overlord,
Shall rest secure, and flourish as our friends.
Assyria sends to you this gilded yoke;
Receive it as the sign of proffered peace.

[*He lays a yoke on the steps of the throne.*]

BENHADAD:

What of the city? Said your king no word
Of our Damascus, and the many folk
That do inhabit her and make her great?
What of the soldiers who have fought for us?
The people who have sheltered 'neath our shield?

WHITE ENVOY:

Of these my royal master did not speak.

BENHADAD:

Strange silence! Must we give them up to him?
Is this the price at which he offers us
The yoke of peace? What if we do refuse?

RED ENYOY: [Stepping forward.]

Then ruthless war! War to the uttermost.

No quarter, no compassion, no escape!
The Bull will gore and trample in his fury
Nobles and priests and king,—none shall be spared!
Before the throne we lay our second gift;
This bloody horn, the symbol of red war.

[*He lays a long bull's horn, stained with blood on the steps of the throne.*]

WHITE ENVOY:

Our message is delivered. Grant us leave
And safe conveyance, that we may return
Unto our master. He will wait three days
To know your royal choice between his gifts.
Keep which you will and send the other back;
The red bull's horn your youngest page may bring;
But with the yoke, best send your mightiest army!

[*The ENVOYS retire, amid confused murmurs of the people, the King silent, his head sunken on his breast.*]

BENHADAD:

Proud words, a bitter message, hard to endure!
We are not now that force which feared no foe;
Our host is weakened, and our old allies
Have left us. Can we face this raging Bull
Alone, and beat him back? Give me your counsel.

[*Many speak at once, confusedly.*]

What babblement is this? Were ye born at Babel?
Give me clear words and reasonable speech.

RAKHAZ: [Pompously]

    O King, I am a reasonable man;
    And there be some who call me very wise
    And prudent; but of this I will not speak,
    For I am also modest. Let me plead,
    Persuade, and reason you to choose for peace.
    This golden yoke may be a bitter draught,
    But better far to fold it in our arms,
    Than risk our cargoes in the savage horn
    Of war. Shall we imperil all our wealth,
    Our valuable lives? Nobles are few,
    Rich men are rare, and wise men rarer still;
    The precious jewels on the tree of life,
    Wherein the common people are but brides
    And clay and rubble. Let the city go,
    But save the corner-stones that float the ship!
    Have I not spoken well?

BENBADAD: [Shaking his head.]

    Excellent well!
    Most eloquent! But misty in the meaning.

HAZAEL: [With cold decision.]

    Then let me speak, O King, in plainer words!
    The days of independent states are past:
    The tide of empire sweeps across the earth;
    Assyria rides it with resistless power
    And thunders on to subjugate the world.
    Oppose her, and we fight with Destiny;
    Submit to her demands, and we shall ride
    With her to victory. Therefore return
    This bloody horn, the symbol of wild war,

With words of soft refusal, and accept
The golden yoke, Assyria's gift of peace.

NAAMAN: [Starting forward eagerly.]
    There is no peace beneath a conqueror's yoke,
    My King, but shame and heaviness of heart!
    For every state that barters liberty
    To win imperial favour, shall be drained
    Of her best blood, henceforth, in endless wars
    To make the empire greater. Here's the choice:
    We fight to-day to keep our country free,
    Or else we fight forevermore to help
    Assyria bind the world as we are bound.
    I am a soldier, and I know the hell
    Of war! But I will gladly ride through hell
    To save Damascus. Master, bid me ride!
    Ten thousand chariots wait for your command;
    And twenty thousand horsemen strain the leash
    Of patience till you let them go; a throng
    Of spearmen, archers, swordsmen, like the sea
    Chafing against a dike, roar for the onset!
    O master, let me launch your mighty host
    Against the Bull,—we'll bring him to his knees!

    [*Cries of "War!" from the soldiers and the people; "peace!" from the courtiers and
        the priests. The King rises, turning toward NAAMAN, and seems about to
        speak. REZON lifts his rod.*]

REZON:
    Shall not the gods decide when mortals doubt?
    Rimmon is master of the city's fate;
    He reigns in secret and his will is law;

We read his will, by our most ancient faith,
In omens and in signs of mystery.
Must we not hearken to his high commands?

BENHADAD: [Sinking hack on the throne, submissively.]
I am the faithful son of Rimmon's House.
Consult the oracle. But who shall read?

REZON:
Tsarpi, the wife of Naaman, who served
Within the temple in her maiden years,
Shall be the mouthpiece of the mighty god,
To-day's high-priestess. Bring the sacrifice!

[*Gongs and cymbals sound: enter priests carrying an altar on which a lamb is bound. The altar is placed in the centre of the hall. TSARPI follows the priests, covered with a long transparent veil of black, sewn with gold stars; RUAHMAH, in white, bears her train. TSARPI stands before the altar, facing it, and lifts her right hand holding a knife. RUAHMAH steps back, near the throne, her hands crossed on her breast, her head bowed. The priests close in around TSARPI and the altar. The knife is seen to strike downward. Gongs and cymbals sound: cries of "Rimmon, hear us." The circle of priests opens, and TSARPI turns slowly to face the King.*]

TSARPI: [Monotonously.]
Black is the blood of the victim,
Rimmon is unfavourable,
Asratu is unfavourable;
They will not war against Asshur,
They will make a league with the God of Nineveh.
Evil is in store for Damascus,
A strong enemy will lay waste the land.

70

Therefore make peace with the Bull;
Hearken to the voice of Rimmon.

[She turns again to the altar, and the priests close in around her. REZON lifts
his rod toward the tower of the temple. A flash of lightning followed by thunder;
smoke rises from the altar; all except NAAMAN and RUAHMAH cover
their faces. The circle of priests opens again, and TSARPI comes forward
slowly, chanting.]

CHANT:
Hear the words of Rimmon! Thus your Maker speaketh:
I, the god of thunder, riding on the whirlwind,
I, the god of lightning leaping from the storm-cloud,
I will smite with vengeance him who dares defy me!
He who leads Damascus into war with Asshur,
Conquering or conquered, bears my curse upon him.
Surely shall my arrow strike his heart in secret,
Burn his flesh with fever, turn his blood to poison,
Brand him with corruption, drive him into darkness;
He alone shall perish, by the doom of Rimmon.

[All are terrified and look toward NAAMAN, shuddering. RUAHMAH alone
seems not to heed the curse, but stands with her eyes fixed on NAAMAN.]

RUAHMAH:
Be not afraid! There is a greater God
Shall cover thee with His almighty wings:
Beneath his shield and buckler shalt thou trust.

BENHADAD:
Repent, my son, thou must not brave this curse.

NAAMAN:

    My King, there is no curse as terrible
    As that which lights a bosom-fire for him
    Who gives away his honour, to prolong
    A craven life whose every breath is shame!
    If I betray the men who follow me,
    The city that has put her trust in me,
    The country to whose service I am bound,
    What king can shield me from my own deep scorn,
    What god release me from that self-made hell?
    The tender mercies of Assyria
    I know; and they are cruel as creeping tigers.
    Give up Damascus, and her streets will run
    Rivers of innocent blood; the city's heart,
    That mighty, labouring heart, wounded and crushed
    Beneath the brutal hooves of the wild Bull,
    Will cry against her captain, sitting safe
    Among the nobles, in some pleasant place.
    I shall be safe,—safe from the threatened wrath
    Of unknown gods, but damned forever by
    The men I know,—that is the curse I fear.

BENHADAD:

    Speak not so high, my son. Must we not bow
    Our heads before the sovereignties of heaven?
    The unseen rulers are Divine.

NAAMAN;

    O King,
    I am unlearned in the lore of priests;
    Yet well I know that there are hidden powers
    About us, working mortal weal and woe

Beyond the force of mortal to control.
And if these powers appear in love and truth,
I think they must be gods, and worship them.
But if their secret will is manifest
In blind decrees of sheer omnipotence,
That punish where no fault is found, and smite
The poor with undeserved calamity,
And pierce the undefended in the dark
With arrows of injustice, and foredoom
The innocent to burn in endless pain,
I will not call this fierce almightiness
Divine. Though I must bear, with every man,
The burden of my life ordained, I'll keep
My soul unterrified, and tread the path
Of truth and honour with a steady heart!
But if I err in this; and if there be
Divinities whose will is cruel, unjust,
Capricious and supreme, I will forswear
The favour of these gods, and take my part
With man to suffer and for man to die.
Have ye not heard, my lords? The oracle
Proclaims to me, to me alone, the doom
Of vengeance if I lead the army out.
"Conquered or conquering!" I grip that chance!
Damascus free, her foes all beaten back,
The people saved from slavery, the King
Upheld in honour on his ancient throne,—
O what's the cost of this? I'll gladly pay
Whatever gods there be, whatever price
They ask for this one victory. Give me
This gilded sign of shame to carry back;
I'll shake it in the face of Asshur's king,

And break it on his teeth.

BENHADAD: [Rising.]
    Then go, my never-beaten captain, go!
    And may the powers that hear thy solemn vow
    Forgive thy rashness for Damascus' sake,
    Prosper thy fighting, and remit thy pledge.

REZON: [Standing beside the altar.]
    The pledge, O King, this man must seal his pledge
    At Rimmon's altar. He must take the cup
    Of soldier-sacrament, and bind himself
    By thrice-performed libation to abide
    The fate he has invoked.

NAAMAN: [Slowly.]
    And so I will.

[He comes down the steps, toward the altar, where REZON is filling the cup
    which TSARPI holds. RUAHMAH throws herself before NAAMAN,
    clasping his knees.]

RUAHMAH: [Passionately and wildly.]
    My lord, I do beseech you, stay! There's death
    Within that cup. It is an offering
    To devils. See, the wine blazes like fire,
    It flows like blood, it is a cursed cup,
    Fulfilled of treachery and hate.
    Dear master, noble master, touch it not!

NAAMAN:

    Poor maid, thy brain is still distraught. Fear not
    But let me go! Here, treat her tenderly!

    [*Gives her into the hands of SABALLIDIN.*]

    Can harm befall me from the wife who bears
    My name? I take the cup of fate from her.
    I greet the unknown powers; [*Pours libation.*]
    I will perform my vow; [*Again.*]
    I will abide my fate; [*Again.*]
    I pledge my life to keep Damascus free.

    [*He drains the cup, and lets it fall.*]

CURTAIN.

ACT II

TIME: *A week later*

The fore-court of the House of Rimmon. At the back the broad steps and double doors of the shrine: above them the tower of the god, its summit invisible. Enter various groups of citizens, talking, laughing, shouting: RAKHAZ, HAZAEL, SHUMAKIM and others.

FIRST CITIZEN:

Great news, glorious news, the Assyrians are beaten!

SECOND CITIZEN:

Naaman is returning, crowned with victory. Glory to our noble captain!

THIRD CITIZEN:

No, he is killed. I had it from one of the camp-followers who saw him fall at the head of the battle. They are bringing his body to bury it with honour. O sorrowful victory!

RAKHAZ;

Peace, my good fellows, you are ignorant, you have not been rightly informed, I will misinform you. The accounts of Naaman's death are overdrawn. He was killed, but his life has been preserved. One of his wounds was mortal, but the other three were curable, and by these the physicians have saved him.

SHUMAKIM: [Balancing himself before RAKHAZ in pretended admiration.]
O wonderful! Most admirable logic! One mortal, and three curable, therefore he must recover as it were, by three to one. Rakhaz, do you know that you are a marvelous man?

RAKHAZ:
Yes, I know it, but I make no boast of my knowledge.

SHUMAKIM:
Too modest, for in knowing this you know what is unknown to any other in Damascus!

[Enter, from the right, SABALLIDIN in armour: from the left, TSARPI with her attendants, among whom is RUAHMAH.]

HAZAEL:
Here is Saballidin, we'll question him;
He was enflamed by Naaman's fiery words,
And rode with him to battle. Good, my lord,
We hail you as a herald of the fight
You helped to win. Give us authentic news
Of your great general! Is he safe and well?
When will he come? Or will he come at all?

[All gather around him, listening eagerly.]

SABALLIDIN:

    He comes but now, returning from the field
    Where he hath gained a crown of deathless fame!
    Three times he led the charge; three times he fell
    Wounded, and the Assyrians beat us back.
    Yet every wound was but a spur to urge
    His valour onward. In the last attack
    He rode before us as the crested wave
    That heads the flood; and lo, our enemies
    Were broken like a dam of river-reeds,
    Burst by the torrent, scattered, swept away!
    But look! the Assyrian king in wavering flight
    Is lodged like driftwood on a little hill,
    Encircled by his guard, and stands at bay.
    Then Naaman, followed hotly by a score
    Of whirlwind riders, hammers through the hedge
    Of spearmen, brandishing the golden yoke:
    "Take back this gift," he cries; and shatters it
    On Shalmaneser's helmet. So the fight
    Dissolves in universal rout: the king,
    His chariots and his horsemen melt away;
    Our captain stands the master of the field,
    And saviour of Damascus! Now he brings,
    First to the king, report of this great triumph.

[Shouts of joy and applause.]

RUAHMAH: [Coming close to SABALLIDIN,]
    But what of him who won it? Fares he well?
    My mistress would receive some word of him.

SABALLIDIN:

    Hath she not heard?

RUAHMAH:

    But one brief message came:
    A tablet saying, "We have fought and conquered,"
    No word of his own person. Fares he well?

SABALLIDIN:

    Alas, most ill! For he is like a man
    Consumed by some strange sickness: wasted, wan,—
    His eyes are dimmed so that scarce can see;
    His ears are dulled; his fearless face is pale
    As one who walks to meet a certain doom
    Yet will not flinch. It is most pitiful,—
    But you shall see.

RUAHMAH:

    Yea, we shall see a man
    Who took upon himself his country's burden, dared
    To hazard all to save the poor and helpless;
    A man who bears the wrath of evil powers
    Unknown, and pays the hero's sacrifice.

    [*Enter BENHADAD with courtiers.*]

BENHADAD:

    Where is my faithful servant Naaman,
    The captain of my host?

SABALLIDIN:

    My lord, he comes.

[*Trumpet sounds. Enter company of soldiers in armour. Then four soldiers bearing captured standards of Asshur. NAAMAN follows, very pale, armour dinted and stained; he is blind, and guides himself by cords from the standards on each side, but walks firmly. The doors of the temple open slightly, and REZON appears at the top of the steps. NAAMAN lets the cords fall, and gropes his way for a few paces.*]

NAAMAN: [Kneeling]
Where is my King?
Master, the bearer of thy sword returns.
The golden yoke thou gavest me I broke
On him who sent it. Asshur's Bull hath fled
Dehorned. The standards of his host are thine!
Damascus is all thine, at peace, and free!

BENHADAD: [Holding out his arms.]
Thou art a mighty man of valour! Come,
And let me fold thy courage to my heart.

REZON: [Lifting his rod.]
Forbear, O King! Stand back from him, all men!
By the great name of Rimmon I proclaim
This man a leper! On his brow I see
The death-white seal, the finger-print of doom!
That tiny spot will spread, eating his flesh,
Gnawing his fingers bone from bone, until
The impious heart that dared defy the gods
Dissolves in the slow death which now begins.
Unclean! unclean! Henceforward he is dead:
No human hand shall touch him, and no home
Of men shall give him shelter. He shall walk
Only with corpses of the selfsame death

80

Down the long path to a forgotten tomb.
Avoid, depart, I do adjure you all,
Leave him to god,—the leper Naaman!

[*All shrink back horrified. REZON retires into the temple; the crowd melts away, wailing: TSARPI is among the first to go, followed by her attendants, except RUAHMAH, who crouches, with her face covered, not far from NAAMAN.*]

BENHADAD: [Lingering and turning back.]
  Alas, my son! O Naaman, my son!
  Why did I let thee go? Thou art cast out
  Irrevocably from the city's life
  Which thou hast saved. Who can resist the gods?
  I must obey the law, and touch thy hand
  Never again. Yet none shall take from thee
  Thy glorious title, captain of my host!
  I will provide for thee, and thou shalt dwell
  With guards of honour in a house of mine
  Always. Damascus never shall forget
  What thou hast done! O miserable words
  Of crowned impotence! O mockery of power
  Given to kings, who cannot even defend
  Their dearest from the secret wrath of heaven!
  Naaman, my son, my son! [*Exit.*]

NAAMAN: [Slowly, passing his hand over his eyes, and looking up.]
  Am I alone
  With thee, inexorable one, whose pride
  Offended takes this horrible revenge?
  I must submit my mortal flesh to thee,
  Almighty, but I will not call thee god!

Yet thou hast found the way to wound my soul
Most deeply through the flesh; and I must find
The way to let my wounded soul escape!

[*Drawing his sword.*]

Come, my last friend, thou art more merciful
Than Rimmon. Why should I endure the doom
He sends me? Irretrievably cut off
From all dear intercourse of human love,
From all the tender touch of human hands,
From all brave comradeship with brother-men,
With eyes that see no faces through this dark,
With ears that hear all voices far away,
Why should I cling to misery, and grope
My long, long way from pain to pain, alone?

RUAHMAH: [At his feet.]
    Nay, not alone, dear lord, for I am here;
    And I will never leave thee, nor forsake thee!

NAAMAN:
    What voice is that? The silence of my tomb
    Is broken by a ray of music,—whose?

RUAHMAH: [Rising.]
    The one who loves thee best in all the world.

NAAMAN:
    Why that should be,—O dare I dream it true?
    Tsarpi, my wife? Have I misjudged thy heart
    As cold and proud? How nobly thou forgivest!

82

Thou com'st to hold me from the last disgrace,—
The coward's flight into the dark. Go back
Unstained, my sword! Life is endurable
While there is one alive on earth who loves us,

RUAHMAH:

My lord,—my lord,—O listen! You have erred,—
You do mistake me now,—this dream—

NAAMAN:

Ah, wake me not! For I can conquer death
Dreaming this dream. Let me at last believe,
Though gods are cruel, a woman can be kind.
Grant me but this! For see,—I ask so little,—
Only to know that thou art faithful,—
Only to lean upon the thought that thou,
My wife, art near me, though I touch thee not,—
O this will hold me up, though it be given
From pity more than love.

RUAHMAH: [Trembling, and speaking slowly.]
Not so, my lord!
My pity is a stream; my pride of thee
Is like the sea that doth engulf the stream;
My love for thee is like the sovran moon
That rules the sea. The tides that fill my soul
Flow unto thee and follow after thee;
And where thou goest I will go; and where
Thou diest I will die,—in the same hour.

[*She lays her hand on his arm. He draws back.*]

NAAMAN:

O touch me not! Thou shall not share my doom.

RUAHMAH:

Entreat me not to go. I will obey
In all but this; but rob me not of this,—
The only boon that makes life worth the living,—
To walk beside thee day by day, and keep
Thy foot from stumbling; to prepare thy food
When thou art hungry, music for thy rest,
And cheerful words to comfort thy black hour;
And so to lead thee ever on, and on,
Through darkness, till we find the door of hope.

NAAMAN:

What word is that? The leper has no hope.

RUAHMAH:

Dear lord, the mark upon thy brow is yet
No broader than my little finger-nail.
Thy force is not abated, and thy step
Is firm. Wilt thou surrender to the enemy
Before thy strength is touched? Why, let me put
A drop of courage from my breast in thine.
There is a hope for thee. The captive maid
Of Israel who dwelt within thy house
Knew of a god very compassionate,
Long-suffering, slow to anger, one who heals
The sick, hath pity on the fatherless,
And saves the poor and him who has no helper.
His prophet dwells nigh to Samaria;
And I have heard that he hath brought the dead

To life again. We'll go to him. The King,
If I beseech him, will appoint a guard
Of thine own soldiers and Saballidin,
Thy friend, to convoy us upon our journey.
He'll give us royal letters to the king
Of Israel to make our welcome sure;
And we will take the open road, beneath
The open sky, to-morrow, and go on
Together till we find the door of hope.
Come, come with me!

[*She grasps his hand.*]

NAAMAN: [Drawing back.]
   Thou must not touch me!

RUAHMAH: [Unclasping her girdle and putting the end in hand.]
   Take my girdle, then!

NAAMAN: [Kissing the clasp of the girdle.]
   I do begin to think there is a God,
   Since love on earth can work such miracles!

CURTAIN.

ACT III

TIME: *A month later: dawn*

SCENE I

NAAMAN'S tent, on high ground among the mountains near Samaria: the city below. In the distance, a wide and splendid landscape. SABALLIDIN and soldiers on guard below the tent. Enter RUAHMAH in hunter's dress, with a lyre slung from her shoulder.

RUAHMAH:
Peace and good health to you, Saballidin.
Good morrow to you all. How fares my lord?

SABALLIDIN:
The curtains of his tent are folded still:
They have not moved since we returned, last night,
And told him what befell us in the city.

RUAHMAH:
Told him! Why did you make report to him.
And not to me? Am I not captain here,
Intrusted by the King's command with care
Of Naaman's life, until he is restored?
'Tis mine to know the first of good or ill

In this adventure: mine to shield his heart
From every arrow of adversity.
What have you told him? Speak!

SABALLIDIN:
Lady, we feared
To bring our news to you. For when the king
Of Israel had read our monarch's letter,
He rent his clothes, and cried, "Am I a god,
To kill and make alive, that I should heal
A leper? Ye have come with false pretence,
Damascus seeks a quarrel with me. Go!"
But when we told our lord, he closed his tent,
And there remains enfolded in his grief.
I trust he sleeps; 't were kind to let him sleep!
For now he doth forget his misery,
And all the burden of his hopeless woe
Is lifted from him by the gentle hand
Of slumber. Oh, to those bereft of hope
Sleep is the only blessing left,—the last
Asylum of the weary, the one sign
Of pity from impenetrable heaven.
Waking is strife: sleep is the truce of God!
Ah, lady, wake him not. The day will be
Full long for him to suffer, and for us
To turn our disappointed faces home
On the long road by which we must return.

RUAHMAH:
Return! Who gave you that command? Not I!
The King made me the leader of this quest,
And bound you all to follow me, because

He knew I never would return without
The thing for which he sent us. I'll go on
Day after day, unto the uttermost parts
Of earth, if need be, and beyond the gates
Of morning, till I find that which I seek,—
New life for Naaman. Are ye ashamed
To have a woman lead you? Then go back
And tell the King, "This huntress went too far
For us to follow; she pursues the trail
Of hope alone, refusing to forsake
The quarry: we grew weary of the chase;
And so we left her and retraced our steps,
Like faithless hounds, to sleep beside the fire."
Did Naaman forsake his soldiers thus
When you went forth to hunt the Assyrian Bull?
Your manly courage is less durable
Than woman's love, it seems. Go, if you will,—
Who bids me now farewell?

SOLDIERS:

Not I, not I!

SABALLIDIN:

Lady, lead on, we'll follow you for ever!

RUAHMAH:

Why, now you speak like men! Brought you no word
Out of Samaria, except that cry
Of impotence and fear from Israel's king?

SABALLIDIN:

    I do remember while he spoke with us
    A rustic messenger came in, and cried
    "Elisha saith, let Naaman come to me
    At Dothan, he shall surely know there is
    A God in Israel."

RUAHMAH:

    What said the King?

SABALLIDIN:

    He only shouted "Go!" more wildly yet,
    And rent his clothes again, as if he were
    Half-maddened by a coward's fear, and thought
    Only of how he might be rid of us.
    What comfort could there be for him, what hope
    For us, in the rude prophet's misty word?

RUAHMAH:

    It is the very word for which I prayed!
    My trust was not in princes; for the crown,
    The sceptre, and the purple robe are not
    Significant of vital power. The man
    Who saves his brother-men is he who lives
    His life with Nature, takes deep hold on truth,
    And trusts in God. A prophet's word is more
    Than all the kings on earth can speak. How far
    Is Dothan?

SOLDIER:

    Lady, 'tis but three hours' ride
    Along the valley northward.

RUAHMAH:

    Near! so near?
    I had not thought to end my task so soon!
    Prepare yourselves with speed to take the road.
    I will awake my lord.

[Exeunt all but SABALLIDIN and RUAHMAH. She goes toward the tent.]

SABALLIDIN;

    Ruahmah, stay! *[She turns back.]*
    I've been your servant in this doubtful quest,
    Obedient, faithful, loyal to your will,—
    What have I earned by this?

RUAHMAH:

    The gratitude
    Of him we both desire to serve: your friend,—
    My master and my lord.

SABALLIDIN:

    No more than this?

RUAHMAH:

    Yes, if you will, take all the thanks my hands
    Can hold, my lips can speak.

SABALLIDIN:

    I would have more.

RUAHMAH:

    My friend, there's nothing more to give to you,
    My service to my lord is absolute.

There's not a drop of blood within my veins
But quickens at the very thought of him;
And not a dream of mine but he doth stand
Within its heart and make it bright. No man
To me is other than his friend or foe.
You are his friend, and I believe you true!

SABALLIDIN:

I have been true to him,—now, I am true
To you.

RUAHMAH:

And therefore doubly true to him!
O let us match our loyalties, and strive
Between us who shall win the higher crown!
Men boast them of a friendship stronger far
Than love of woman. Prove it! I'll not boast,
But I'll contend with you on equal terms
In this brave race: and if you win the prize
I'll hold you next to him: and if I win
He'll hold you next to me; and either way
We'll not be far apart. Do you accept
My challenge?

SABALLIDIN:

Yes! For you enforce my heart
By honour to resign its great desire,
And love itself to offer sacrifice
Of all disloyal dreams on its own altar.
Yet love remains; therefore I pray you, think
How surely you must lose in our contention.
For I am known to Naaman: but you

He blindly takes for Tsarpi. 'Tis to her
He gives his gratitude: the praise you win
Endears her name.

RUAHMAH:

Her name? Why, what is that?
A name is but an empty shell, a mask
That does not change the features of the face
Beneath it. Can a name rejoice, or weep,
Or hope? Can it be moved by tenderness
To daily services of love, or feel the warmth
Of dear companionship? How many things
We call by names that have no meaning: kings
That cannot rule; and gods that are not good;
And wives that do not love! It matters not
What syllables he utters when he calls,
'Tis I who come,—'tis I who minister
Unto my lord, and mine the living heart
That feels the comfort of his confidence,
The thrill of gladness when he speaks to me,—
I do not hear the name!

SABALLIDIN:

And yet, be sure
There's danger in this error,—and no gain!

RUAHMAH:

I seek no gain; I only tread the path
Marked for me daily by the hand of love.
And if his blindness spared my lord one pang
Of sorrow in his black, forsaken hour,—
And if this error makes his burdened heart

More quiet, and his shadowed way less dark,
Whom do I rob? Not her who chose to stay
At ease in Rimmon's House! Surely not him!
Only myself? And that enriches me.
Why trouble we the master? Let it go,—
To-morrow he must know the truth,—and then
He shall dispose of me e'en as he will!

SABALLIDIN:
  To-morrow?

RUAHMAH:
  Yes, for I will tarry here,
While you conduct him to Elisha's house
To find the promised healing. I forebode
A sudden danger from the craven king
Of Israel, or else a secret ambush
From those who hate us in Damascus. Go,
But leave me twenty men: this mountain-pass
Protects the road behind you. Make my lord
Obey the prophet's word, whatever he commands,
And come again in peace. Farewell!

[*Exit SABALLIDIN. RUAHMAH goes toward the tent, then pauses and
  turns back. She takes her lyre and sings.*]

SONG.

Above the edge of dark appear the lances of the sun;
Along the mountain-ridges clear his rosy heralds run;
The vapours down the valley go
Like broken armies, dark and low.

Look up, my heart, from every hill
In folds of rose and daffodil
The sunrise banners flow.

O fly away on silent wing, ye boding owls of night!
O welcome little birds that sing the coming-in of light!
For new, and new, and ever-new,
The golden bud within the blue;
And every morning seems to say:
"There's something happy on the way,
And God sends love to you!"

NAAMAN: [Appearing at the entrance of his tent.]
　　O let me ever wake to music! For the soul
　　Returns most gently then, and finds its way
　　By the soft, winding clue of melody,
　　Out of the dusky labyrinth of sleep,
　　Into the light. My body feels the sun
　　Though I behold naught that his rays reveal.
　　Come, thou who art my daydawn and my sight,
　　Sweet eyes, come close, and make the sunrise mine!

RUAHMAH: [Coming near.]
　　A fairer day, dear lord, was never born
　　In Paradise! The sapphire cup of heaven
　　Is filled with golden wine: the earth, adorned
　　With jewel-drops of dew, unveils her face
　　A joyful bride, in welcome to her king.
　　And look! He leaps upon the Eastern hills
　　All ruddy fire, and claims her with a kiss.
　　Yonder the snowy peaks of Hermon float

Unmoving as a wind-dropt cloud. The gulf
Of Jordan, filled with violet haze, conceals
The rivers winding trail with wreaths of mist.
Below us, marble-crowned Samaria thrones
Upon her emerald hill amid the Vale
Of Barley, while the plains to northward change
Their colour like the shimmering necks of doves.
The lark springs up, with morning on her wings,
To climb her singing stairway in the blue,
And all the fields are sprinkled with her joy!

NAAMAN:
Thy voice is magical: thy words are visions!
I must content myself with them, for now
My only hope is lost: Samaria's king
Rejects our monarch's message,—hast thou heard?
"Am I a god that I should cure a leper?"
He sends me home unhealed, with angry words,
Back to Damascus and the lingering death.

RUAHMAH:
What matter where he sends? No god is he
To slay or make alive. Elisha bids
You come to him at Dothan, there to learn
There is a God in Israel.

NAAMAN:
I fear
That I am grown mistrustful of all gods;
Their secret counsels are implacable.

RUAHMAH:

Fear not! There's One who rules in righteousness
High over all.

NAAMAN:

What knowest thou of Him?

RUAHMAH:

Oh, I have heard,—the maid of Israel,—
Rememberest thou? She often said her God
Was merciful and kind, and slow to wrath,
And plenteous in forgiveness, pitying us
Like as a father pitieth his children.

NAAMAN:

If there were such a God, I'd worship Him
For ever!

RUAHMAH:

Then make haste to hear the word
His prophet promises to speak to thee!
Obey it, my dear lord, and thou shalt lose
This curse that burdens thee. This tiny spot
Of white that mars the beauty of thy brow
Shall melt like snow; thine eyes be filled with light.
Thou wilt not need my leading any more,—
Nor me,—for thou wilt see me, all unveiled,—
I tremble at the thought.

NAAMAN:

Why, what is this?
Why shouldst thou tremble? Art thou not mine own?

RUAHMAH: [Turning to him.]
    Surely I am! But take me, take me now!
    For I belong to thee in body and soul;
    The very pulses of my heart are thine.
    Wilt thou not feel how tenderly they beat?
    Wilt thou not lie like myrrh between my breasts
    And satisfy thy lonely lips with love?
    Thou art opprest, and I would comfort thee
    While yet thy sorrow weighs upon thy life.
    To-morrow? No, to-day! The crown of love
    Is sacrifice; I have not given thee
    Enough! Ah, fold me in thine arms,—take all!

[*She takes his hands and puts them around her neck; he holds her from him, with one hand on her shoulder, the other behind her head.*]

NAAMAN:
    Thou art too dear to injure with a kiss,—
    Too dear for me to stain thy purity,
    Or leave one touch upon thee to regret!
    How should I take a gift may bankrupt thee,
    Or drain the fragrant chalice of thy love
    With lips that may be fatal? Tempt me not
    To sweet dishonour; strengthen me to wait
    Until thy prophecy is all fulfilled,
    And I can claim thee with a joyful heart.

RUAHMAH: [Turning away.]
    Thou wilt not need me then,—and I shall be
    No more than the faint echo of a song
    Heard half asleep. We shall go back to where
    We stood before this journey.

NAAMAN:

Never again!
For thou art changed by some deep miracle.
The flower of womanhood hath bloomed in thee,—
Art thou not changed?

RUAHMAH:

Yea, I am changed,—and changed
Again,—bewildered,—till there's nothing clear
To me but this: I am the instrument
In an Almighty hand to rescue thee
From death. This will I do,—and afterward—

[*A trumpet is blown, without.*]

Hearken, the trumpet sounds, the chariot waits.
Away, dear lord, follow the road to light!

SCENE II.[1]

The house of Elisha, upon a terraced hillside. A low stone cottage with vine-trellises and flowers; a flight of steps, at the foot of which is NAAMAN'S chariot. He is standing in it; SABALLIDIN beside it. Two soldiers come down the steps.

FIRST SOLDIER:

We have delivered my lord's greeting and his message.

---

1   Note that this scene is not intended to be put upon the stage, the effect of the action upon the drama being given at the beginning of Act IV.

98

SECOND SOLDIER:

Yes, and near lost our noses in the doing of it! For the servant slammed the door in our faces. A most unmannerly reception!

FIRST SOLDIER:

But I take that as a good omen. It is mark of holy men to keep ill-conditioned servants. Look, the door opens, the prophet is coming.

SECOND SOLDIER:

No, by my head, it's that notable mark of his master's holiness, that same lantern-jawed lout of a servant.

[*GEHAZI loiters down the steps and comes to NAAMAN with a slight obeisance.*]

GEHAZI:

My master, the prophet of Israel, sends word to Naaman the Syrian,— are you he?—"Go wash in Jordan seven times and be healed."

[*GEHAZI turns and goes slowly up the steps.*]

NAAMAN:

What insolence is this? Am I a man
To be put off with surly messengers?
Has not Damascus rivers more renowned
Than this rude, torrent Jordan? Crystal streams,
Abana! Pharpar! flowing smoothly through
A paradise of roses? Might I not
Have bathed in them and been restored at ease?
Come up, Saballidin, and guide me home!

SABALLIDIN:

Bethink thee, master, shall we lose our quest
Because a servant is uncouth? The road
That seeks the mountain leads us through the vale.
The prophet's word is friendly after all;
For had it been some mighty task he set,
Thou wouldst perform it. How much rather then
This easy one? Hast thou not promised her
Who waits for thy return? Wilt thou go back
To her unhealed?

NAAMAN:

No! not for all my pride!
I'll make myself most humble for her sake,
And stoop to anything that gives me hope
Of having her. Make haste, Saballidin,
Bring me to Jordan. I will cast myself
Into that river's turbulent embrace
A hundred times, until I save my life
Or lose it!

[*Exeunt. The light fades: musical interlude. The light increases again with ruddy
sunset shining on the door of ELISHA'S house. The prophet appears and looks
off, shading his eyes with his hand as he descends the steps slowly. Trumpet blows,—
NAAMAN'S call;—sound of horses galloping and men shouting. NAAMAN
enters joyously, followed by SABALLIDIN and soldiers, with gifts.*]

NAAMAN:

Behold a man delivered from the grave
By thee! I rose from Jordan's waves restored
To youth and vigour, as the eagle mounts
Upon the sunbeam and renews his strength!

O mighty prophet deign to take from me
These gifts too poor to speak my gratitude;
Silver and gold and jewels, damask robes,—

ELISHA: [Interrupting.]
    As thy soul liveth I will not receive
    A gift from thee, my son! Give all to Him
    Whose mercy hath redeemed thee from thy plague.

NAAMAN:
    He is the only God! I worship Him!
    Grant me a portion of the blessed soil
    Of this most favoured land where I have found
    His mercy; in Damascus will I build
    An altar to His name, and praise Him there
    Morning and night. There is no other God
    In all the world.

ELISHA:
                        Thou needest not
    This load of earth to build a shrine for Him;
    Yet take it if thou wilt. But be assured
    God's altar is in every loyal heart,
    And every flame of love that kindles there
    Ascends to Him and brightens with His praise.
    There is no other God! But evil Powers
    Make war against Him in the darkened world;
    And many temples have been built to them.

NAAMAN:
    I know them well! Yet when my master goes
    To worship in the House of Rimmon, I

Must enter with him; for he trusts me, leans
Upon my hand; and when he bows himself
I cannot help but make obeisance too,—
But not to Rimmon! To my country's king
I'll bow in love and honour. Will the Lord
Pardon thy servant in this thing?

ELISHA:

My son,
Peace has been granted thee. 'Tis thine to find
The only way to keep it. Go in peace.

NAAMAN:

Thou hast not answered me,—may I bow down?

ELISHA:

The answer must be thine. The heart that knows
The perfect peace of gratitude and love,
Walks in the light and needs no other rule.
Take counsel with thy heart and go in peace!

CURTAIN.

ACT IV

SCENE I

The interior of NAAMAN'S tent, at night. RUAHMAH alone, sleeping on the ground. A vision appears to her through the curtains of the font: ELISHA standing on the hillside at Dothan: NAAMAN, restored to sight, comes in and kneels before him. ELISHA blesses him, and he goes out rejoicing. The vision of the prophet turns to RUAHMAH and lifts his hand in warning.

ELISHA:
    Daughter of Israel, what dost thou here?
    Thy prayer is granted. Naaman is healed:
    Mar not true service with a selfish thought.
    Nothing remains for thee to do, except
    Give thanks, and go whither the Lord commands.
    Obey,—obey! Ere Naaman returns
    Thou must depart to thine own house in Shechem.

    [The vision vanishes.]

RUAHMAH: [Waking and rising slowly.]
    A dream, a dream, a messenger of God!
    O dear and dreadful vision, art thou true?
    Then am I glad with all my broken heart.

Nothing remains,—nothing remains but this,—
Give thanks, obey, depart,—and so I do.
Farewell, my master's sword! Farewell to you,
My amulet! I lay you on the hilt
His hand shall clasp again: bid him farewell
For me, since I must look upon his face
No more for ever!—Hark, what sound was that?

[*Enter soldier hurriedly.*]

SOLDIER:

Mistress, an arméd troop, footmen and horse,
Mounting the hill!

RUAHMAH:

My lord returns in triumph.

SOLDIER:

Not so, for these are enemies; they march
In haste and silence, answering not our cries.

RUAHMAH:

Our enemies? Then hold your ground,—on guard!
Fight! fight! Defend the pass, and drive them down.

[*Exit soldier. RUAHMAH draws NAAMAN'S sword from the scabbard
and hurries out of the tent. Confused noise of fighting outside. Three or four
soldiers are driven in by a troop of men in disguise. RUAHMAH follows: she
is beaten to her knees, and her sword is broken.*]

REZON: [Throwing aside the cloth which covers his face.]
Hold her! So, tiger-maid, we've found your lair

104

And trapped you. Where is Naaman,
Your master?

RUAHMAH: [Rising, her arms held by two of REZON'S followers.]
He is far beyond your reach.

REZON:
Brave captain! He has saved himself, the leper,
And left you here?

RUAHMAH:
The leper is no more.

REZON:
What mean you?

RUAHMAH:
He has gone to meet his God.

REZON:
Dead? Dead? Behold how Rimmon's wrath is swift!
Damascus shall be mine: I'll terrify
The King with this, and make my terms. But no!
False maid, you sweet-faced harlot, you have lied
To save him,—speak.

RUAHMAH:
I am not what you say,
Nor have I lied, nor will I ever speak
A word to you, vile servant of a traitor-god.

REZON:

> Break off this little flute of blasphemy,
> This ivory neck,—twist it, I say!
> Give her a swift despatch after her leper!
> But stay,—if he still lives he'll follow her,
> And so we may ensnare him. Harm her not!
> Bind her! Away with her to Rimmon's House!
> Is all this carrion dead? There's one that moves,—
> A spear,—fasten him down! All quiet now?
> Then back to our Damascus! Rimmon's face
> Shall be made bright with sacrifice.

> [*Exeunt forcing RUAHMAH with them. Musical interlude. A wounded soldier crawls from a dark corner of the tent and finds the chain with NAAMAN's seal, which has fallen to the ground in the struggle.*]

WOUNDED SOLDIER:

> This signet of my lord, her amulet!
> Lost, lost! Ah, noble lady,—let me die
> With this upon my breast.

> [*The tent is dark. Enter NAAMAN and his company in haste, with torches.*]

NAAMAN:

> What bloody work
> Is here? God, let me live to punish him
> Who wrought this horror! Treacherously slain
> At night, by unknown hands, my brave companions:
> Tsarpi, my best beloved, light of my soul,
> Put out in darkness! O my broken lamp
> Of life, where art thou? Nay, I cannot find her.

WOUNDED SOLDIER: [Raising himself on his arm.]
Master!

NAAMAN: [Kneels beside him.]
One living? Quick, a torch this way!
Lift up his head,—so,—carefully!
Courage, my friend, your captain is beside you.
Call back your soul and make report to him.

WOUNDED SOLDIER:
Hail, captain! O my captain,—here!

NAAMAN:
Be patient,—rest in peace,—the fight is done.
Nothing remains but render your account.

WOUNDED SOLDIER:
They fell upon us suddenly,—we fought
Our fiercest,—every man,—our lady fought
Fiercer than all. They beat us down,—she's gone.
Rezon has carried her away a captive. See,—
Her amulet,—I die for you, my captain.

NAAMAN: [He gently lays the dead soldier on the ground, and rises.]
Farewell. This last report was brave; but strange
Beyond my thought! How came the High Priest here?
And what is this? my chain, my seal! But this
Has never been in Tsarpi's hand. I gave
This signet to a captive maid one night,—
A maid of Israel. How long ago?
Ruahmah was her name,—almost forgotten!

107

So long ago,—how comes this token here?
What is this mystery, Saballidin?

SABALLIDIN:

Ruahmah is her name who brought you hither.

NAAMAN:

Where then is Tsarpi?

SABALLIDIN:

In Damascus.
She left you when the curse of Rimmon fell,—
Took refuge in his House,—and there she waits
Her lord's return,—Rezon's return.

NAAMAN:

'Tis false!

SABALLIDIN:

The falsehood is in her. She hath been friend
With Rezon in his priestly plot to win
Assyria's favour,—friend to his design
To sell his country to enrich his temple,—
And friend to him in more,—I will not name it.

NAAMAN:

Nor will I credit it. Impossible!

SABALLIDIN:

Did she not plead with you against the war,
Counsel surrender, seek to break your will?

NAAMAN:

She did not love my work, a soldier's task.
She never seemed to be at one with me
Until I was a leper.

SABALLIDIN:

From whose hand
Did you receive the sacred cup?

NAAMAN:

From hers.

SABALLIDIN:

And from that hour the curse began to work.

NAAMAN:

But did she not have pity when she saw
Me smitten? Did she not beseech the King
For letters and a guard to make this journey?
Has she not been the fountain of my hope,
My comforter and my most faithful guide
In this adventure of the dark? All this
Is proof of perfect love that would have shared
A leper's doom rather than give me up.
Can I doubt her who dared to love like this?

SABALLIDIN:

O master, doubt her not,—but know her name;
Ruahmah! It was she alone who wrought
This wondrous work of love. She won the King
By the strong pleading of resistless hope

To furnish forth this company. She led
Our march, kept us in heart, fought off despair,
Offered herself to you as to her god,
Watched over you as if you were her child,
Prepared your food, your cup, with her own hands,
Sang you asleep at night, awake at dawn,—

NAAMAN: [Interrupting.]
Enough! I do remember every hour
Of that sweet comradeship! And now her voice
Wakens the echoes in my lonely breast;
The perfume of her presence fills my sense
With longing. All my soul cries out in vain
For her embracing, satisfying love,
her eyes and called her my Ruahmah!

[*To his soldiers.*]

Away! away! I burn to take the road
That leads me back to Rimmon's House,—
But not to bow,—by God, never to bow!

TIME: *Three days later*

SCENE II

Inner court of the House of Rimmon; a temple with huge pillars at each side. In the right foreground the seat of the King; at the left, of equal height, the seat of the High Priest. In the background a broad flight of steps, rising to a curtain of cloudy gray, embroidered with two gigantic hands holding thunderbolts. The temple is in half darkness at first. Enter KHAMMA and NUBTA, robed as Kharimati, or religious dancers, in gowns of black gauze with yellow embroideries and mantles.

KHAMMA:

> All is ready for the rites of worship; our lady will play a great part in them. She has put on her Tyrian robes, and all her ornaments.

NUBTA:

> That is a sure sign of a religious purpose. She is most devout, our lady Tsarpi!

KHAMMA:

> A favourite of Rimmon, too! The High Priest has assured her of it. He is a great man,—next to the King, now that Naaman is gone.

NUBTA:

> But if Naaman should come back, healed of the leprosy?

KHAMMA:

> How can he come back? The Hebrew slave that went away with him, when they caught her, said that he was dead. The High Priest has shut her up in the prison of the temple, accusing her of her master's death.

NUBTA:

Yet I think he does not believe it, for I heard him telling our mistress what to do if Naaman should return.

KHAMMA:

What, then?

NUBTA:

She will claim him as her husband. Was she not wedded to him before the god? That is a sacred bond. Only the High Priest can loose it. She will keep her hold on Naaman for the sake of the House of Rimmon. A wife knows her husband's secrets, she can tell—

[*Enter SHUMAKIM, with his flagon, walking unsteadily.*]

KHAMMA:

Hush! here comes the fool Shumakim. He is never sober.

SHUMAKIM: [Laughing.]

Are there two of you? I see two, but that is no proof. I think there is only one, but beautiful enough for two. What were you talking to yourself about, fairest one!

KHAMMA:

About the lady Tsarpi, fool, and what she would do if her husband returned.

SHUMAKIM:

Fie! fie! That is no talk for an innocent fool to hear. Has she a husband?

NUBTA:

You know very well that she is the wife of Lord Naaman.

SHUMAKIM:

I remember that she used to wear his name and his jewels. But I thought he had exchanged her,—for a leprosy.

KHAMMA:

You must have heard that he went away to Samaria to look for healing. Some say that he died on the journey; but others say he has been cured, and is on his way home to his wife.

SHUMAKIM:

It may be, for this is a mad world, and men never know when they are well off,—except us fools. But he must come soon if he would find his wife as he parted from her,—or the city where he left it. The Assyrians have returned with a greater army, and this time they will make an end of us. There is no Naaman how, and the Bull will devour Damascus like a bunch of leeks, flowers and all,—flowers and all, my double-budded fair one! Are you not afraid?

NUBTA:

We belong to the House of Rimmon. He will protect us.

SHUMAKIM:

What? The mighty one who hides behind the curtain there, and tells his secrets to Rezon? No doubt he will take care of you, and of himself. Whatever game is played, the gods never lose. But for the protection, of the common people and the rest of us fools, I would rather have Naaman at the head of an army than all the sacred images between here and Babylon.

KHAMMA:

You are a wicked old man. You mock the god. He will punish you.

SHUMAKIM: [Bitterly.]

How can he punish me? Has he not already made me a fool? Hark, here comes my brother the High Priest, and my brother the King. Rimmon made us all; but nobody knows who made Rimmon, except the High Priest; and he will never tell.

[*Gongs and cymbals sound. Enter REZON with priests, and the King with courtiers. They take their seats. A throng of Khali and Kharimati come in, TSARPI presiding; a sacred dance is performed with torches, burning incense, and chanting, in which TSARPI leads.*]

CHANT.

Hail, mighty Rimmon, ruler of the whirl-storm,
Hail, shaker of mountains, breaker-down of forests,
Hail, thou who roarest terribly in the darkness,
Hail, thou whose arrows flame across the heavens!
Hail, great destroyer, lord of flood and tempest,
In thine anger almighty, in thy wrath eternal,
Thou who delightest in ruin, maker of desolations,
Immeru, Addu, Barku, Rimmon!
See we tremble before thee, low we bow at thine altar,
Have mercy upon us, be favourable unto us,
Save us from our enemy, accept our sacrifice,
Barku, Immeru, Addu, Rimmon!

[*Silence follows, all bowing down.*]

REZON:

O King, last night the counsel from above
Was given in answer to our divination.
Ambassadors must go forthwith to crave
Assyria's pardon, and a second offer
Of the same terms of peace we did reject
Not long ago.

BENHADAD:

Dishonour! Yet I see
No other way! Assyria will refuse,
Or make still harder terms. Disaster, shame
For this gray head, and ruin for Damascus!

REZON:

Yet may we trust Rimmon will favour us,
If we adhere devoutly to his worship.
He will incline his brother-god, the Bull,
To spare us, if we supplicate him now
With costly gifts. Therefore I have prepared
A sacrifice: Rimmon shall be well pleased
With the red blood that bathes his knees to-night!

BENHADAD:

My mind is dark with doubt,—I do forebode
Some horror! Let me go,—I am an old man,—
If Naaman my captain were alive!
But he is dead,—the glory is departed!

[*He rises, trembling, to leave the throne. Trumpet sounds,—NAAMAN'S call;—
enter NAAMAN, followed by soldiers; he kneels at the foot of the throne.*]

BENHADAD: [Half-whispering.]
   Art thou a ghost escaped from Allatu?
   How didst thou pass the seven doors of death?
   O noble ghost I am afraid of thee,
   And yet I love thee,—let me hear thy voice!

NAAMAN:
   No ghost, my King, but one who lives to serve
   Thee and Damascus with his heart and sword
   As in the former days. The only God
   Has healed my leprosy: my life is clean
   To offer to my country and my King.

BENHADAD: [Starting toward him.]
   O welcome to thy King! Thrice welcome!

REZON; [Leaving his seat and coming toward NAAMAN.]
   Stay!
   The leper must appear before the priest,
   The only one who can pronounce him clean.

   [*NAAMAN turns; they stand looking each other in the face.*]

   Yea,—thou art cleansed: Rimmon hath pardoned thee,—
   In answer to the daily prayers of her
   Whom he restores to thine embrace,—thy wife.

   [*TSARPI comes slowly toward NAAMAN.*]

NAAMAN:

　　From him who rules this House will I receive
　　Nothing! I seek no pardon from his priest,
　　No wife of mine among his votaries!

TSARPI: [Holding out her hands.]

　　Am I not yours? Will you renounce our vows?

NAAMAN:

　　The vows were empty,—never made you mine
　　In aught but name. A wife is one who shares
　　Her husband's thought, incorporates his heart
　　With hers by love, and crowns him with her trust.
　　She is God's remedy for loneliness,
　　And God's reward for all the toil of life.
　　This you have never been to me,—and so
　　I give you back again to Rimmon's House
　　Where you belong. Claim what you will of mine,—
　　Not me! I do renounce you,—or release you,—
　　According to the law. If you demand
　　A further cause than what I have declared,
　　I will unfold it fully to the King.

REZON: [Interposing hurriedly.]

　　No need of that! This duteous lady yields
　　To your caprice as she has ever done;
　　She stands a monument of loyalty
　　And woman's meekness.

NAAMAN:

　　　　　　Let her stand for that!
　　Adorn your temple with her piety!

But you in turn restore to me the treasure
You stole at midnight from my tent.

REZON:

What treasure? I have stolen none from you.

NAAMAN:

The very jewel of my soul,—Ruahmah!
My King, the captive maid of Israel,
To whom thou didst commit my broken life
With letters to Samaria,—my light,
My guide, my saviour in this pilgrimage,—
Dost thou remember?

BENHADAD:

I recall the maid,—
But dimly,—for my mind is old and weary.
She was a fearless maid, I trusted her
And gave thee to her charge. Where is she now?

NAAMAN:

This robber fell upon my camp by night,—
While I was with Elisha at the Jordan,—
Slaughtered my soldiers, carried off the maid,
And holds her somewhere in imprisonment.
O give this jewel back to me, my King,
And I will serve thee with a grateful heart
For ever. I will fight for thee, and lead
Thine armies on to glorious victory
Over all foes! Thou shalt no longer fear
The host of Asshur, for thy throne shall stand
Encompassed with a wall of dauntless hearts,

And founded on a mighty people's love,
And guarded by the God of righteousness.

BENHADAD:
    I feel the flame of courage at thy breath
    Leap up among the ashes of despair.
    Thou hast returned to save us! Thou shalt have
    The maid; and thou shalt lead my host again!
    Priest, I command you give her back to him.

REZON:
    O master, I obey thy word as thou
    Hast ever been obedient to the voice
    Of Rimmon. Let thy fiery captain wait
    Until the sacrifice has been performed,
    And he shall have the jewel that he claims.
    Must we not first placate the city's god
    With due allegiance, keep the ancient faith,
    And pay our homage to the Lord of Wrath?

BENHADAD: [Sinking hack upon his throne in fear.]
    I am the faithful son of Rimmon's House,—
    And lo, these many years I worship him!
    My thoughts are troubled,—I am very old,
    But still a King! O Naaman, be patient!
    Priest, let the sacrifice be offered.

[*The High Priest lifts his rod. Gongs and cymbals sound. The curtain is rolled
    back, disclosing the image of Rimmon; a gigantic and hideous idol, with a cruel
    human face, four horns, the mane of a lion, and huge paws stretched in front of
    him enclosing a low altar of black stone. RUAHMAH stands on the altar,*

chained, her arms are bare and folded on her breast. The people prostrate themselves in silence, with signs of astonishment and horror.]

REZON:

Behold the sacrifice! Bow down, bow down!

NAAMAN: [Stabbing him.]

Bow thou, black priest! Down,—down to hell!
Ruahmah! do not die! I come to thee,

[*NAAMAN rushes toward her, attacked by the priests, crying "Sacrilege! Kill him!" But the soldiers stand on the steps and beat them back. He springs upon the altar and clasps her by the hand. Tumult and confusion. The King rises and speaks with a loud voice, silence follows.*]

BENHADAD:

Peace, peace! The King commands all weapons down!
O Naaman, what wouldst thou do? Beware
Lest thou provoke the anger of a god.

NAAMAN:

There is no God but one, the Merciful,
Who gave this perfect woman to my soul
That I might learn through her to worship Him,
And know the meaning of immortal Love.
Whom God hath joined together, all the Powers
Of hate and falsehood never shall divide.

BENHADAD: [Agitated.]

Yet she is consecrated, bound, and doomed
To sacrificial death; but thou art sworn
To live and lead my host,—Hast thou not sworn?

120

NAAMAN:

    Only if thou wilt keep thy word to me!
    Break with this idol of iniquity
    Whose shadow makes a darkness in the land;
    Give her to me who gave me back to thee;
    And I will lead thine army to renown
    And plant thy banners on the hill of triumph.
    But if she dies, I die with her, defying Rimmon.

[Cries of "Spare them! Release her! Give us back our Captain!" and "Sacrilege!
Let them die!" Then silence, all turning toward the King.]

BENHADAD:

    Is this the choice? Must we destroy the bond
    Of ancient faith, or slay the city's living hope!
    I am an old, old man,—and yet the King!
    Must I decide?—O let me ponder it!

[His head sinks upon his breast. All stand eagerly looking at him.]

NAAMAN; [Holding her in his arms.]
    Ruahmah, my Ruahmah! I have come
    To thee at last! And art thou satisfied?

RUAHMAH: [Looking into his face.]
    Belovéd, my belovéd, I am glad
    Forever! Come what may, the only God
    Is Love,—and He will never part us.

SONGS OUT OF DOORS

I.

OF BIRDS AND FLOWERS

THE VEERY

The moonbeams over Arno's vale in silver flood were pouring,
When first I heard the nightingale a long-lost love deploring.
So passionate, so full of pain, it sounded strange and eerie;
I longed to hear a simpler strain,—the woodnotes of the veery.

The laverock sings a bonny lay above the Scottish heather;
It sprinkles down from far away like light and love together;
He drops the golden notes to greet his brooding mate, his dearie;
I only know one song more sweet,—the vespers of the veery.

In English gardens, green and bright and full of fruity treasure,
I heard the blackbird with delight repeat his merry measure:
The ballad was a pleasant one, the tune was loud and cheery,
And yet, with every setting sun, I listened for the veery.

But far away, and far away, the tawny thrush is singing;
New England woods, at close of day, with that clear chant are ringing:
And when my light of life is low, and heart and flesh are weary,
I fain would hear, before I go, the wood-notes of the veery.

1895.

THE SONG-SPARROW

There is a bird I know so well,
 It seems as if he must have sung
 Beside my crib when I was young;
Before I knew the way to spell
 The name of even the smallest bird,
 His gentle-joyful song I heard.
Now see if you can tell, my dear,
What bird it is that, every year,
Sings *"Sweet—sweet—sweet—very merry cheer."*

He comes in March, when winds are strong,
 And snow returns to hide the earth;
 But still he warms his heart with mirth,
And waits for May. He lingers long
 While flowers fade; and every day
 Repeats his small, contented lay;
As if to say, we need not fear
The season's change, if love is here
With *"Sweet—sweet—sweet—very merry cheer."*

He does not wear a Joseph's-coat
 Of many colours, smart and gay;
 His suit is Quaker brown and gray,
With darker patches at his throat.
 And yet of all the well-dressed throng
 Not one can sing so brave a song.
It makes the pride of looks appear
A vain and foolish thing, to hear
His *"Sweet—sweet—sweet—very merry cheer."*

126

A lofty place he does not love,
    But sits by choice, and well at ease,
    In hedges, and in little trees
That stretch their slender arms above
    The meadow-brook; and there he sings
    Till all the field with pleasure rings;
And so he tells in every ear,
That lowly homes to heaven are near
In *"Sweet—sweet—sweet—very merry cheer."*

I like the tune, I like the words;
    They seem so true, so free from art,
    So friendly, and so full of heart,
That if but one of all the birds
    Could be my comrade everywhere,
    My little brother of the air,
I'd choose the song-sparrow, my dear,
Because he'd bless me, every year,
With *"Sweet—sweet—sweet—very merry cheer."*

1895.

THE MARYLAND YELLOW-THROAT

When May bedecks the naked trees
With tassels and embroideries,
And many blue-eyed violets beam
Along the edges of the stream,
I hear a voice that seems to say,
Now near at hand, now far away,
    "Witchery—witchery—witchery."

An incantation so serene,
So innocent, befits the scene:
There's magic in that small bird's note—
See, there he flits—the Yellow-throat;
A living sunbeam, tipped with wings,
A spark of light that shines and sings
    "Witchery—witchery—witchery."

You prophet with a pleasant name,
If out of Mary-land you came,
You know the way that thither goes
Where Mary's lovely garden grows:
Fly swiftly back to her, I pray,
And try to call her down this way,
    "Witchery—witchery—witchery."

Tell her to leave her cockle-shells,
And all her little silver bells
That blossom into melody,
And all her maids less fair than she.
She does not need these pretty things,
For everywhere she comes, she brings
    "Witchery—witchery—witchery."

The woods are greening overhead,
And flowers adorn each mossy bed;
The waters babble as they run—
One thing is lacking, only one:
If Mary were but here to-day,
I would believe your charming lay,
    "Witchery—witchery—witchery."

Along the shady road I look—
Who's coming now across the brook?
A woodland maid, all robed in white—
The leaves dance round her with delight,
The stream laughs out beneath her feet—
Sing, merry bird, the charm's complete,
   "Witchery—witchery—witchery!"

1895.

THE WHIP-POOR-WILL

Do you remember, father,—
It seems so long ago,—
The day we fished together
Along the Pocono?
At dusk I waited for you,
Beside the lumber-mill,
And there I heard a hidden bird
That chanted, "whip-poor-will,"
"Whippoorwill! whippoorwill!"
Sad and shrill,—*"whippoorwill!"*

The place was all deserted;
The mill-wheel hung at rest;
The lonely star of evening
Was throbbing in the west;
The veil of night was falling;
The winds were folded still;
And everywhere the trembling air
   Re-echoed "whip-poor-will!"

"Whippoorwill! whippoorwill!"
Sad and shrill,—*"whippoorwill!"*

You seemed so long in coming,
   I felt so much alone;
The wide, dark world was round me,
   And life was all unknown;
The hand of sorrow touched me,
   And made my senses thrill
With all the pain that haunts the strain
   Of mournful whip-poor-will.
"Whippoorwill! whippoorwill!"
   Sad and shrill,—*"whippoorwill!"*

What knew I then of trouble?
   An idle little lad,
I had not learned the lessons
   That make men wise and sad.
I dreamed of grief and parting,
   And something seemed to fill
My heart with tears, while in my ears
   Resounded "whip-poor-will."
"Whippoorwill! whippoorwill!"
   Sad and shrill,—*"whippoorwill!"*

'Twas but a cloud of sadness,
   That lightly passed away;
But I have learned the meaning
   Of sorrow, since that day.
For nevermore at twilight,
   Beside the silent mill,

130

I'll wait for you, in the falling dew,
    And hear the whip-poor-will.
    "Whippoorwill! whippoorwill!"
    Sad and shrill,—*"whippoorwill!"*

But if you still remember
    In that fair land of light,
The pains and fears that touch us
    Along this edge of night,
I think all earthly grieving,
    And all our mortal ill,
To you must seem like a sad boy's dream
    Who hears the whip-poor-will.
    "Whippoorwill! whippoorwill!"
    A passing thrill,—*"whippoorwill!"*

1894.

WINGS OF A DOVE

I

At sunset, when the rosy light was dying
    Far down the pathway of the west,
I saw a lonely dove in silence flying,
        To be at rest.

Pilgrim of air, I cried, could I but borrow
    Thy wandering wings, thy freedom blest,
I'd fly away from every careful sorrow,
        And find my rest.

But when the filmy veil of dusk was falling,
   Home flew the dove to seek his nest,
Deep in the forest where his mate was calling
      To love and rest.

Peace, heart of mine! no longer sigh to wander;
   Lose not thy life in barren quest.
There are no happy islands over yonder;
         Come home and rest.

1874.

THE HERMIT THRUSH

O wonderful! How liquid clear
The molten gold of that ethereal tone,
Floating and falling through the wood alone,
A hermit-hymn poured out for God to hear!

O holy, holy! holy! Hyaline,
Long light, low light, glory of eventide!
Love far away, far up,—love divine!
Little love, too, for ever, ever near,
Warm love, earth love, tender love of mine,
In the leafy dark where you hide,
You are mine,—mine,—mine!

Ah, my belovèd, do you feel with me
The hidden virtue of that melody,

The rapture and the purity of love,
The heavenly joy that can not find the word?

Then, while we wait again to hear the bird,
Come very near to me, and do not move,—
Now, hermit of the woodland, fill anew
The cool, green cup of air with harmony,
And we will drink the wine of love with you.

May, 1908.

SEA-GULLS OF MANHATTAN

Children of the elemental mother,
    Born upon some lonely island shore
Where the wrinkled ripples run and whisper,
    Where the crested billows plunge and roar;
Long-winged, tireless roamers and adventurers,
    Fearless breasters of the wind and sea,
In the far-off solitary places
    I have seen you floating wild and free!

Here the high-built cities rise around you;
    Here the cliffs that tower east and west,
Honeycombed with human habitations,
    Have no hiding for the sea-bird's nest:
Here the river flows begrimed and troubled;
    Here the hurrying, panting vessels fume,
Restless, up and down the watery highway,
    While a thousand chimneys vomit gloom.

Toil and tumult, conflict and confusion,
    Clank and clamour of the vast machine
Human hands have built for human bondage—
    Yet amid it all you float serene;
Circling, soaring, sailing, swooping lightly
    Down to glean your harvest from the wave;
In your heritage of air and water,
    You have kept the freedom Nature gave.

Even so the wild-woods of Manhattan
    Saw your wheeling flocks of white and gray;
Even so you fluttered, followed, floated,
    Round the *Half-Moon* creeping up the bay;
Even so your voices creaked and chattered,
    Laughing shrilly o'er the tidal rips,
While your black and beady eyes were glistening
    Round the sullen British prison-ships.

Children of the elemental mother,
    Fearless floaters 'mid the double blue,
From the crowded boats that cross the ferries
    Many a longing heart goes out to you.
Though the cities climb and close around us,
    Something tells us that our souls are free,
While the sea-gulls fly above the harbour,
    While the river flows to meet the sea!

December, 1905.

THE RUBY-CROWNED KINGLET

I

Where's your kingdom, little king?
　　Where the land you call your own,
　　Where your palace and your throne?
Fluttering lightly on the wing
　　Through the blossom-world of May,
　　Whither lies your royal way,
　　　　　　　Little king?

Far to northward lies a land
Where the trees together stand
Closely as the blades of wheat
When the summer is complete.
Rolling like an ocean wide
Over vale and mountainside,
Balsam, hemlock, spruce and pine,—
All those mighty trees are mine.
There's a river flowing free,—
All its waves belong to me.
There's a lake so clear and bright
Stars shine out of it all night;
Rowan-berries round it spread
Like a belt of coral red.
Never royal garden planned
Fair as my Canadian land!
There I build my summer nest,
There I reign and there I rest,
While from dawn to dark I sing,
Happy kingdom! Lucky king!

Back again, my little king!
　　Is your happy kingdom lost
　　To the rebel knave, Jack Frost?
Have you felt the snow-flakes sting?
　　Houseless, homeless in October,
　　Whither now? Your plight is sober,
　　　　Exiled king!

Far to southward lie the regions
Where my loyal flower-legions
Hold possession of the year,
Filling every month with cheer.
Christmas wakes the winter rose;
New Year daffodils unclose;
Yellow jasmine through the wood
Flows in February flood,
Dropping from the tallest trees
Golden streams that never freeze.
Thither now I take my flight
Down the pathway of the night,
Till I see the southern moon
Glisten on the broad lagoon,
Where the cypress' dusky green,
And the dark magnolia's sheen,
Weave a shelter round my home.
There the snow-storms never come;
There the bannered mosses gray
Like a curtain gently sway,
Hanging low on every side
Round the covert inhere I bide,

Till the March azalea glows,
Royal red and heavenly rose,
Through the Carolina glade
Where my winter home is made.
There I hold my southern court,
Full of merriment and sport:
There I take my ease and sing,
Happy kingdom! Lucky king!

III

Little boaster, vagrant king,
   Neither north nor south is yours,
   You've no kingdom that endures!
Wandering every fall and spring,
With your ruby crown so slender,
Are you only a Pretender,
            Landless king?

Never king by right divine
Ruled a richer realm than mine!
What are lands and golden crowns,
Armies, fortresses and towns,
Jewels, sceptres, robes and rings,—
What are these to song and wings?
Everywhere that I can fly,
There I own the earth and sky;
Everywhere that I can sing,
There I'm happy as a king.

1900.

THE ANGLER'S REVEILLE

What time the rose of dawn is laid across the lips of night,
And all the little watchman-stars have fallen asleep in light,
'Tis then a merry wind awakes, and runs from tree to tree,
And borrows words from all the birds to sound the reveille.

This is the carol the Robin throws
        Over the edge of the valley;
Listen how boldly it flows,
        Sally on sally:
                Tirra-lirra,
                Early morn,
                New born!
                Day is near,
                Clear, clear.
                Down the river
                All a-quiver,
                Fish are breaking;
                Time for waking,
                Tup, tup, tup!
                Do you hear?
                All clear—
                Wake up!

The phantom flood of dreams has ebbed and vanished with the
    dark,
And like a dove the heart forsakes the prison of the ark;
Now forth she fares thro' friendly woods and diamond-fields of
    dew,
While every voice cries out "Rejoice!" as if the world were new.

This is the ballad the Bluebird sings,
 Unto his mate replying,
Shaking the tune from his wings
 While he is flying:
  Surely, surely, surely,
   Life is dear
   Even here.
   Blue above,
   You to love,
   Purely, purely, purely.

There's wild azalea on the hill, and iris down the dell,
And just one spray of lilac still abloom beside the well;
The columbine adorns the rocks, the laurel buds grow pink,
Along the stream white arums gleam, and violets bend to drink.

This is the song of the Yellow-throat,
 Fluttering gaily beside you;
Hear how each voluble note
 Offers to guide you:

   Which way, sir?
   I say, sir,
   Let me teach you,
   I beseech you!
   Are you wishing
   Jolly fishing?
   This way, sir!
   I'll teach you.

Then come, my friend, forget your foes and leave your fears behind,
And wander forth to try your luck, with cheerful, quiet mind;
For be your fortune great or small, you take what God will give,
And all the day your heart will say, "'Tis luck enough to live."

This is the song the Brown Thrush flings
        Out of his thicket of roses;
Hark how it bubbles and rings,
        Mark how it closes:

> *Luck, luck,*
> *What luck?*
> *Good enough for me,*
> *I'm alive, you see!*
> *Sun shining,*
> *No repining;*
> *Never borrow*
> *Idle sorrow;*
> *Drop it!*
> *Cover it up!*
> *Hold your cup!*
> *Joy will fill it,*
> *Don't spill it,*
> *Steady, be ready,*
> *Good luck!*

1899.

A NOVEMBER DAISY

Afterthought of summer's bloom!
Late arrival at the feast,

Coming when the songs have ceased
And the merry guests departed,
Leaving but an empty room,
Silence, solitude, and gloom,—
Are you lonely, heavy-hearted;
You, the last of all your kind,
Nodding in the autumn wind;
Now that all your friends are flown,
Blooming late and all alone?

Nay, I wrong you, little flower,
Reading mournful mood of mine
In your looks, that give no sign
Of a spirit dark and cheerless!
You possess the heavenly power
That rejoices in the hour.
Glad, contented, free, and fearless,
Lift a sunny face to heaven
When a sunny day is given!
Make a summer of your own,
Blooming late and all alone!

Once the daisies gold and white
Sea-like through the meadow rolled:
Once my heart could hardly hold
All its pleasures. I remember,
In the flood of youth's delight
Separate joys were lost to sight.
That was summer! Now November
Sets the perfect flower apart;
Gives each blossom of the heart

Meaning, beauty, grace unknown,—
Blooming late and all alone.

November, 1899.

THE LILY OF YORROW

Deep in the heart of the forest the lily of Yorrow is growing;
Blue is its cup as the sky, and with mystical odour o'erflowing;
Faintly it falls through the shadowy glades when the south wind is
    blowing.

Sweet are the primroses pale and the violets after a shower;
Sweet are the borders of pinks and the blossoming grapes on the
    bower;
Sweeter by far is the breath of that far-away woodland flower.

Searching and strange in its sweetness, it steals like a perfume
    enchanted
Under the arch of the forest, and all who perceive it are haunted,
Seeking and seeking for ever, till sight of the lily is granted.

Who can describe how it grows, with its chalice of lazuli leaning
Over a crystalline spring, where the ferns and the mosses are
    greening?
Who can imagine its beauty, or utter the depth of its meaning?

Calm of the journeying stars, and repose of the mountains olden,
Joy of the swift-running rivers, and glory of sunsets golden,
Secrets that cannot be told in the heart of the flower are holden.

Surely to see it is peace and the crown of a lifelong endeavour;
Surely to pluck it is gladness,—but they who have found it can never
Tell of the gladness and peace: they are hid from our vision for ever.

'Twas but a moment ago that a comrade was walking near me:
Turning aside from the pathway he murmured a greeting to cheer
    me,—
Then he was lost in the shade, and I called but he did not hear me.

Why should I dream he is dead, and bewail him with passionate
    sorrow?
Surely I know there is gladness in finding the lily of Yorrow:
He has discovered it first, and perhaps I shall find it to-morrow.

1894.

II.

OF SKIES AND SEASONS

IF ALL THE SKIES

If all the skies were sunshine,
  Our faces would be fain
To feel once more upon them
  The cooling plash of rain.

If all the world were music,
  Our hearts would often long
For one sweet strain of silence,
  To break the endless song.

If life were always merry,
  Our souls would seek relief,
And rest from weary laughter
  In the quiet arms of grief.

THE AFTER-ECHO

How long the echoes love to play
  Around the shore of silence, as a wave
  Retreating circles down the sand!

144

One after one, with sweet delay,
The mellow sounds that cliff and island gave,
    Have lingered in the crescent bay,
    Until, by lightest breezes fanned,
They float far off beyond the dying day
            And leave it still as death.
                    But hark,—
            Another singing breath
Comes from the edge of dark;
            A note as clear and slow
        As falls from some enchanted bell,
        Or spirit, passing from the world below,
                That whispers back, Farewell.
    So in the heart,
When, fading slowly down the past,
    Fond memories depart,
And each that leaves it seems the last;
Long after all the rest are flown,
Returns a solitary tone,—
The after-echo of departed years,—
And touches all the soul to tears.

                                        1871.

DULCIORA

A tear that trembles for a little while
Upon the trembling eyelid, till the world
Wavers within its circle like a dream,
Holds more of meaning in its narrow orb
Than all the distant landscape that it blurs.

A smile that hovers round a mouth beloved,
Like the faint pulsing of the Northern Light,
And grows in silence to an amber dawn
Born in the sweetest depths of trustful eyes,
Is dearer to the soul than sun or star.

A joy that falls into the hollow heart
From some far-lifted height of love unseen,
Unknown, makes a more perfect melody
Than hidden brooks that murmur in the dusk,
Or fall athwart the cliff with wavering gleam.

Ah, not for their own sake are earth and sky
And the fair ministries of Nature dear,
But as they set themselves unto the tune
That fills our life; as light mysterious
Flows from within and glorifies the world.

For so a common wayside blossom, touched
With tender thought, assumes a grace more sweet
Than crowns the royal lily of the South;
And so a well-remembered perfume seems
The breath of one who breathes in Paradise.

1872.

MATINS

Flowers rejoice when night is done,
Lift their heads to greet the sun;
Sweetest looks and odours raise,
In a silent hymn of praise.

So my heart would turn away
From the darkness to the day;
Lying open in God's sight
Like a flower in the light.

THE PARTING AND THE COMING GUEST

Who watched the worn-out Winter die?
   Who, peering through the window-pane
   At nightfall, under sleet and rain
Saw the old graybeard totter by?
Who listened to his parting sigh,
   The sobbing of his feeble breath,
   His whispered colloquy with Death,
   And when his all of life was done
Stood near to bid a last good-bye?
   Of all his former friends not one
Saw the forsaken Winter die.

Who welcomed in the maiden Spring?
   Who heard her footfall, swift and light
   As fairy-dancing in the night?
Who guessed what happy dawn would bring
The flutter of her bluebird's wing,
The blossom of her mayflower-face
   To brighten every shady place?
   One morning, down the village street,
"Oh, here am I," we heard her sing,—
   And none had been awake to greet
The coming of the maiden Spring.

But look, her violet eyes are wet
  With bright, unfallen, dewy tears;
  And in her song my fancy hears
A note of sorrow trembling yet.
Perhaps, beyond the town, she met
  Old Winter as he limped away
  To die forlorn, and let him lay
  His weary head upon her knee,
And kissed his forehead with regret
  For one so gray and lonely,—see,
Her eyes with tender tears are wet.

And so, by night, while we were all at rest,
I think the coming sped the parting guest.

1873.

WHEN TULIPS BLOOM

I

When tulips bloom in Union Square,
And timid breaths of vernal air
  Go wandering down the dusty town,
Like children lost in Vanity Fair;

When every long, unlovely row
Of westward houses stands aglow,
  And leads the eyes to sunset skies
Beyond the hills where green trees grow;

Then weary seems the street parade,
And weary books, and weary trade:
   I'm only wishing to go a-fishing;
For this the month of May was made.

II

I guess the pussy-willows now
Are creeping out on every bough
   Along the brook; and robins look
For early worms behind the plough.

The thistle-birds have changed their dun,
For yellow coats, to match the sun;
   And in the same array of flame
The Dandelion Show's begun.

The flocks of young anemones
Are dancing round the budding trees:
   Who can help wishing to go a-fishing
In days as full of joy as these?

III

I think the meadow-lark's clear sound
Leaks upward slowly from the ground,
   While on the wing the bluebirds ring
Their wedding-bells to woods around.

The flirting chewink calls his dear
Behind the bush; and very near,

Where water flows, where green grass grows,
Song-sparrows gently sing, "Good cheer."

And, best of all, through twilight's calm
The hermit-thrush repeats his psalm.
　　How much I'm wishing to go a-fishing
In days so sweet with music's balm!

IV

'Tis not a proud desire of mine;
I ask for nothing superfine;
　　No heavy weight, no salmon great,
To break the record, or my line.

Only an idle little stream,
Whose amber waters softly gleam,
　　Where I may wade through woodland shade,
And cast the fly, and loaf, and dream:

Only a trout or two, to dart
From foaming pools, and try my art:
　　'Tis all I'm wishing—old-fashioned fishing,
And just a day on Nature's heart.

1894.

SPRING IN THE NORTH

I

Ah, who will tell me, in these leaden days,
Why the sweet Spring delays,
And where she hides,—the dear desire
    Of every heart that longs
For bloom, and fragrance, and the ruby fire
Of maple-buds along the misty hills,
And that immortal call which fills
    The waiting wood with songs?
The snow-drops came so long ago,
    It seemed that Spring was near!
    But then returned the snow
With biting winds, and earth grew sere,
    And sullen clouds drooped low
To veil the sadness of a hope deferred:
Then rain, rain, rain, incessant rain
    Beat on the window-pane,

Through which I watched the solitary bird
That braved the tempest, buffeted and tossed
With rumpled feathers down the wind again.
    Oh, were the seeds all lost
When winter laid the wild flowers in their tomb?
    I searched the woods in vain
For blue hepaticas, and trilliums white,
And trailing arbutus, the Spring's delight,
Starring the withered leaves with rosy bloom.
    But every night the frost
To all my longing spoke a silent nay,

And told me Spring was far away.
Even the robins were too cold to sing,
Except a broken and discouraged note,—
Only the tuneful sparrow, on whose throat
Music has put her triple finger-print,
Lifted his head and sang my heart a hint,—
"Wait, wait, wait! oh, wait a while for Spring!"

II

But now, Carina, what divine amends
For all delay! What sweetness treasured up,
    What wine of joy that blends
A hundred flavours in a single cup,
Is poured into this perfect day!
For look, sweet heart, here are the early flowers
    That lingered on their way,
Thronging in haste to kiss the feet of May,
Entangled with the bloom of later hours,—
Anemones and cinque-foils, violets blue
And white, and iris richly gleaming through
The grasses of the meadow, and a blaze
Of butter-cups and daisies in the field,
    Filling the air with praise,
As if a chime of golden bells had pealed!
    The frozen songs within the breast
Of silent birds that hid in leafless woods,
    Melt into rippling floods
    Of gladness unrepressed.
Now oriole and bluebird, thrush and lark,
Warbler and wren and vireo,
Mingle their melody; the living spark

Of love has touched the fuel of desire,
And every heart leaps up in singing fire.

It seems as if the land
Were breathing deep beneath the sun's caress,
Trembling with tenderness,
While all the woods expand,
In shimmering clouds of rose and gold and green,
To veil a joy too sacred to be seen.

III

Come, put your hand in mine,
True love, long sought and found at last,
And lead me deep into the Spring divine
That makes amends for all the wintry past.
For all the flowers and songs I feared to miss
Arrive with you;
And in the lingering pressure of your kiss
My dreams come true;
And in the promise of your generous eyes
I read the mystic sign
Of joy more perfect made
Because so long delayed,
And bliss enhanced by rapture of surprise.

Ah, think not early love alone is strong;
He loveth best whose heart has learned to wait:
Dear messenger of Spring that tarried long,
You're doubly dear because you come so late.

SPRING IN THE SOUTH

Now in the oak the sap of life is welling,
　Tho' to the bough the rusty leafage clings;
Now on the elm the misty buds are swelling;
　Every little pine-wood grows alive with wings;
Blue-jays are fluttering, yodeling and crying,
　Meadow-larks sailing low above the faded grass,
Red-birds whistling clear, silent robins flying,—
　Who has waked the birds up? What has come to pass?

Last year's cotton-plants, desolately bowing,
　Tremble in the March-wind, ragged and forlorn,
Red are the hillsides of the early ploughing,
　Gray are the lowlands, waiting for the corn.
Earth seems asleep, but she is only feigning;
　Deep in her bosom thrills a sweet unrest;
Look where the jasmine lavishly is raining
　Jove's golden shower into Danäe's breast!

Now on the plum-tree a snowy bloom is sifted,
　Now on the peach-tree, the glory of the rose,
Far o'er the hills a tender haze is drifted,
　Full to the brim the yellow river flows.
Dark cypress boughs with vivid jewels glisten,
　Greener than emeralds shining in the sun.
Whence comes the magic? Listen, sweetheart, listen!
　The mocking-bird is singing: Spring is begun.

Hark, in his song no tremor of misgiving!
　All of his heart he pours into his lay,—
"Love, love, love, and pure delight of living:

Winter is forgotten: here's a happy day!"
Fair in your face I read the flowery presage,
    Snowy on your brow and rosy on your mouth:
Sweet in your voice I hear the season's message,—
    Love, love, love, and Spring in the South!

1904.

HOW SPRING COMES TO SHASTA JIM

I never seen no "red gods"; I dunno wot's a "lure";
But if it's sumpin' takin', then Spring has got it sure;
An' it doesn't need no Kiplins, ner yet no London Jacks,
To make up guff about it, w'ile settin' in their shacks.

It's sumpin' very simple 'at happens in the Spring,
But it changes all the lookin's of every blessed thing;
The buddin' woods look bigger, the mounting twice as high,
But the house looks kindo smaller, tho I couldn't tell ye why.

It's cur'ous wot a show-down the month of April makes,
Between the reely livin', an' the things 'at's only fakes!
Machines an' barns an' buildin's, they never give no sign;
But the livin' things look lively w'en Spring is on the line.

She doesn't come too suddin, ner she doesn't come too slow;
Her gaits is some cayprishus, an' the next ye never know,—
A single-foot o' sunshine, a buck o' snow er hail—
But don't be disapp'inted, fer Spring ain't goin' ter fail.

She's loopin' down the hillside,—the driffs is fadin' out.
She's runnin' down the river,—d'ye see them risin' trout?

155

She's loafin' down the canyon,—the squaw-bed's growin' blue,
An' the teeny Johnny-jump-ups is jest a-peekin' thru.

A thousan' miles o' pine-trees, with Douglas firs between,
Is waitin' fer her fingers to freshen up their green;
With little tips o' brightness the firs 'ill sparkle thick,
An' every yaller pine-tree, a giant candlestick!

The underbrush is risin' an' spreadin' all around,
Jest like a mist o' greenness 'at hangs above the ground;
A million manzanitas 'ill soon be full o' pink;
So saddle up, my sonny,—it's time to ride, I think!

We'll ford er swim the river, becos there ain't no bridge;
We'll foot the gulches careful, an' lope along the ridge;
We'll take the trail to Nowhere, an' travel till we tire,
An' camp beneath a pine-tree, an' sleep beside the fire.

We'll see the blue-quail chickens, an' hear 'em pipin' clear;
An' p'raps we'll sight a brown-bear, er else a bunch o' deer;
But nary a heathen goddess or god 'ill meet our eyes;
For why? There isn't any! They're jest a pack o' lies!

Oh, wot's the use o' "red gods," an' "Pan," an' all that stuff?
The natcheral facts o' Springtime is wonderful enuff!
An' if there's Someone made 'em I guess He understood,
To be alive in Springtime would make a man feel good.

California, 1913.

THE FIRST BIRD O' SPRING

TO OLIVE WHEELER

Winter on Mount Shasta,
April down below;
Golden hours of glowing sun
Sudden showers of snow!
Under leafless thickets
Early wild-flowers cling;
But, oh, my dear, I'm fain to hear
The first bird o' Spring!

Alders are in tassel,
Maples are in bud;
Waters of the blue McCloud
Shout in joyful flood;
Through the giant pine-trees
Flutters many a wing;
But, oh, my dear, I long to hear
The first bird o' Spring!

Candle-light and fire-light
Mingle at "the Bend";
'Neath the roof of Bo-hai-pan
Light and shadow blend.
Sweeter than a wood-thrush
A maid begins to sing;
And, oh, my dear, I'm glad to hear
The first bird o' Spring!

The Bend, California, April 29, 1913.

A BUNCH OF TROUT-FLIES

FOR ARCHIE RUTLEDGE

Here's a half-a-dozen flies,
Just about the proper size
For the trout of Dickey's Run,—
Luck go with them every one!

Dainty little feathered beauties,
Listen now, and learn your duties:
Not to tangle in the box;
Not to catch on logs or rocks,
Boughs that wave or weeds that float,
Nor in the angler's "pants" or coat!
Not to lure the glutton frog
From his banquet in the bog;
Nor the lazy chub to fool,
Splashing idly round the pool;
Nor the sullen horned pout
From the mud to hustle out!

None of this vulgarian crew,
Dainty flies, is game for you.
Darting swiftly through the air
Guided by the angler's care,
Light upon the flowing stream
Like a winged fairy dream;
Float upon the water dancing,
Through the lights and shadows glancing,
Till the rippling current brings you,
And with quiet motion swings you,

Where a speckled beauty lies
Watching you with hungry eyes.

Here's your game and here's your prize!
Hover near him, lure him, tease him,
Do your very best to please him,
Dancing on the water foamy,
Like the frail and fair Salome,
Till the monarch yields at last,
Rises, and you have him fast!
Then remember well your duty,—
Do not lose, but land, your booty;
For the finest fish of all is
Salvelinus Fontinalis.

So, you plumed illusions, go,
Let my comrade Archie know
Every day he goes a-fishing
I'll be with him in well-wishing.
Most of all when lunch is laid
In the dappled orchard shade,
With Will, Corinne, and Dixie too,
Sitting as we used to do
Round the white cloth on the grass
While the lazy hours pass,
And the brook's contented tune
Lulls the sleepy afternoon,—
Then's the time my heart will be
With that pleasant company!

June 17, 1913.

159

A NOON-SONG

There are songs for the morning and songs for the night,
　　For sunrise and sunset, the stars and the moon;
But who will give praise to the fulness of light,
　　And sing us a song of the glory of noon?
　　　　Oh, the high noon, the clear noon,
　　　　The noon with golden crest;
　　　　When the blue sky burns, and the great sun turns
　　　　With his face to the way of the west!

How swiftly he rose in the dawn of his strength!
　　How slowly he crept as the morning wore by!
Ah, steep was the climbing that led him at length
　　To the height of his throne in the wide summer sky.
　　　　Oh, the long toil, the slow toil,
　　　　The toil that may not rest,
　　　　Till the sun looks down from his journey's crown,
　　　　To the wonderful way of the west!

Then a quietness falls over meadow and hill,
　　The wings of the wind in the forest are furled,
The river runs softly, the birds are all still,
　　The workers are resting all over the world.
　　　　Oh, the good hour, the kind hour,
　　　　The hour that calms the breast!
　　　　Little inn half-way on the road of the day,
　　　　Where it follows the turn to the west!

There's a plentiful feast in the maple-tree shade,
　　The lilt of a song to an old-fashioned tune,
The talk of a friend, or the kiss of a maid,

160

To sweeten the cup that we drink to the noon.
Oh, the deep noon, the full noon,
  Of all the day the best!
When the blue sky burns, and the great sun turns
  To his home by the way of the west!

1906.

TURN O' THE TIDE

The tide flows in to the harbour,—
  The bold tide, the gold tide, the flood o' the sunlit sea,—
And the little ships riding at anchor,
  Are swinging and slanting their prows to the ocean, panting
    To lift their wings to the wide wild air,
    And venture a voyage they know not where,—
  To fly away and be free!

The tide runs out of the harbour,—
  The low tide, the slow tide, the ebb o' the moonlit bay,—
And the little ships rocking at anchor,
  Are rounding and turning their bows to the landward, yearning
    To breathe the breath of the sun-warmed strand,
    To rest in the lee of the high hill land,—
To hold their haven and stay!

My heart goes round with the vessels,—
  My wild heart, my child heart, in love with the sea and the land,—
And the turn o' the tide passes through it,
  In rising and falling with mystical currents, calling
    At morn, to range where the far waves foam,

At night, to a harbour in love's true home,
   With the hearts that understand!

Seal Harbour, August 12, 1911.

SIERRA MADRE

O mother mountains! billowing far to the snowlands,
   Robed in aërial amethyst, silver, and blue,
Why do ye look so proudly down on the lowlands?
   What have their groves and gardens to do with you?

Theirs is the languorous charm of the orange and myrtle,
   Theirs are the fruitage and fragrance of Eden of old,—
Broad-boughed oaks in the meadows fair and fertile,
   Dark-leaved orchards gleaming with globes of gold.

You, in your solitude standing, lofty and lonely,
   Bear neither garden nor grove on your barren breasts;
Rough is the rock-loving growth of your canyons, and only
   Storm-battered pines and fir-trees cling to your crests.

Why are ye throned so high, and arrayed in splendour
   Richer than all the fields at your feet can claim?
What is your right, ye rugged peaks, to the tender
   Queenly promise and pride of the mother-name?

Answered the mountains, dim in the distance dreaming:
   "Ours are the forests that treasure the riches of rain;
Ours are the secret springs and the rivulets gleaming
   Silverly down through the manifold bloom of the plain.

"Vain were the toiling of men in the dust of the dry land,
    Vain were the ploughing and planting in waterless fields,
Save for the life-giving currents we send from the sky land,
    Save for the fruit our embrace with the storm-cloud yields."

O mother mountains, Madre Sierra, I love you!
    Rightly you reign o'er the vale that your bounty fills,—
Kissed by the sun, or with big, bright stars above you,—
    I murmur your name and lift up mine eyes to the hills.

Pasadena, March, 1913.

SCHOOL

I put my heart to school
In the world where men grow wise:
"Go out," I said, "and learn the rule;
'Come back when you win a prize.'"

My heart came back again:
"Now where is the prize?" I cried.—
"The rule was false, and the prize was pain,
And the teacher's name was Pride."

I put my heart to school
In the woods where veeries sing
And brooks run clear and cool,
In the fields where wild flowers spring.

"And why do you stay so long
My heart, and where do you roam?"

163

The answer came with a laugh and a song,—
"I find this school is home."

April, 1901.

INDIAN SUMMER

A silken curtain veils the skies,
And half conceals from pensive eyes
    The bronzing tokens of the fall;
A calmness broods upon the hills,
And summer's parting dream distils
    A charm of silence over all.

The stacks of corn, in brown array,
Stand waiting through the tranquil day,
    Like tattered wigwams on the plain;
The tribes that find a shelter there
Are phantom peoples, forms of air,
    And ghosts of vanished joy and pain.

At evening when the crimson crest
Of sunset passes down the West,
    I hear the whispering host returning;
On far-off fields, by elm and oak,
I see the lights, I smell the smoke,—
    The Camp-fires of the Past are burning.

Tertius and Henry van Dyke.

November, 1903.

LIGHT BETWEEN THE TREES

Long, long, long the trail
   Through the brooding forest-gloom,
Down the shadowy, lonely vale
   Into silence, like a room
      Where the light of life has fled,
   And the jealous curtains close
   Round the passionless repose
Of the silent dead.

Plod, plod, plod away,
   Step by step in mouldering moss;
Thick branches bar the day
   Over languid streams that cross
      Softly, slowly, with a sound
   Like a smothered weeping,
   In their aimless creeping
      Through enchanted ground.

"Yield, yield, yield thy quest,"
   Whispers through the woodland deep:
"Come to me and be at rest;
I am slumber, I am sleep."
      Then the weary feet would fail,
   But the never-daunted will
   Urges "Forward, forward still!
      Press along the trail!"

Breast, breast, breast the slope
   See, the path is growing steep.
Hark! a little song of hope

Where the stream begins to leap.
   Though the forest, far and wide,
Still shuts out the bending blue,
We shall finally win through,
   Cross the long divide.

On, on, on we tramp!
   Will the journey never end?
Over yonder lies the camp;
   Welcome waits us there, my friend,
      Can we reach it ere the night?
   Upward, upward, never fear!
   Look, the summit must be near;
      See the line of light!

Red, red, red the shine
   Of the splendour in the west,
Glowing through the ranks of pine,
   Clear along the mountain-crest!
   Long, long, long the trail
   Out of sorrow's lonely vale;
      But at last the traveller sees
      Light between the trees!

March, 1904.

THE FALL OF THE LEAVES

I

In warlike pomp, with banners flowing,
   The regiments of autumn stood:

I saw their gold and scarlet glowing
   From every hillside, every wood.

Above the sea the clouds were keeping
   Their secret leaguer, gray and still;
They sent their misty vanguard creeping
   With muffled step from hill to hill.

All day the sullen armies drifted
   Athwart the sky with slanting rain;
At sunset for a space they lifted,
   With dusk they settled down again.

II

At dark the winds began to blow
With mutterings distant, low;
   From sea and sky they called their strength,
      Till with an angry, broken roar,
      Like billows on an unseen shore,
   Their fury burst at length.

I heard through the night
   The rush and the clamour;
The pulse of the fight
   Like blows of Thor's hammer;
The pattering flight
Of the leaves, and the anguished
Moan of the forest vanquished.

At daybreak came a gusty song:
"Shout! the winds are strong.

The little people of the leaves are fled.
Shout! The Autumn is dead!"

III

The storm is ended! The impartial sun
   Laughs down upon the battle lost and won,
And crowns the triumph of the cloudy host
   In rolling lines retreating to the coast.

But we, fond lovers of the woodland shade,
   And grateful friends of every fallen leaf,
Forget the glories of the cloud-parade,
   And walk the ruined woods in quiet grief.

For ever so our thoughtful hearts repeat
   On fields of triumph dirges of defeat;
And still we turn on gala-days to tread
   Among the rustling memories of the dead.

1874.

THREE ALPINE SONNETS

I

THE GLACIER

At dawn in silence moves the mighty stream,
   The silver-crested waves no murmur make;
   But far away the avalanches wake

The rumbling echoes, dull as in a dream;
Their momentary thunders, dying, seem
  To fall into the stillness, flake by flake,
  And leave the hollow air with naught to break
The frozen spell of solitude supreme.

At noon unnumbered rills begin to spring
  Beneath the burning sun, and all the walls
Of all the ocean-blue crevasses ring
  With liquid lyrics of their waterfalls;
As if a poet's heart had felt the glow
Of sovereign love, and song began to flow.

Zermatt, 1872.

II

THE SNOW-FIELD

White Death had laid his pall upon the plain,
  And crowned the mountain-peaks like monarchs dead;
  The vault of heaven was glaring overhead
With pitiless light that filled my eyes with pain;
And while I vainly longed, and looked in vain
  For sign or trace of life, my spirit said,
  "Shall any living thing that dares to tread
This royal lair of Death escape again?"

But even then I saw before my feet
  A line of pointed footprints in the snow:
  Some roving chamois, but an hour ago,

Had passed this way along his journey fleet,
And left a message from a friend unknown
To cheer my pilgrim-heart, no more alone.

Zermatt, 1872.

III

MOVING BELLS

I love the hour that comes, with dusky hair
    And dewy feet, along the Alpine dells,
     To lead the cattle forth. A thousand bells
Go chiming after her across the fair
And flowery uplands, while the rosy flare
     Of sunset on the snowy mountain dwells,
     And valleys darken, and the drowsy spells
Of peace are woven through the purple air.

Dear is the magic of this hour: she seems
     To walk before the dark by falling rills,
And lend a sweeter song to hidden streams;
     She opens all the doors of night, and fills
With moving bells the music of my dreams,
     That wander far among the sleeping hills.

Gstaad, August, 1909.

A SNOW-SONG

Does the snow fall at sea?
    Yes, when the north winds blow,

When the wild clouds fly low,
Out of each gloomy wing,
Silently glimmering,
Over the stormy sea
    Falleth the snow.

Does the snow hide the sea?
  Nay, on the tossing plains
  Never a flake remains;
Drift never resteth there;
Vanishing everywhere,
Into the hungry sea
    Falleth the snow.

What means the snow at sea?
  Whirled in the veering blast,
Thickly the flakes drive past;
Each like a childish ghost
Wavers, and then is lost;
In the forgetful sea
  Fadeth the snow.

1875.

ROSLIN AND HAWTHORNDEN

Fair Roslin Chapel, how divine
The art that reared thy costly shrine!
Thy carven columns must have grown
By magic, like a dream in stone.

Yet not within thy storied wall
Would I in adoration fall,
So gladly as within the glen
That leads to lovely Hawthornden.

A long-drawn aisle, with roof of green
And vine-clad pillars, while between,
The Esk runs murmuring on its way,
In living music night and day.

Within the temple of this wood
The martyrs of the covenant stood,
And rolled the psalm, and poured the prayer,
From Nature's solemn altar-stair.

Edinburgh, 1877.

THE HEAVENLY HILLS OF HOLLAND

The heavenly hills of Holland,—
    How wondrously they rise
Above the smooth green pastures
    Into the azure skies!
With blue and purple hollows,
    With peaks of dazzling snow,
Along the far horizon
    The clouds are marching slow.

No mortal foot has trodden
    The summits of that range,
Nor walked those mystic valleys

Whose colours ever change;
Yet we possess their beauty,
  And visit them in dreams,
While ruddy gold of sunset
  From cliff and canyon gleams.

In days of cloudless weather
  They melt into the light;
When fog and mist surround us
  They're hidden from our sight;
But when returns a season
  Clear shining after rain,
While the northwest wind is blowing,
  We see the hills again.

The old Dutch painters loved them,
  Their pictures show them fair,—
Old Hobbema and Ruysdael,
  Van Goyen and Vermeer.
Above the level landscape,
  Rich polders, long-armed mills,
Canals and ancient cities,—
  Float Holland's heavenly hills.

The Hague, November, 1916.

FLOOD-TIDE OF FLOWERS

IN HOLLAND

The laggard winter ebbed so slow
With freezing rain and melting snow,

It seemed as if the earth would stay
Forever where the tide was low,
In sodden green and watery gray.

But now from depths beyond our sight,
The tide is turning in the night,
And floods of colour long concealed
Come silent rising toward the light,
Through garden bare and empty field.

And first, along the sheltered nooks,
The crocus runs in little brooks
Of joyance, till by light made bold
They show the gladness of their looks
In shining pools of white and gold.

The tiny scilla, sapphire blue,
Is gently seeping in, to strew
The earth with heaven; and sudden rills
Of sunlit yellow, sweeping through,
Spread into lakes of daffodils.

The hyacinths, with fragrant heads,
Have overflowed their sandy beds,
And fill the earth with faint perfume,
The breath that Spring around her she
And now the tulips break in bloom!

A sea, a rainbow-tinted sea,
A splendour and a mystery,
Floods o'er the fields of faded gray:

174

The roads are full of folks in glee,
For lo,—to-day is Easter Day!

April, 1916.

SALUTE TO THE TREES

Many a tree is found in the wood
And every tree for its use is good:
Some for the strength of the gnarled root,
Some for the sweetness of flower or fruit;
Some for shelter against the storm,
And some to keep the hearth-stone warm;
Some for the roof, and some for the beam,
And some for a boat to breast the stream;—
In the wealth of the wood since the world began
The trees have offered their gifts to man.

But the glory of trees is more than their gifts:
'Tis a beautiful wonder of life that lifts,
From a wrinkled seed in an earth-bound clod,
A column, an arch in the temple of God,
A pillar of power, a dome of delight,
A shrine of song, and a joy of sight!
Their roots are the nurses of rivers in birth;
Their leaves are alive with the breath of the earth;
They shelter the dwellings of man; and they bend
O'er his grave with the look of a loving friend.

I have camped in the whispering forest of pines,
I have slept in the shadow of olives and vines;
In the knees of an oak, at the foot of a palm

I have found good rest and slumber's balm.
And now, when the morning gilds the boughs
Of the vaulted elm at the door of my house,
I open the window and make salute:
"God bless thy branches and feed thy root!
Thou hast lived before, live after me,
Thou ancient, friendly, faithful tree."

February, 1920.

III.

OF THE UNFAILING LIGHT

THE GRAND CANYON

DAYBREAK

What makes the lingering Night so cling to thee?
Thou vast, profound, primeval hiding-place
Of ancient secrets,—gray and ghostly gulf
Cleft in the green of this high forest land,
And crowded in the dark with giant forms!
Art thou a grave, a prison, or a shrine?

A stillness deeper than the dearth of sound
Broods over thee: a living silence breathes
Perpetual incense from thy dim abyss.
The morning-stars that sang above the bower
Of Eden, passing over thee, are dumb
With trembling bright amazement; and the Dawn
Steals through the glimmering pines with naked feet,
Her hand upon her lips, to look on thee!

She peers into thy depths with silent prayer
For light, more light, to part thy purple veil.
O Earth, swift-rolling Earth, reveal, reveal,—
Turn to the East, and show upon thy breast
The mightiest marvel in the realm of Time!
'Tis done,—the morning miracle of light,—
The resurrection of the world of hues
That die with dark, and daily rise again
With every rising of the splendid Sun!

Be still, my heart! Now Nature holds her breath
To see the solar flood of radiance leap
Across the chasm, and crown the western rim
Of alabaster with a far-away
Rampart of pearl, and flowing down by walls
Of changeful opal, deepen into gold
Of topaz, rosy gold of tourmaline,
Crimson of garnet, green and gray of jade,
Purple of amethyst, and ruby red,
Beryl, and sard, and royal porphyry;
Until the cataract of colour breaks
Upon the blackness of the granite floor.

How far below! And all between is cleft
And carved into a hundred curving miles
Of unimagined architecture! Tombs,
Temples, and colonnades are neighboured there
By fortresses that Titans might defend,
And amphitheatres where Gods might strive.
Cathedrals, buttressed with unnumbered tiers

Of ruddy rock, lift to the sapphire sky
A single spire of marble pure as snow;
And huge aerial palaces arise
Like mountains built of unconsuming flame.
Along the weathered walls, or standing deep
In riven valleys where no foot may tread,
Are lonely pillars, and tall monuments
Of perished aeons and forgotten things.
My sight is baffled by the wide array
Of countless forms: my vision reels and swims
Above them, like a bird in whirling winds.
Yet no confusion fills the awful chasm;
But spacious order and a sense of peace
Brood over all. For every shape that looms
Majestic in the throng, is set apart
From all the others by its far-flung shade,
Blue, blue, as if a mountain-lake were there.

How still it is! Dear God, I hardly dare
To breathe, for fear the fathomless abyss
Will draw me down into eternal sleep.

What force has formed this masterpiece of awe?
What hands have wrought these wonders in the waste?
O river, gleaming in the narrow rift
Of gloom that cleaves the valley's nether deep,—
Fierce Colorado, prisoned by thy toil,
And blindly toiling still to reach the sea,—
Thy waters, gathered from the snows and springs
Amid the Utah hills, have carved this road
Of glory to the California Gulf.

But now, O sunken stream, thy splendour lost,
'Twixt iron walls thou rollest turbid waves,
Too far away to make their fury heard!

At sight of thee, thou sullen labouring slave
Of gravitation,—yellow torrent poured
From distant mountains by no will of thine,
Through thrice a hundred centuries of slow
Fallings and liftings of the crust of Earth,—
At sight of thee my spirit sinks and fails.
Art thou alone the Maker? Is the blind
Unconscious power that drew thee dumbly down
To cut this gash across the layered globe,
The sole creative cause of all I see?
Are force and matter all? The rest a dream?

Then is thy gorge a canyon of despair,
A prison for the soul of man, a grave
Of all his dearest daring hopes! The world
Wherein we live and move is meaningless,
No spirit here to answer to our own!
The stars without a guide: The chance-born
     Earth
Adrift in space, no Captain on the ship:
Nothing in all the universe to prove
Eternal wisdom and eternal love!
And man, the latest accident of Time,—
Who thinks he loves, and longs to understand,
Who vainly suffers, and in vain is brave,
Who dupes his heart with immortality,—
Man is a living lie,—a bitter jest
Upon himself,—a conscious grain of sand

Lost in a desert of unconsciousness,
Thirsting for God and mocked by his own thirst.

Spirit of Beauty, mother of delight,
Thou fairest offspring of Omnipotence
Inhabiting this lofty lone abode,
Speak to my heart again and set me free
From all these doubts that darken earth and
        heaven!
Who sent thee forth into the wilderness
To bless and comfort all who see thy face?
Who clad thee in this more than royal robe
Of rainbows? Who designed these jeweled thrones
For thee, and wrought these glittering palaces?
Who gave thee power upon the soul of man
To lift him up through wonder into joy?
God! let the radiant cliffs bear witness, God!
Let all the shining pillars signal, God!
He only, on the mystic loom of light,
Hath woven webs of loveliness to clothe
His most majestic works: and He alone
Hath delicately wrought the cactus-flower
To star the desert floor with rosy bloom.

O Beauty, handiwork of the Most High,
Where'er thou art He tells his Love to man,
And lo, the day breaks, and the shadows flee!

Now, far beyond all language and all art
In thy wild splendour, Canyon marvellous,
The secret of thy stillness lies unveiled
In worldless worship! This is holy ground;

Thou art no grave, no prison, but a shrine.
Garden of Temples filled with Silent Praise,
If God were blind thy Beauty could not be!

February 24-26, 1913.

GOD OF THE OPEN AIR

I

Thou who hast made thy dwelling fair
    With flowers below, above with starry lights
And set thine altars everywhere,—
        On mountain heights,
In woodlands dim with many a dream,
        In valleys bright with springs,
And on the curving capes of every stream:
Thou who hast taken to thyself the wings
        Of morning, to abide
Upon the secret places of the sea,
    And on far islands, where the tide
Visits the beauty of untrodden shores,
Waiting for worshippers to come to thee
        In thy great out-of-doors!
To thee I turn, to thee I make my prayer,
        God of the open air.

II

Seeking for thee, the heart of man
        Lonely and longing ran,
In that first, solitary hour,

When the mysterious power
To know and love the wonder of the morn
Was breathed within him, and his soul was born;
And thou didst meet thy child,
Not in some hidden shrine,
But in the freedom of the garden wild,
And take his hand in thine,—
There all day long in Paradise he walked,
And in the cool of evening with thee talked.

III

Lost, long ago, that garden bright and pure,
Lost, that calm day too perfect to endure,
And lost the child-like love that worshipped and was sure!
For men have dulled their eyes with sin,
And dimmed the light of heaven with doubt,
And built their temple walls to shut thee in,
And framed their iron creeds to shut thee out.
But not for thee the closing of the door,
O Spirit unconfined!
Thy ways are free
As is the wandering wind,
And thou hast wooed thy children, to restore
Their fellowship with thee,
In peace of soul and simpleness of mind.

IV

Joyful the heart that, when the flood rolled by,
Leaped up to see the rainbow in the sky;
And glad the pilgrim, in the lonely night,

For whom the hills of Haran, tier on tier,
Built up a secret stairway to the height
Where stars like angel eyes were shining clear.
From mountain-peaks, in many a land and age,
 Disciples of the Persian seer
Have hailed the rising sun and worshipped thee;
And wayworn followers of the Indian sage
Have found the peace of God beneath a spreading tree.

V

 But One, but One,—ah, Son most dear,
And perfect image of the Love Unseen,—
 Walked every day in pastures green,
And all his life the quiet waters by,
Reading their beauty with a tranquil eye.
To him the desert was a place prepared
 For weary hearts to rest;
 The hillside was a temple blest;
 The grassy vale a banquet-room
Where he could feed and comfort many a guest.
 With him the lily shared
The vital joy that breathes itself in bloom;
And every bird that sang beside the nest
Told of the love that broods o'er every living thing.

He watched the shepherd bring
His flock at sundown to the welcome fold,
The fisherman at daybreak fling
His net across the waters gray and cold,
And all day long the patient reaper swing
His curving sickle through the harvest gold.

So through the world the foot-path way he trod,
Breathing the air of heaven in every breath;
And in the evening sacrifice of death
Beneath the open sky he gave his soul to God.
Him will I trust, and for my Master take;
Him will I follow; and for his dear sake,
God of the open air,
To thee I make my prayer.

VI

From the prison of anxious thought that greed has builded,
From the fetters that envy has wrought and pride has gilded,
From the noise of the crowded ways and the fierce confusion,
From the folly that wastes its days in a world of illusion,
(Ah, but the life is lost that frets and languishes there!)
I would escape and be free in the joy of the open air.
By the breadth of the blue that shines in silence o'er me,
By the length of the mountain-lines that stretch before me,
By the height of the cloud that sails, with rest in motion,
Over the plains and the vales to the measureless ocean,
(Oh, how the sight of the greater things enlarges the eyes!)
Draw me away from myself to the peace of the hills and skies.

While the tremulous leafy haze on the woodland is spreading,
And the bloom on the meadow betrays where May has been
    treading;
While the birds on the branches above, and the brooks flowing under,
Are singing together of love in a world full of wonder,
(Lo, in the magic of Springtime, dreams are changed into truth!)
Quicken my heart, and restore the beautiful hopes of youth.

By the faith that the wild-flowers show when they bloom unbidden,
By the calm of the river's flow to a goal that is hidden,
By the strength of the tree that clings to its deep foundation,
By the courage of birds' light wings on the long migration,
(Wonderful spirit of trust that abides in Nature's breast!)
Teach me how to confide, and live my life, and rest.

For the comforting warmth of the sun that my body embraces,
For the cool of the waters that run through the shadowy places,
For the balm of the breezes that brush my face with their fingers,
For the vesper-hymn of the thrush when the twilight lingers,
For the long breath, the deep breath, the breath of a heart without
    care,—
I will give thanks and adore thee, God of the open air!

VII

        These are the gifts I ask
        Of thee, Spirit serene:
        Strength for the daily task,
        Courage to face the road,
Good cheer to help me bear the traveller's load,
And, for the hours of rest that come between,
An inward joy in all things heard and seen.
    These are the sins I fain
    Would have thee take away:
    Malice, and cold disdain,
    Hot anger, sullen hate,
Scorn of the lowly, envy of the great,
And discontent that casts a shadow gray
On all the brightness of the common day.
        These are the things I prize

And hold of dearest worth:
    Light of the sapphire skies,
    Peace of the silent hills,
Shelter of forests, comfort of the grass,
Music of birds, murmur of little rills,
Shadows of cloud that swiftly pass,
      And, after showers,
      The smell of flowers
  And of the good brown earth,—
And best of all, along the way, friendship and mirth.
     So let me keep
  These treasures of the humble heart
In true possession, owning them by love;
And when at last I can no longer move
  Among them freely, but must part
From the green fields and from the waters clear,
    Let me not creep
Into some darkened room and hide
From all that makes the world so bright and dear;
    But throw the windows wide
    To welcome in the light;
  And while I clasp a well-belovèd hand,
    Let me once more have sight
  Of the deep sky and the far-smiling land,—
    Then gently fall on sleep,
And breathe my body back to Nature's care,
My spirit out to thee, God of the open air.

1904.

IV.

WAYFARING PSALMS IN PALESTINE

THE DISTANT ROAD

Blessed is the man that beholdeth the face of a friend in a far country,
The darkness of his heart is melted by the dawning of day within him,

It is like the sound of a sweet music heard long ago and half
    forgotten:
It is like the coming back of birds to a wood when the winter is ended.

I knew not the sweetness of the fountain till I found it flowing in the
    desert,
Nor the value of a friend till we met in a land that was crowded and
    lonely.

The multitude of mankind had bewildered me and oppressed me,
And I complained to God, Why hast thou made the world so wide?

But when my friend came the wideness of the world had no more
    terror,
Because we were glad together among men to whom we were
    strangers.

It seemed as if I had been reading a book in a foreign language,
And suddenly I came upon a page written in the tongue of my
   childhood.

This was the gentle heart of my friend who quietly understood me,
The open and loving heart whose meaning was clear without a word.

O thou great Companion who carest for all thy pilgrims and strangers,
I thank thee heartily for the comfort of a comrade on the distant road.

THE WELCOME TENT

This is the thanksgiving of the weary,
The song of him that is ready to rest.

It is good to be glad when the day is declining,
And the setting of the sun is like a word of peace.

The stars look kindly on the close of a journey,
The tent says welcome when the day's march is done.

For now is the time of the laying down of burdens,
And the cool hour cometh to them that have borne the heat.

I have rejoiced greatly in labour and adventure;
My heart hath been enlarged in the spending of my strength.

Now it is all gone, yet I am not impoverished,
For thus only I inherit the treasure of repose.

Blessed be the Lord that teacheth my fingers to loosen,
And cooleth my feet with water after the dust of the way.

Blessed be the Lord that giveth me hunger at nightfall,
And filleth my evening cup with the wine of good cheer.

Blessed be the Lord that maketh me happy to be quiet,
Even as a child that cometh softly to his mother's lap.

O God, thy strength is never worn away with labour:
But it is good for us to be weary and receive thy gift of rest.

THE GREAT CITIES

How wonderful are the cities that man hath builded:
Their walls are compacted of heavy stones,
And their lofty towers rise above the tree-tops.

Rome, Jerusalem, Cairo, Damascus,—
Venice, Constantinople, Moscow, Pekin,—
London, New York, Berlin, Paris, Vienna,—

These are the names of mighty enchantments,
They have called to the ends of the earth,
They have secretly summoned a host of servants.

They shine from far sitting beside great waters,
They are proudly enthroned upon high hills,
They spread out their splendour along the rivers.

Yet are they all the work of small patient fingers,
Their strength is in the hand of man,
He hath woven his flesh and blood into their glory.

The cities are scattered over the world like anthills,
Every one of them is full of trouble and toil,
And their makers run to and fro within them.

Abundance of riches is laid up in their treasuries,
But they are tormented with the fear of want,
The cry of the poor in their streets is exceeding bitter.

Their inhabitants are driven by blind perturbations,
They whirl sadly in the fever of haste,
Seeking they know not what, they pursue it fiercely.

The air is heavy-laden with their breathing,
The sound of their coming and going is never still,
Even in the night I hear them whispering and crying.

Beside every ant-hill I behold a monster crouching:
This is the ant-lion Death,
He thrusteth forth his tongue and the people perish.

O God of wisdom thou hast made the country:
Why hast thou suffered man to make the town?

Then God answered, Surely I am the maker of man:
And in the heart of man I have set the city.

THE FRIENDLY TREES

I will sing of the bounty of the big trees,
They are the green tents of the Almighty,
He hath set them up for comfort and for shelter.

Their cords hath he knotted in the earth,
He hath driven their stakes securely,
Their roots take hold of the rocks like iron.

He sendeth into their bodies the sap of life,
They lift themselves lightly toward the heavens.
They rejoice in the broadening of their branches.

Their leaves drink in the sunlight and the air,
They talk softly together when the breeze bloweth,
Their shadow in the noon-day is full of coolness.

The tall palm-trees of the plain are rich in fruit,
While the fruit ripeneth the flower unfoldeth,
The beauty of their crown is renewed on high forever.

The cedars of Lebanon are fed by the snow,
Afar on the mountain they grow like giants,
In their layers of shade a thousand years are dreaming.

How fair are the trees that befriend the home of man,
The oak, and the terebinth, and the sycamore,
The broad-leaved fig-tree and the delicate silvery olive.

In them the Lord is loving to his little birds,
The linnets and the finches and the nightingales,
They people his pavilions with nests and with music.

The cattle also are very glad of a great tree,
They chew the cud beneath it while the sun is burning,
And there the panting sheep lie down around their shepherd.

He that planteth a tree is a servant of God,
He provideth a kindness for many generations,
And faces that he hath not seen shall bless him.

Lord, when my spirit shall return to thee,
At the foot of a friendly tree let my body be buried,
That this dust may rise and rejoice among the branches.

THE PATHWAY OF RIVERS

The rivers of God are full of water,
They are wonderful in the renewal of their strength,
He poureth them out from a hidden fountain.

They are born among the hills in the high places,
Their cradle is in the bosom of the rocks,
The mountain is their mother and the forest is their father.

They are nourished among the long grasses,
They receive the tribute of a thousand springs,
The rain and the snow provide their inheritance.

They are glad to be gone from their birthplace,
With a joyful noise they hasten away,
They are going forever and never departed.

The courses of the rivers are all appointed;
They roar loudly but they follow the road,
For the finger of God hath marked their pathway.

The rivers of Damascus rejoice among their gardens;
The great river of Egypt is proud of his ships;
The Jordan is lost in the Lake of Bitterness.

Surely the Lord guideth them every one in his wisdom,
In the end he gathereth all their drops on high,
And sendeth them forth again in the clouds of mercy.

O my God, my life floweth away like a river:
Guide me, I beseech thee, in a pathway of good:
Let me run in blessing to my rest in thee.

THE GLORY OF RUINS

The lizard rested on the rock while I sat among the ruins,
And the pride of man was like a vision of the night.

Lo, the lords of the city have disappeared into darkness,
The ancient wilderness hath swallowed up all their work.

There is nothing left of the city but a heap of fragments;
The bones of a vessel broken by the storm.

Behold the waves of the desert wait hungrily for man's dwellings,
And the tides of desolation return upon his toil.

All that he hath painfully built up is shaken down in a moment,
The memory of his glory is buried beneath the billows of sand.

Then a voice said, Look again upon the ruins,
These broken arches have taught generations to build.

Moreover the name of this city shall be remembered,
For here a poor man spoke a word that shall not die.

This is the glory that is stronger than the desert;
God hath given eternity to the thought of man.

THE TRIBE OF THE HELPERS

The ways of the world are full of haste and turmoil;
I will sing of the tribe of the helpers who travel in peace.

He that turneth from the road to rescue another,
Turneth toward his goal:
He shall arrive in time by the foot-path of mercy,
God will be his guide.

He that taketh up the burden of the fainting,
Lighteneth his own load:
The Almighty will put his arms underneath him,
He shall lean upon the Lord.

He that speaketh comfortable words to mourners,
Healeth his own hurt;
In the time of grief they will come to his remembrance.
God will use them for balm.

He that careth for a wounded brother,
Watcheth not alone:
There are three in the darkness together,
And the third is the Lord.

Blessed is the way of the helpers,
The companions of the Christ.

GOOD TEACHER

The Lord is my teacher,
I shall not lose the way.

He leadeth me in the lowly path of learning,
He prepareth a lesson for me every day;
He bringeth me to the clear fountains of instruction,
Little by little he showeth me the beauty of truth.

The world is a great book that he hath written,
He turneth the leaves for me slowly;
They are inscribed with images and letters,
He poureth light on the pictures and the words.

He taketh me by the hand to the hill-top of vision,
And my soul is glad when I perceive his meaning;
In the valley also he walketh beside me,
In the dark places he whispereth to my heart.

Even though my lesson be hard it is not hopeless,
For the Lord is patient with his slow scholar;
He will wait awhile for my weakness,
And help me to read the truth through tears.

THE CAMP-FIRES OF MY FRIEND

Thou hast taken me into thy tent of the world, O God,
Beneath thy blue canopy I have found shelter,
Therefore thou wilt not deny me the right of a guest.

Naked and poor I arrived at thy door before sunset:
Thou hast refreshed me with beautiful bowls of milk,
As a great chief thou hast set forth food in abundance.

I have loved the daily delights of thy dwelling,
Thy moon and thy stars have lighted me to my bed,
In the morning I have made merry with thy servants.

Surely thou wilt not send me away in the darkness?
There the enemy Death is lying in wait for my soul:
Thou art the host of my life and I claim thy protection.

Then the Lord of the tent of the world made answer:
The right of a guest endureth for a certain time,
After three days and nights cometh the day of departure.

Yet hearken to me since thou fearest to go in the dark:
I will make with thee a new covenant of hospitality,
Behold I will come unto thee as a stranger and be thy guest.

Poor and needy will I come that thou mayest entertain me,
Meek and lowly will I come that thou mayest find a friend,
With mercy and with truth will I come to give thee comfort.

Therefore open thy heart to me and bid me welcome,
In this tent of the world I will be thy brother of the bread,
And when thou farest forth I will be thy companion forever.

Then my soul rested in the word of the Lord;
And I saw that the curtains of the world were shaken,
But I looked beyond them to the stars,
The camp-fires of my eternal friend.

THE STORY OF THE OTHER WISE MAN

THE STORY OF OTHER WISE MAN.

Who seeks for heaven alone to save his soul,
May keep the path, but will not reach the goal;
While he who walks in love may wander far,
Yet God will bring him where the blessed are.

You know the story of the Three Wise Men of the East, and how they travelled from far away to offer their gifts at the manger-cradle in Bethlehem. But have you ever heard the story of the Other Wise Man, who also saw the star in its rising, and set out to follow it, yet did not arrive with his brethren in the presence of the young child Jesus? Of the great desire of this fourth pilgrim, and how it was denied, yet accomplished in the denial; of his many wanderings and the probations of his soul; of the long way of his seeking, and the strange way of his finding, the One whom he sought—I would tell the tale as I have heard fragments of it in the Hall of Dreams, in the palace of the Heart of Man.

THE SIGN IN THE SKY

In the days when Augustus Caesar was master of many kings and Herod reigned in Jerusalem, there lived in the city of Ecbatana, among the mountains of Persia, a certain man named Artaban, the Median. His house stood close to the outermost of the seven walls which encircled the royal treasury. From his roof he could look over the rising battlements of black and white and crimson and blue and red and silver and gold, to the hill where the summer palace of the Parthian emperors glittered like a jewel in a sevenfold crown.

Around the dwelling of Artaban spread a fair garden, a tangle of flowers and fruit-trees, watered by a score of streams descending from the slopes of Mount Orontes, and made musical by innumerable birds. But all colour was lost in the soft and odorous darkness of the late September night, and all sounds were hushed in the deep charm of its silence, save the plashing of the water, like a voice half sobbing and half laughing under the shadows. High above the trees a dim glow of light shone through the curtained arches of the upper chamber, where the master of the house was holding council with his friends.

He stood by the doorway to greet his guests—a tall, dark man of about forty years, with brilliant eyes set near together under his broad brow, and firm lines graven around his fine, thin lips; the brow of a dreamer and the mouth of a soldier, a man of sensitive feeling but inflexible will—one of those who, in whatever age they may live, are born for inward conflict and a life of quest.

His robe was of pure white wool, thrown over a tunic of silk; and a white, pointed cap, with long lapels at the sides, rested on his flowing

203

black hair. It was the dress of the ancient priesthood of the Magi, called the fire-worshippers.

"Welcome!" he said, in his low, pleasant voice, as one after another entered the room—"welcome, Abdus; peace be with you, Rhodaspes and Tigranes, and with you my father, Abgarus. You are all welcome, and this house grows bright with the joy of your presence."

There were nine of the men, differing widely in age, but alike in the richness of their dress of many-coloured silks, and in the massive golden collars around their necks, marking them as Parthian nobles, and in the winged circles of gold resting upon their breasts, the sign of the followers of Zoroaster.

They took their places around a small black altar at the end of the room, where a tiny flame was burning. Artaban, standing beside it, and waving a barsom of thin tamarisk branches above the fire, fed it with dry sticks of pine and fragrant oils. Then he began the ancient chant of the Yasna, and the voices of his companions joined in the beautiful hymn to Ahura-Mazda:

> We worship the Spirit Divine,
>   all wisdom and goodness possessing,
> Surrounded by Holy Immortals,
>   the givers of bounty and blessing.
> We joy in the works of His hands,
>   His truth and His power confessing.
>
> We praise all the things that are pure,
>   for these are His only Creation;
> The thoughts that are true, and the words
>   and deeds that have won approbation;
> These are supported by Him,
>   and for these we make adoration.

Hear us, O Mazda! Thou livest
    in truth and in heavenly gladness;
Cleanse us from falsehood, and keep us
    from evil and bondage to badness;
Pour out the light and the joy of Thy life
    on our darkness and sadness.

Shine on our gardens and fields,
    Shine on our working and weaving;
Shine on the whole race of man,
    Believing and unbelieving;
    Shine on us now through the night,
    Shine on us now in Thy might,
The flame of our holy love
    and the song of our worship receiving.

The fire rose with the chant, throbbing as if it were made of musical flame, until it cast a bright illumination through the whole apartment, revealing its simplicity and splendour.

The floor was laid with tiles of dark blue veined with white; pilasters of twisted silver stood out against the blue walls; the clearstory of round-arched windows above them was hung with azure silk; the vaulted ceiling was a pavement of sapphires, like the body of heaven in its clearness, sown with silver stars. From the four corners of the roof hung four golden magic-wheels, called the tongues of the gods. At the eastern end, behind the altar, there were two dark-red pillars of porphyry; above them a lintel of the same stone, on which was carved the figure of a winged archer, with his arrow set to the string and his bow drawn.

The doorway between the pillars, which opened upon the terrace of the roof, was covered with a heavy curtain of the colour of a ripe pomegranate, embroidered with innumerable golden rays shooting upward from the floor. In effect the room was like a quiet, starry night, all azure and silver, flushed in the East with rosy promise of the dawn. It was, as the house of a man should be, an expression of the character and spirit of the master.

He turned to his friends when the song was ended, and invited them to be seated on the divan at the western end of the room.

"You have come to-night," said he, looking around the circle, "at my call, as the faithful scholars of Zoroaster, to renew your worship and rekindle your faith in the God of Purity, even as this fire has been rekindled on the altar. We worship not the fire, but Him of whom it is the chosen symbol, because it is the purest of all created things. It speaks to us of one who is Light and Truth. Is it not so, my father?"

"It is well said, my son," answered the venerable Abgarus. "The enlightened are never idolaters. They lift the veil of the form and go in to the shrine of the reality, and new light and truth are coming to them continually through the old symbols." "Hear me, then, my father and my friends," said Artaban, very quietly, "while I tell you of the new light and truth that have come to me through the most ancient of all signs. We have searched the secrets of nature together, and studied the healing virtues of water and fire and the plants. We have read also the books of prophecy in which the future is dimly foretold in words that are hard to understand. But the highest of all learning is the knowledge of the stars. To trace their courses is to untangle the threads of the mystery of life from the beginning to the end. If we could follow them perfectly, nothing would be hidden from us. But is not our knowledge of them still incomplete? Are there not many stars still beyond our horizon—lights that are known only to the dwellers in the far south-land, among the spice-trees of Punt and the gold mines of Ophir?"

There was a murmur of assent among the listeners.

"The stars," said Tigranes, "are the thoughts of the Eternal. They are numberless. But the thoughts of man can be counted, like the years of his life. The wisdom of the Magi is the greatest of all wisdoms on earth, because it knows its own ignorance. And that is the secret of power. We keep men always looking and waiting for a new sunrise. But we ourselves know that the darkness is equal to the light, and that the conflict between them will never be ended."

"That does not satisfy me," answered Artaban, "for, if the waiting must be endless, if there could be no fulfilment of it, then it would not be wisdom to look and wait. We should become like those new teachers of the Greeks, who say that there is no truth, and that the only wise men are those who spend their lives in discovering and exposing the lies that have been believed in the world. But the new sunrise will certainly dawn in the appointed time. Do not our own books tell us that this will come to pass, and that men will see the brightness of a great light?"

"That is true," said the voice of Abgarus; "every faithful disciple of Zoroaster knows the prophecy of the Avesta and carries the word in his heart. 'In that day Sosiosh the Victorious shall arise out of the number of the prophets in the east country. Around him shall shine a mighty brightness, and he shall make life everlasting, incorruptible, and immortal, and the dead shall rise again.'"

"This is a dark saying," said Tigranes, "and it may be that we shall never understand it. It is better to consider the things that are near at hand, and to increase the influence of the Magi in their own country, rather than to look for one who may be a stranger, and to whom we must resign our power."

The others seemed to approve these words. There was a silent feeling of agreement manifest among them; their looks responded with that indefinable expression which always follows when a speaker has uttered the thought that has been slumbering in the hearts of his listeners. But Artaban turned to Abgarus with a glow on his face, and said:

"My father, I have kept this prophecy in the secret place of my soul. Religion without a great hope would be like an altar without a living fire. And now the flame has burned more brightly, and by the light of it I have read other words which also have come from the fountain of

Truth, and speak yet more clearly of the rising of the Victorious One in his brightness."

He drew from the breast of his tunic two small rolls of fine linen, with writing upon them, and unfolded them carefully upon his knee.

"In the years that are lost in the past, long before our fathers came into the land of Babylon, there were wise men in Chaldea, from whom the first of the Magi learned the secret of the heavens. And of these Balaam the son of Beor was one of the mightiest. Hear the words of his prophecy: 'There shall come a star out of Jacob, and a sceptre shall arise out of Israel.'"

The lips of Tigranes drew downward with contempt, as he said:

"Judah was a captive by the waters of Babylon, and the sons of Jacob were in bondage to our kings. The tribes of Israel are scattered through the mountains like lost sheep, and from the remnant that dwells in Judea under the yoke of Rome neither star nor sceptre shall arise."

"And yet," answered Artaban, "it was the Hebrew Daniel, the mighty searcher of dreams, the counsellor of kings, the wise Belteshazzar, who was most honored and beloved of our great King Cyrus. A prophet of sure things and a reader of the thoughts of God, Daniel proved himself to our people. And these are the words that he wrote." (Artaban read from the second roll:) "'Know, therefore, and understand that from the going forth of the commandment to restore Jerusalem, unto the Anointed One, the Prince, the time shall be seven and threescore and two weeks.'"

"But, my son," said Abgarus, doubtfully, "these are mystical numbers. Who can interpret them, or who can find the key that shall unlock their meaning?"

Artaban answered: "It has been shown to me and to my three companions among the Magi—Caspar, Melchior, and Balthazar. We have searched the ancient tablets of Chaldea and computed the time. It falls in this year. We have studied the sky, and in the spring of the year we saw two of the greatest stars draw near together in the sign of the Fish, which is the house of the Hebrews. We also saw a new star there, which shone for one night and then vanished. Now again the two great planets are meeting. This night is their conjunction. My three brothers are watching at the ancient temple of the Seven Spheres, at Borsippa, in Babylonia, and I am watching here. If the star shines again, they will wait ten days for me at the temple, and then we will set out together for Jerusalem, to see and worship the promised one who shall be born King of Israel. I believe the sign will come. I have made ready for the journey. I have sold my house and my possessions, and bought these three jewels—a sapphire, a ruby, and a pearl—to carry them as tribute to the King. And I ask you to go with me on the pilgrimage, that we may have joy together in finding the Prince who is worthy to be served."

While he was speaking he thrust his hand into the inmost fold of his girdle and drew out three great gems—one blue as a fragment of the night sky, one redder than a ray of sunrise, and one as pure as the peak of a snow mountain at twilight—and laid them on the outspread linen scrolls before him.

But his friends looked on with strange and alien eyes. A veil of doubt and mistrust came over their faces, like a fog creeping up from the marshes to hide the hills. They glanced at each other with looks of wonder and pity, as those who have listened to incredible sayings, the story of a wild vision, or the proposal of an impossible enterprise.

At last Tigranes said: "Artaban, this is a vain dream. It comes from too much looking upon the stars and the cherishing of lofty thoughts. It would be wiser to spend the time in gathering money for the new fire-temple at Chala. No king will ever rise from the broken race of Israel, and no end will ever come to the eternal strife of light and darkness. He who looks for it is a chaser of shadows. Farewell."

And another said: "Artaban, I have no knowledge of these things, and my office as guardian of the royal treasure binds me here. The quest is not for me. But if thou must follow it, fare thee well."

And another said: "In my house there sleeps a new bride, and I cannot leave her nor take her with me on this strange journey. This quest is not for me. But may thy steps be prospered wherever thou goest. So, farewell."

And another said: "I am ill and unfit for hardship, but there is a man among my servants whom I will send with thee when thou goest, to bring me word how thou farest."

But Abgarus, the oldest and the one who loved Artaban the best, lingered after the others had gone, and said, gravely: "My son, it may be that the light of truth is in this sign that has appeared in the skies, and then it will surely lead to the Prince and the mighty brightness. Or it may be that it is only a shadow of the light, as Tigranes has said, and then he who follows it will have only a long pilgrimage and an empty search. But it is better to follow even the shadow of the best than to remain content with the worst. And those who would see wonderful things must often be ready to travel alone. I am too old for this journey, but my heart shall be a companion of the pilgrimage day and night, and I shall know the end of thy quest. Go in peace."

So one by one they went out of the azure chamber with its silver stars, and Artaban was left in solitude.

He gathered up the jewels and replaced them in his girdle. For a long time he stood and watched the flame that flickered and sank upon the altar. Then he crossed the hall, lifted the heavy curtain, and passed out between the dull red pillars of porphyry to the terrace on the roof.

The shiver that thrills through the earth ere she rouses from her night sleep had already begun, and the cool wind that heralds the daybreak was drawing downward from the lofty snow-traced ravines of Mount Orontes. Birds, half awakened, crept and chirped among the rustling leaves, and the smell of ripened grapes came in brief wafts from the arbours.

Far over the eastern plain a white mist stretched like a lake. But where the distant peak of Zagros serrated the western horizon the sky was clear.

Jupiter and Saturn rolled together like drops of lambent flame about to blend in one.

As Artaban watched them, behold, an azure spark was born out of the darkness beneath, rounding itself with purple splendours to a crimson sphere, and spiring upward through rays of saffron and orange into a point of white radiance. Tiny and infinitely remote, yet perfect in every part, it pulsated in the enormous vault as if the three jewels in the Magian's breast had mingled and been transformed into a living heart of light. He bowed his head. He covered his brow with his hands.

"It is the sign," he said. "The King is coming, and I will go to meet him."

BY THE WATERS OF BABYLON

All night long Vasda, the swiftest of Artaban's horses, had been waiting, saddled and bridled, in her stall, pawing the ground impatiently, and shaking her bit as if she shared the eagerness of her master's purpose, though she knew not its meaning.

Before the birds had fully roused to their strong, high, joyful chant of morning song, before the white mist had begun to lift lazily from the plain, the other wise man was in the saddle, riding swiftly along the high-road, which skirted the base of Mount Orontes, westward.

How close, how intimate is the comradeship between a man and his favourite horse on a long journey. It is a silent, comprehensive friendship, an intercourse beyond the need of words. They drink at the same way-side springs, and sleep under the same guardian stars. They are conscious together of the subduing spell of nightfall and the quickening joy of daybreak. The master shares his evening meal with his hungry companion, and feels the soft, moist lips caressing the palm of his hand as they close over the morsel of bread. In the gray dawn he is roused from his bivouac by the gentle stir of a warm, sweet breath over his sleeping face, and looks up into the eyes of his faithful fellow-traveller, ready and waiting for the toil of the day. Surely, unless he is a pagan and an unbeliever, by whatever name he calls upon his God, he will thank Him for this voiceless sympathy, this dumb affection, and his morning prayer will embrace a double blessing—God bless us both, and keep our feet from falling and our souls from death!

And then, through the keen morning air, the swift hoofs beat their spirited music along the road, keeping time to the pulsing of two hearts that are moved with the same eager desire—to conquer space, to devour the distance, to attain the goal of the journey.

Artaban must indeed ride wisely and well if he would keep the appointed hour with the other Magi; for the route was a hundred and fifty parasangs, and fifteen was the utmost that he could travel in a day. But he knew Vasda's strength, and pushed forward without anxiety, making the fixed distance every day, though he must travel late into the night, and in the morning long before sunrise.

He passed along the brown slopes of Mt. Orontes, furrowed by the rocky courses of a hundred torrents.

He crossed the level plains of the Nisaeans, where the famous herds of horses, feeding in the wide pastures, tossed their heads at Vasda's approach, and galloped away with a thunder of many hoofs, and flocks of wild birds rose suddenly from the swampy meadows, wheeling in great circles with a shining flutter of innumerable wings and shrill cries of surprise.

He traversed the fertile fields of Concabar, where the dust from the threshing-floors filled the air with a golden mist, half hiding the huge temple of Astarte with its four hundred pillars.

At Baghistan, among the rich gardens watered by fountains from the rock, he looked up at the mountain thrusting its immense rugged brow out over the road, and saw the figure of King Darius trampling upon his fallen foes, and the proud list of his wars and conquests graven high upon the face of the eternal cliff.

Over many a cold and desolate pass, crawling painfully across the wind-swept shoulders of the hills; down many a black mountain-gorge, where the river roared and raced before him like a savage guide; across many a smiling vale, with terraces of yellow limestone full of vines and fruit-trees; through the oak-groves of Carine and the dark Gates of Zagros, walled in by precipices; into the ancient city of Chala, where the people of Samaria had been kept in captivity long ago; and out again by the mighty portal, riven through the encircling hills, where he saw the image of the High Priest of the Magi sculptured on the wall of rock, with hand uplifted as if to bless the centuries of pilgrims; past the entrance of the narrow defile, filled from end to end with orchards of peaches and figs, through which the river Gyndes foamed down to meet him; over the broad rice-fields, where the autumnal vapours spread their deathly mists; following along the course of the river, under tremulous shadows of poplar and tamarind, among the lower hills; and out upon the flat plain, where the road ran straight as an arrow through the stubble-fields and parched meadows; past the city of Ctesiphon, where the Parthian emperors reigned, and the vast metropolis of Seleucia which Alexander built; across the swirling floods of Tigris and the many channels of Euphrates, flowing yellow through the corn-lands—Artaban pressed onward until he arrived, at nightfall of the tenth day, beneath the shattered walls of populous Babylon.

Vasda was almost spent, and he would gladly have turned into the city to find rest and refreshment for himself and for her. But he knew that it was three hours' journey yet to the Temple of the Seven Spheres, and he must reach the place by midnight if he would find his comrades waiting. So he did not halt, but rode steadily across the stubble-fields.

A grove of date-palms made an island of gloom in the pale yellow sea. As she passed into the shadow Vasda slackened her pace, and began to pick her way more carefully.

Near the farther end of the darkness an access of caution seemed to fall upon her. She scented some danger or difficulty; it was not in her heart to fly from it—only to be prepared for it, and to meet it wisely, as a good horse should do. The grove was close and silent as the tomb; not a leaf rustled, not a bird sang.

She felt her steps before her delicately, carrying her head low, and sighing now and then with apprehension. At last she gave a quick breath of anxiety and dismay, and stood stock-still, quivering in every muscle, before a dark object in the shadow of the last palm-tree.

Artaban dismounted. The dim starlight revealed the form of a man lying across the road. His humble dress and the outline of his haggard face showed that he was probably one of the poor Hebrew exiles who still dwelt in great numbers in the vicinity. His pallid skin, dry and yellow as parchment, bore the mark of the deadly fever which ravaged the marshlands in autumn. The chill of death was in his lean hand, and, as Artaban released it, the arm fell back inertly upon the motionless breast.

He turned away with a thought of pity, consigning the body to that strange burial which the Magians deem most fitting—the funeral of the desert, from which the kites and vultures rise on dark wings, and the beasts of prey slink furtively away, leaving only a heap of white bones in the sand.

But, as he turned, a long, faint, ghostly sigh came from the man's lips. The brown, bony fingers closed convulsively on the hem of the Magian's robe and held him fast.

Artaban's heart leaped to his throat, not with fear, but with a dumb resentment at the importunity of this blind delay. How could he stay here in the darkness to minister to a dying stranger? What claim had this unknown fragment of human life upon his compassion or his service? If he lingered but for an hour he could hardly reach Borsippa at the appointed time. His companions would think he had given up the journey. They would go without him. He would lose his quest.

But if he went on now, the man would surely die. If he stayed, life might be restored. His spirit throbbed and fluttered with the urgency of the crisis. Should he risk the great reward of his divine faith for the sake of a single deed of human love? Should he turn aside, if only for a moment, from the following of the star, to give a cup of cold water to a poor, perishing Hebrew?

"God of truth and purity," he prayed, "direct me in the holy path, the way of wisdom which Thou only knowest."

Then he turned back to the sick man. Loosening the grasp of his hand, he carried him to a little mound at the foot of the palm-tree. He unbound the thick folds of the turban and opened the garment above the sunken breast. He brought water from one of the small canals near by, and moistened the sufferer's brow and mouth. He mingled a draught of one of those simple but potent remedies which he carried always in his girdle—for the Magians were physicians as well as astrologers—and poured it slowly between the colourless lips. Hour after hour he labored as only a skilful healer of disease can do; and, at last, the man's strength returned; he sat up and looked about him.

"Who art thou?" he said, in the rude dialect of the country, "and why hast thou sought me here to bring back my life?"

"I am Artaban the Magian, of the city of Ecbatana, and I am going to Jerusalem in search of one who is to be born King of the Jews, a great Prince and Deliverer for all men. I dare not delay any longer upon my journey, for the caravan that has waited for me may depart without me. But see, here is all that I have left of bread and wine, and here is a potion of healing herbs. When thy strength is restored thou can'st find the dwellings of the Hebrews among the houses of Babylon."

The Jew raised his trembling hands solemnly to heaven.

"Now may the God of Abraham and Isaac and Jacob bless and prosper the journey of the merciful, and bring him in peace to his desired haven. But stay; I have nothing to give thee in return—only this: that I can tell thee where the Messiah must be sought. For our prophets have said that he should be born not in Jerusalem, but in Bethlehem of Judah. May the Lord bring thee in safety to that place, because thou hast had pity upon the sick."

It was already long past midnight. Artaban rode in haste, and Vasda, restored by the brief rest, ran eagerly through the silent plain and swam the channels of the river. She put forth the remnant of her strength, and fled over the ground like a gazelle.

But the first beam of the sun sent her shadow before her as she entered upon the final stadium of the journey, and the eyes of Artaban anxiously scanning the great mound of Nimrod and the Temple of the Seven Spheres, could discern no trace of his friends.

The many-coloured terraces of black and orange and red and yellow and green and blue and white, shattered by the convulsions of nature, and crumbling under the repeated blows of human violence, still glittered like a ruined rainbow in the morning light.

Artaban rode swiftly around the hill. He dismounted and climbed to the highest terrace, looking out towards the west.

The huge desolation of the marshes stretched away to the horizon and the border of the desert. Bitterns stood by the stagnant pools and jackals skulked through the low bushes; but there was no sign of the caravan of the wise men, far or near.

At the edge of the terrace he saw a little cairn of broken bricks, and under them a piece of parchment. He caught it up and read: "We have waited past the midnight, and can delay no longer. We go to find the King. Follow us across the desert." Artaban sat down upon the ground and covered his head in despair.

"How can I cross the desert," said he, "with no food and with a spent horse? I must return to Babylon, sell my sapphire, and buy a train of camels, and provision for the journey. I may never overtake my friends. Only God the merciful knows whether I shall not lose the sight of the King because I tarried to show mercy."

FOR THE SAKE OF A LITTLE CHILD

There was a silence in the Hall of Dreams, where I was listening to the story of the other wise man. And through this silence I saw, but very dimly, his figure passing over the dreary undulations of the desert, high upon the back of his camel, rocking steadily onward like a ship over the waves.

The land of death spread its cruel net around him. The stony wastes bore no fruit but briers and thorns. The dark ledges of rock thrust themselves above the surface here and there, like the bones of perished monsters. Arid and inhospitable mountain ranges rose before him, furrowed with dry channels of ancient torrents, white and ghastly as scars on the face of nature. Shifting hills of treacherous sand were heaped like tombs along the horizon. By day, the fierce heat pressed its intolerable burden on the quivering air; and no living creature moved, on the dumb, swooning earth, but tiny jerboas scuttling through the parched bushes, or lizards vanishing in the clefts of the rock. By night the jackals prowled and barked in the distance, and the lion made the black ravines echo with his hollow roaring, while a bitter, blighting chill followed the fever of the day. Through heat and cold, the Magian moved steadily onward.

Then I saw the gardens and orchards of Damascus, watered by the streams of Abana and Pharpar, with their sloping swards inlaid with bloom, and their thickets of myrrh and roses. I saw also the long, snowy ridge of Hermon, and the dark groves of cedars, and the valley of the Jordan, and the blue waters of the Lake of Galilee, and the fertile plain of Esdraelon, and the hills of Ephraim, and the highlands of Judah. Through all these I followed the figure of Artaban moving steadily onward, until he arrived at Bethlehem. And it was the third day after the three wise men had come to that place and had found Mary and Joseph, with the young child, Jesus, and had laid their gifts of gold and frankincense and myrrh at his feet.

Then the other wise man drew near, weary, but full of hope, bearing his ruby and his pearl to offer to the King. "For now at last," he said, "I shall surely find him, though it be alone, and later than my brethren. This is the place of which the Hebrew exile told me that the prophets had spoken, and here I shall behold the rising of the great light. But I must inquire about the visit of my brethren, and to what house the star directed them, and to whom they presented their tribute."

The streets of the village seemed to be deserted, and Artaban wondered whether the men had all gone up to the hill-pastures to bring down their sheep. From the open door of a low stone cottage he heard the sound of a woman's voice singing softly. He entered and found a young mother hushing her baby to rest. She told him of the strangers from the far East who had appeared in the village three days ago, and how they said that a star had guided them to the place where Joseph of Nazareth was lodging with his wife and her new-born child, and how they had paid reverence to the child and given him many rich gifts.

"But the travellers disappeared again," she continued, "as suddenly as they had come. We were afraid at the strangeness of their visit. We could not understand it. The man of Nazareth took the babe and his mother and fled away that same night secretly, and it was whispered that they were going far away to Egypt. Ever since, there has been a spell upon the village; something evil hangs over it. They say that the Roman soldiers are coming from Jerusalem to force a new tax from us, and the men have driven the flocks and herds far back among the hills, and hidden themselves to escape it."

Artaban listened to her gentle, timid speech, and the child in her arms looked up in his face and smiled, stretching out its rosy hands to grasp at the winged circle of gold on his breast. His heart warmed to the touch. It seemed like a greeting of love and trust to one who had journeyed long in loneliness and perplexity, fighting with his own doubts and fears, and following a light that was veiled in clouds.

"Might not this child have been the promised Prince?" he asked within himself, as he touched its soft cheek. "Kings have been born ere now in lowlier houses than this, and the favourite of the stars may rise even from a cottage. But it has not seemed good to the God of wisdom to reward my search so soon and so easily. The one whom I seek has gone before me; and now I must follow the King to Egypt."

The young mother laid the babe in its cradle, and rose to minister to the wants of the strange guest that fate had brought into her house. She set food before him, the plain fare of peasants, but willingly offered, and therefore full of refreshment for the soul as well as for the body. Artaban accepted it gratefully; and, as he ate, the child fell into a happy slumber, and murmured sweetly in its dreams, and a great peace filled the quiet room.

But suddenly there came the noise of a wild confusion and uproar in the streets of the village, a shrieking and wailing of women's voices, a clangor of brazen trumpets and a clashing of swords, and a desperate cry: "The soldiers! the soldiers of Herod! They are killing our children."

The young mother's face grew white with terror. She clasped her child to her bosom, and crouched motionless in the darkest corner of the room, covering him with the folds of her robe, lest he should wake and cry.

But Artaban went quickly and stood in the doorway of the house. His broad shoulders filled the portal from side to side, and the peak of his white cap all but touched the lintel.

The soldiers came hurrying down the street with bloody hands and dripping swords. At the sight of the stranger in his imposing dress they hesitated with surprise. The captain of the band approached the threshold to thrust him aside. But Artaban did not stir. His face was as calm as though he were watching the stars, and in his eyes there burned that steady radiance before which even the half-tamed hunting leopard

220

shrinks, and the fierce bloodhound pauses in his leap. He held the soldier silently for an instant, and then said in a low voice:

"There is no one in this place but me, and I am waiting to give this jewel to the prudent captain who will leave me in peace."

He showed the ruby, glistening in the hollow of his hand like a great drop of blood.

The captain was amazed at the splendour of the gem. The pupils of his eyes expanded with desire, and the hard lines of greed wrinkled around his lips. He stretched out his hand and took the ruby.

"March on!" he cried to his men, "there is no child here. The house is still."

The clamour and the clang of arms passed down the street as the headlong fury of the chase sweeps by the secret covert where the trembling deer is hidden. Artaban re-entered the cottage. He turned his face to the east and prayed:

"God of truth, forgive my sin! I have said the thing that is not, to save the life of a child. And two of my gifts are gone. I have spent for man that which was meant for God. Shall I ever be worthy to see the face of the King?"

But the voice of the woman, weeping for joy in the shadow behind him, said very gently:

"Because thou hast saved the life of my little one, may the Lord bless thee and keep thee; the Lord make His face to shine upon thee and be gracious unto thee; the Lord lift up His countenance upon thee and give thee peace."

IN THE HIDDEN WAY OF SORROW

Then again there was a silence in the Hall of Dreams, deeper and more mysterious than the first interval, and I understood that the years of Artaban were flowing very swiftly under the stillness of that clinging fog, and I caught only a glimpse, here and there, of the river of his life shining through the shadows that concealed its course.

I saw him moving among the throngs of men in populous Egypt, seeking everywhere for traces of the household that had come down from Bethlehem, and finding them under the spreading sycamore-trees of Heliopolis, and beneath the walls of the Roman fortress of New Babylon beside the Nile—traces so faint and dim that they vanished before him continually, as footprints on the hard river-sand glisten for a moment with moisture and then disappear.

I saw him again at the foot of the pyramids, which lifted their sharp points into the intense saffron glow of the sunset sky, changeless monuments of the perishable glory and the imperishable hope of man. He looked up into the vast countenance of the crouching Sphinx and vainly tried to read the meaning of her calm eyes and smiling mouth. Was it, indeed, the mockery of all effort and all aspiration, as Tigranes had said—the cruel jest of a riddle that has no answer, a search that never can succeed? Or was there a touch of pity and encouragement in that inscrutable smile—a promise that even the defeated should attain a victory, and the disappointed should discover a prize, and the ignorant should be made wise, and the blind should see, and the wandering should come into the haven at last?

I saw him again in an obscure house of Alexandria, taking counsel with a Hebrew rabbi. The venerable man, bending over the rolls of parchment on which the prophecies of Israel were written, read aloud the pathetic words which foretold the sufferings of the promised Messiah—the despised and rejected of men, the man of sorrows and the acquaintance of grief.

"And remember, my son," said he, fixing his deep-set eyes upon the face of Artaban, "the King whom you are seeking is not to be found in a palace, nor among the rich and powerful. If the light of the world and the glory of Israel had been appointed to come with the greatness of earthly splendour, it must have appeared long ago. For no son of Abraham will ever again rival the power which Joseph had in the palaces of Egypt, or the magnificence of Solomon throned between the lions in Jerusalem. But the light for which the world is waiting is a new light, the glory that shall rise out of patient and triumphant suffering. And the kingdom which is to be established forever is a new kingdom, the royalty of perfect and unconquerable love. I do not know how this shall come to pass, nor how the turbulent kings and peoples of earth shall be brought to acknowledge the Messiah and pay homage to him. But this I know. Those who seek Him will do well to look among the poor and the lowly, the sorrowful and the oppressed."

So I saw the other wise man again and again, travelling from place to place, and searching among the people of the dispersion, with whom the little family from Bethlehem might, perhaps, have found a refuge. He passed through countries where famine lay heavy upon the land, and the poor were crying for bread. He made his dwelling in plague-stricken cities where the sick were languishing in the bitter companionship of helpless misery. He visited the oppressed and the afflicted in the gloom of subterranean prisons, and the crowded wretchedness of slave-markets, and the weary toil of galley-ships. In all this populous and intricate world of anguish, though he found none to worship, he found many to help. He fed the hungry, and clothed the naked, and healed the sick, and comforted the captive; and his years went by more swiftly than the weaver's shuttle that flashes back and forth through the loom while the web grows and the invisible pattern is completed.

It seemed almost as if he had forgotten his quest. But once I saw him for a moment as he stood alone at sunrise, waiting at the gate of a Roman prison. He had taken from a secret resting-place in his bosom the pearl, the last of his jewels. As he looked at it, a mellower lustre, a soft and iridescent light, full of shifting gleams of azure and rose, trembled upon its surface. It seemed to have absorbed some reflection of the colours of the lost sapphire and ruby. So the profound, secret purpose of a noble life draws into itself the memories of past joy and past sorrow. All that has helped it, all that has hindered it, is transfused by a subtle magic into its very essence. It becomes more luminous and precious the longer it is carried close to the warmth of the beating heart. Then, at last, while I was thinking of this pearl, and of its meaning, I heard the end of the story of the other wise man.

A PEARL OF GREAT PRICE

Three-and-thirty years of the life of Artaban had passed away, and he was still a pilgrim and a seeker after light. His hair, once darker than the cliffs of Zagros, was now white as the wintry snow that covered them. His eyes, that once flashed like flames of fire, were dull as embers smouldering among the ashes.

Worn and weary and ready to die, but still looking for the King, he had come for the last time to Jerusalem. He had often visited the holy city before, and had searched through all its lanes and crowded hovels and black prisons without finding any trace of the family of Nazarenes who had fled from Bethlehem long ago. But now it seemed as if he must make one more effort, and something whispered in his heart that, at last, he might succeed. It was the season of the Passover. The city was thronged with strangers. The children of Israel, scattered in far lands all over the world, had returned to the Temple for the great feast, and there had been a confusion of tongues in the narrow streets for many days.

But on this day there was a singular agitation visible in the multitude. The sky was veiled with a portentous gloom, and currents of excitement seemed to flash through the crowd like the thrill which shakes the forest on the eve of a storm. A secret tide was sweeping them all one way. The clatter of sandals, and the soft, thick sound of thousands of bare feet shuffling over the stones, flowed unceasingly along the street that leads to the Damascus gate.

Artaban joined company with a group of people from his own country, Parthian Jews who had come up to keep the Passover, and inquired of them the cause of the tumult, and where they were going.

"We are going," they answered, "to the place called Golgotha, outside the city walls, where there is to be an execution. Have you not heard what has happened? Two famous robbers are to be crucified, and with them another, called Jesus of Nazareth, a man who has done many wonderful works among the people, so that they love him greatly. But the priests and elders have said that he must die, because he gave himself out to be the Son of God. And Pilate has sent him to the cross because he said that he was the 'King of the Jews.'"

How strangely these familiar words fell upon the tired heart of Artaban! They had led him for a lifetime over land and sea. And now they came to him darkly and mysteriously like a message of despair. The King had arisen, but he had been denied and cast out. He was about to perish. Perhaps he was already dying. Could it be the same who had been born in Bethlehem, thirty-three years ago, at whose birth the star had appeared in heaven, and of whose coming the prophets had spoken?

Artaban's heart beat unsteadily with that troubled, doubtful apprehension which is the excitement of old age. But he said within himself, "The ways of God are stranger than the thoughts of men, and it may be that I shall find the King, at last, in the hands of His enemies, and shall come in time to offer my pearl for His ransom before He dies."

So the old man followed the multitude with slow and painful steps towards the Damascus gate of the city. Just beyond the entrance of the guard-house a troop of Macedonian soldiers came down the street, dragging a young girl with torn dress and dishevelled hair. As the Magian paused to look at her with compassion, she broke suddenly from the hands of her tormentors, and threw herself at his feet, clasping him around the knees. She had seen his white cap and the winged circle on his breast.

"Have pity on me," she cried, "and save me, for the sake of the God of Purity! I also am a daughter of the true religion which is taught by the Magi. My father was a merchant of Parthia, but he is dead, and I

226

am seized for his debts to be sold as a slave. Save me from worse than death!"

Artaban trembled.

It was the old conflict in his soul, which had come to him in the palm-grove of Babylon and in the cottage at Bethlehem—the conflict between the expectation of faith and the impulse of love. Twice the gift which he had consecrated to the worship of religion had been drawn from his hand to the service of humanity. This was the third trial, the ultimate probation, the final and irrevocable choice.

Was it his great opportunity, or his last temptation? He could not tell. One thing only was clear in the darkness of his mind—it was inevitable. And does not the inevitable come from God?

One thing only was sure to his divided heart—to rescue this helpless girl would be a true deed of love. And is not love the light of the soul?

He took the pearl from his bosom. Never had it seemed so luminous, so radiant, so full of tender, living lustre. He laid it in the hand of the slave.

"This is thy ransom, daughter! It is the last of my treasures which I kept for the King."

While he spoke the darkness of the sky thickened, and shuddering tremors ran through the earth, heaving convulsively like the breast of one who struggles with mighty grief.

The walls of the houses rocked to and fro. Stones were loosened and crashed into the street. Dust clouds filled the air. The soldiers fled in terror, reeling like drunken men. But Artaban and the girl whom he had ransomed crouched helpless beneath the wall of the Praetorium.

What had he to fear? What had he to live for? He had given away the last remnant of his tribute for the King. He had parted with the last hope of finding Him. The quest was over, and it had failed. But, even in that thought, accepted and embraced, there was peace. It was not resignation. It was not submission. It was something more profound and searching. He knew that all was well, because he had done the best that he could, from day to day. He had been true to the light that had been given to him. He had looked for more. And if he had not found it, if a failure was all that came out of his life, doubtless that was the best that was possible. He had not seen the revelation of "life everlasting, incorruptible and immortal." But he knew that even if he could live his earthly life over again, it could not be otherwise than it had been.

One more lingering pulsation of the earthquake quivered through the ground. A heavy tile, shaken from the roof, fell and struck the old man on the temple. He lay breathless and pale, with his gray head resting on the young girl's shoulder, and the blood trickling from the wound. As she bent over him, fearing that he was dead, there came a voice through the twilight, very small and still, like music sounding from a distance, in which the notes are clear but the words are lost. The girl turned to see if some one had spoken from the window above them, but she saw no one.

Then the old man's lips began to move, as if in answer, and she heard him say in the Parthian tongue:

"Not so, my Lord! For when saw I thee an hungered, and fed thee? Or thirsty, and gave thee drink? When saw I thee a stranger, and took thee in? Or naked, and clothed thee? When saw I thee sick or in prison, and came unto thee? Three-and-thirty years have I looked for thee; but I have never seen thy face, nor ministered to thee, my King."

He ceased, and the sweet voice came again. And again the maid heard it, very faintly and far away. But now it seemed as though she understood the words:

"*Verily I say unto thee, inasmuch as thou hast done it unto one of the least of these my brethren, thou hast done it unto me.*"

A calm radiance of wonder and joy lighted the pale face of Artaban like the first ray of dawn on a snowy mountain-peak. One long, last breath of relief exhaled gently from his lips.

His journey was ended. His treasures were accepted. The other Wise Man had found the King.

THE AMERICANISM OF WASHINGTON

Hard is the task of the man who at this late day attempts to say anything new about Washington. But perhaps it may be possible to unsay some of the things which have been said, and which, though they were at one time new, have never at any time been strictly true.

The character of Washington, emerging splendid from the dust and tumult of those great conflicts in which he played the leading part, has passed successively into three media of obscuration, from each of which his figure, like the sun shining through vapors, has received some disguise of shape and color. First came the mist of mythology, in which we discerned the new St. George, serene, impeccable, moving through an orchard of ever-blooming cherry-trees, gracefully vanquishing dragons with a touch, and shedding fragrance and radiance around him. Out of that mythological mist we groped our way, to find ourselves beneath the rolling clouds of oratory, above which the head of the hero was pinnacled in remote grandeur, like a sphinx poised upon a volcanic peak, isolated and mysterious. That altitudinous figure still dominates the cloudy landscapes of the after-dinner orator; but the frigid, academic mind has turned away from it, and looking through the fog of criticism has descried another Washington, not really an American, not amazingly a hero, but a very decent English country gentleman, honorable, courageous, good, shrewd, slow, and above all immensely lucky.

Now here are two of the things often said about Washington which need, if I mistake not, to be unsaid: first, that he was a solitary and inexplicable phenomenon of greatness; and second, that he was not an American.

Solitude, indeed, is the last quality that an intelligent student of his career would ascribe to him. Dignified and reserved he was, undoubtedly; and as this manner was natural to him, he won more true friends by using it than if he had disguised himself in a forced familiarity and worn his heart upon his sleeve. But from first to last he was a man who did his work in the bonds of companionship, who trusted his comrades in the great enterprise even though they were not his intimates, and who neither sought nor occupied a lonely eminence of unshared glory. He was not of the jealous race of those who

"Bear, like the Turk, no brother near the throne";

nor of the temper of George III., who chose his ministers for their vacuous compliancy. Washington was surrounded by men of similar though not of equal strength—Franklin, Hamilton, Knox, Greene, the Adamses, Jefferson, Madison. He stands in history not as a lonely pinnacle like Mount Shasta, elevated above the plain

"By drastic lift of pent volcanic fires";

but as the central summit of a mountain range, with all his noble fellowship of kindred peaks about him, enhancing his unquestioned supremacy by their glorious neighborhood and their great support.

Among these men whose union in purpose and action made the strength and stability of the republic, Washington was first, not only in the largeness of his nature, the loftiness of his desires, and the vigor of his will, but also in that representative quality which makes a man able to stand as the true hero of a great people. He had an instinctive power to divine, amid the confusions of rival interests and the cries of factional strife, the new aims and hopes, the vital needs and aspirations, which were the common inspiration of the people's cause and the creative forces of

230

the American nation. The power to understand this, the faith to believe in it, and the unselfish courage to live for it, was the central factor of Washington's life, the heart and fountain of his splendid Americanism.

It was denied during his lifetime, for a little while, by those who envied his greatness, resented his leadership, and sought to shake him from his lofty place. But he stood serene and imperturbable, while that denial, like many another blast of evil-scented wind, passed into nothingness, even before the disappearance of the party strife out of whose fermentation it had arisen. By the unanimous judgment of his countrymen for two generations after his death he was hailed as *Pater Patriae*; and the age which conferred that title was too ingenuous to suppose that the father could be of a different race from his own offspring.

But the modern doubt is more subtle, more curious, more refined in its methods. It does not spring, as the old denial did, from a partisan hatred, which would seek to discredit Washington by an accusation of undue partiality for England, and thus to break his hold upon the love of the people. It arises, rather, like a creeping exhalation, from a modern theory of what true Americanism really is: a theory which goes back, indeed, for its inspiration to Dr. Johnson's somewhat crudely expressed opinion that "the Americans were a race whom no other mortals could wish to resemble"; but which, in its later form, takes counsel with those British connoisseurs who demand of their typical American not depravity of morals but deprivation of manners, not vice of heart but vulgarity of speech, not badness but bumptiousness, and at least enough of eccentricity to make him amusing to cultivated people.

Not a few of our native professors and critics are inclined to accept some features of this view, perhaps in mere reaction from the unamusing character of their own existence. They are not quite ready to subscribe to Mr. Kipling's statement that the real American is

"Unkempt, disreputable, vast,"

I remember reading somewhere that Tennyson had an idea that Longfellow, when he met him, would put his feet upon the table. And it is precisely because Longfellow kept his feet in their proper place, in society as well as in verse, that some critics, nowadays, would have us believe that he was not a truly American poet.

Traces of this curious theory of Americanism in its application to Washington may now be found in many places. You shall hear historians describe him as a transplanted English commoner, a second edition of John Hampden. You shall read, in a famous poem, of Lincoln as

"New birth of our new soil, the *first* American."

He knew it, I say: and by what divination? By a test more searching than any mere peculiarity of manners, dress, or speech; by a touchstone able to divide the gold of essential character from the alloy of superficial characteristics; by a standard which disregarded alike Franklin's fur cap and Putnam's old felt hat, Morgan's leather leggings and Witherspoon's black silk gown and John Adams's lace ruffles, to recognize and approve, beneath these various garbs, the vital sign of America woven into the very souls of the men who belonged to her by a spiritual birthright.

For what is true Americanism, and where does it reside? Not on the tongue, nor in the clothes, nor among the transient social forms, refined or rude, which mottle the surface of human life. The log cabin has no monopoly of it, nor is it an immovable fixture of the stately pillared mansion. Its home is not on the frontier nor in the populous city, not among the trees of the wild forest nor the cultured groves of Academe. Its dwelling is in the heart. It speaks a score of dialects but one language, follows a hundred paths to the same goal, performs a thousand kinds of service in loyalty to the same ideal which is its life. True Americanism is this:

232

To believe that the inalienable rights of man to life, liberty, and the pursuit of happiness are given by God.

To believe that any form of power that tramples on these rights is unjust.

To believe that taxation without representation is tyranny, that government must rest upon the consent of the governed, and that the people should choose their own rulers.

To believe that freedom must be safeguarded by law and order, and that the end of freedom is fair play for all.

To believe not in a forced equality of conditions and estates, but in a true equalization of burdens, privileges, and opportunities.

To believe that the selfish interests of persons, classes, and sections must be subordinated to the welfare of the commonwealth.

To believe that union is as much a human necessity as liberty is a divine gift.

To believe, not that all people are good, but that the way to make them better is to trust the whole people.

To believe that a free state should offer an asylum to the oppressed, and an example of virtue, sobriety, and fair dealing to all nations.

To believe that for the existence and perpetuity of such a state a man should be willing to give his whole service, in property, in labor, and in life.

That is Americanism; an ideal embodying itself in a people; a creed heated white hot in the furnace of conviction and hammered into shape on the anvil of life; a vision commanding men to follow it whithersoever it may lead them. And it was the subordination of the personal self to that ideal, that creed, that vision, which gave eminence and glory to Washington and the men who stood with him.

This is the truth that emerges, crystalline and luminous, from the conflicts and confusions of the Revolution. The men who were able to surrender themselves and all their interests to the pure and loyal service of their ideal were the men who made good, the victors crowned with glory and honor. The men who would not make that surrender, who sought selfish ends, who were controlled by personal ambition and the love of gain, who were willing to stoop to crooked means to advance their own fortunes, were the failures, the lost leaders, and, in some cases, the men whose names are embalmed in their own infamy. The ultimate secret of greatness is neither physical nor intellectual, but moral. It is the capacity to lose self in the service of something greater. It is the faith to recognize, the will to obey, and the strength to follow, a star.

Washington, no doubt, was pre-eminent among his contemporaries in natural endowments. Less brilliant in his mental gifts than some, less eloquent and accomplished than others, he had a rare balance of large powers which justified Lowell's phrase of "an imperial man." His athletic vigor and skill, his steadiness of nerve restraining an intensity of passion, his undaunted courage which refused no necessary risks and his prudence which took no unnecessary ones, the quiet sureness with which he grasped large ideas and the pressing energy with which he executed small details, the breadth of his intelligence, the depth of his convictions, his power to apply great thoughts and principles to every-day affairs, and his singular superiority to current prejudices and illusions—these were gifts in combination which would have made him distinguished in any company, in any age.

But what was it that won and kept a free field for the exercise of these gifts? What was it that secured for them a long, unbroken opportunity of development in the activities of leadership, until they reached the summit of their perfection? It was a moral quality. It was the evident magnanimity of the man, which assured the people that he was no self-seeker who would betray their interests for his own glory or rob them for his own gain. It was the supreme magnanimity of the man, which made the best spirits of the time trust him implicitly, in war and peace, as one who would never forget his duty or his integrity in the sense of his own greatness.

234

From the first, Washington appears not as a man aiming at prominence or power, but rather as one under obligation to serve a cause. Necessity was laid upon him, and he met it willingly. After Washington's marvellous escape from death in his first campaign for the defence of the colonies, the Rev. Samuel Davies, fourth president of Princeton College, spoke of him in a sermon as "that heroic youth, Colonel Washington, whom I can but hope Providence has hitherto preserved in so signal a manner for some important service to his country." It was a prophetic voice, and Washington was not disobedient to the message. Chosen to command the Army of the Revolution in 1775, he confessed to his wife his deep reluctance to surrender the joys of home, acknowledged publicly his feeling that he was not equal to the great trust committed to him, and then, accepting it as thrown upon him "by a kind of destiny," he gave himself body and soul to its fulfilment refusing all pay beyond the mere discharge of his expenses, of which he kept a strict account, and asking no other reward than the success of the cause which he served.

"Ah, but he was a rich man," cries the carping critic; "he could afford to do it." How many rich men to-day avail themselves of their opportunity to indulge in this kind of extravagance, toiling tremendously without a salary, neglecting their own estate for the public benefit, seeing their property diminished without complaint, and coming into serious financial embarrassment, even within sight of bankruptcy, as Washington did, merely for the gratification of a desire to serve the people? This is indeed a very singular and noble form of luxury. But the wealth which makes it possible neither accounts for its existence nor detracts from its glory. It is the fruit of a manhood superior alike to riches and to poverty, willing to risk all, and to use all, for the common good.

Was it in any sense a misfortune for the people of America, even the poorest among them, that there was a man able to advance sixty-four thousand dollars out of his own purse, with no other security but his own faith in their cause, to pay his daily expenses while he was leading their armies? This unsecured loan was one of the very things, I doubt not, that helped to inspire general confidence. Even so the prophet Jeremiah purchased a field in Anathoth, in the days when Judah was captive unto Babylon, paying down the money, seventeen shekels of silver, as a token of his faith that the land would some day be delivered from the enemy and restored to peaceful and orderly habitation.

Washington's substantial pledge of property to the cause of liberty was repaid by a grateful country at the close of the war. But not a dollar of payment for the tremendous toil of body and mind, not a dollar for work "overtime," for indirect damages to his estate, for commissions on the benefits which he secured for the general enterprise, for the use of his name or the value of his counsel, would he receive.

A few years later, when his large sagacity perceived that the development of internal commerce was one of the first needs of the new country, at a time when he held no public office, he became president of a company for the extension of navigation on the rivers James and Potomac. The Legislature of Virginia proposed to give him a hundred and fifty shares of stock. Washington refused this, or any other kind of pay, saying that he could serve the people better in the enterprise if he were known to have no selfish interest in it. He was not the kind of a man to reconcile himself to a gratuity (which is the Latinized word for a "tip" offered to a person not in livery), and if the modern methods of "coming in on the ground-floor" and "taking a rake-off" had been explained and suggested to him, I suspect that he would have described them in language more notable for its force than for its elegance.

It is true, of course, that the fortune which he so willingly imperilled and impaired recouped itself again after peace was established, and his industry and wisdom made him once more a rich man for those days. But what injustice was there in that? It is both natural and right that men who have risked their all to secure for the country at large what they could have secured for themselves by other means, should share in the general prosperity attendant upon the success of their efforts and sacrifices for the common good.

I am sick of the shallow judgment that ranks the worth of a man by his poverty or by his wealth at death. Many a selfish speculator dies poor. Many an unselfish patriot dies prosperous. It is not the possession of the dollar that cankers the soul, it is the worship of it. The true test of a man is this: Has he labored for his own interest, or for the general welfare? Has he earned his money fairly or unfairly? Does he use it greedily or generously? What does it mean to him, a personal advantage over his fellow-men, or a personal opportunity of serving them?

There are a hundred other points in Washington's career in which the same supremacy of character, magnanimity focussed on service to an ideal, is revealed in conduct. I see it in the wisdom with which he, a son of the South, chose most of his generals from the North, that he might secure immediate efficiency and unity in the army. I see it in the generosity with which he praised the achievements of his associates, disregarding jealous rivalries, and ever willing to share the credit of victory as he was to bear the burden of defeat. I see it in the patience with which he suffered his fame to be imperilled for the moment by reverses and retreats, if only he might the more surely guard the frail hope of ultimate victory for his country. I see it in the quiet dignity with which he faced the Conway Cabal, not anxious to defend his own reputation and secure his own power, but nobly resolute to save the army from being crippled and the cause of liberty from being wrecked. I see it in the splendid self-forgetfulness which cleansed his mind of all temptation to take personal revenge upon those who had sought to injure him in that base intrigue. I read it in his letter of consolation and encouragement to the wretched Gates after the defeat at Camden. I hear the prolonged reechoing music of it in his letter to General Knox in 1798, in regard to military appointments, declaring his wish to "avoid feuds with those who are embarked in the same general enterprise with myself."

Listen to the same spirit as it speaks in his circular address to the governors of the different States, urging them to "forget their local prejudices and policies; to make those mutual concessions which are requisite to the general prosperity, and in some instances to sacrifice their individual advantages to the interest of the community." Watch how it guides him unerringly through the critical period of American history which lies between the success of the Revolution and the establishment of the nation, enabling him to avoid the pitfalls of sectional and partisan strife, and to use his great influence with the people in leading them out of the confusion of a weak confederacy into the strength of an indissoluble union of sovereign States.

See how he once more sets aside his personal preferences for a quiet country life, and risks his already secure popularity, together with his reputation for consistency, by obeying the voice which calls him to be a candidate for the Presidency. See how he chooses for the cabinet and for the Supreme Court, not an exclusive group of personal friends, but men who can be trusted to serve the great cause of Union with fidelity and power—Jefferson, Randolph, Hamilton, Knox, John Jay, Wilson, Cushing, Rutledge. See how patiently and indomitably he gives himself to the toil of office, deriving from his exalted station no gain "beyond the lustre which may be reflected from its connection with a power of promoting human felicity." See how he retires, at last, to the longed-for joys of private life, confessing that his career has not been without errors of judgment, beseeching the Almighty that they may bring no harm to his country, and asking no other reward for his labors than to partake, "in the midst of my fellow-citizens, the benign influence of good laws under a free government, the ever favorite object of my heart."

Oh, sweet and stately words, revealing, through their calm reserve, the inmost secret of a life that did not flare with transient enthusiasm but glowed with unquenchable devotion to a cause! "The ever favorite object of my heart"—how quietly, how simply he discloses the source and origin of a sublime consecration, a lifelong heroism! Thus speaks the victor in calm retrospect of the long battle. But if you would know the depth and the intensity of the divine fire that burned within his breast you must go back to the dark and icy days of Valley Forge, and hear

238

him cry in passion unrestrained: "If I know my own mind, I could offer myself a living sacrifice to the butchering enemy, provided that would contribute to the people's ease. I would be a living offering to the savage fury and die by inches to save the people."

"*The ever favorite object of my heart*." I strike this note again and again, insisting upon it, harping upon it; for it is the key-note of the music. It is the capacity to find such an object in the success of the people's cause, to follow it unselfishly, to serve it loyally, that distinguishes the men who stood with Washington and who deserve to share his fame. I read the annals of the Revolution, and I find everywhere this secret and searching test dividing the strong from the weak, the noble from the base, the heirs of glory from the captives of oblivion and the inheritors of shame. It was the unwillingness to sink and forget self in the service of something greater that made the failures and wrecks of those tempestuous times, through which the single-hearted and the devoted pressed on to victory and honor.

Turn back to the battle of Saratoga. There were two Americans on that field who suffered under a great personal disappointment: Philip Schuyler, who was unjustly supplanted in command of the army by General Gates; and Benedict Arnold, who was deprived by envy of his due share in the glory of winning the battle. Schuyler forgot his own injury in loyalty to the cause, offered to serve Gates in any capacity, and went straight on to the end of his noble life giving all that he had to his country. But in Arnold's heart the favorite object was not his country, but his own ambition, and the wound which his pride received at Saratoga rankled and festered and spread its poison through his whole nature, until he went forth from the camp, "a leper white as snow."

What was it that made Charles Lee, as fearless a man as ever lived, play the part of a coward in order to hide his treason at the battle of Monmouth? It was the inward eating corruption of that selfish vanity which caused him to desire the defeat of an army whose command he had wished but failed to attain. He had offered his sword to America for his own glory, and when that was denied him, he withdrew the offering, and died, as he had lived, to himself.

What was it that tarnished the fame of Gates and Wilkinson and Burr and Conway? What made their lives, and those of men like them, futile and inefficient compared with other men whose natural gifts were less? It was the taint of dominant selfishness that ran through their careers, now hiding itself, now breaking out in some act of malignity or treachery. Of the common interest they were reckless, provided they might advance their own. Disappointed in that "ever favorite object of their hearts," they did not hesitate to imperil the cause in whose service they were enlisted.

Turn to other cases, in which a charitable judgment will impute no positive betrayal of trusts, but a defect of vision to recognize the claim of the higher ideal. Tory or Revolutionist a man might be, according to his temperament and conviction; but where a man begins with protests against tyranny and ends with subservience to it, we look for the cause. What was it that separated Joseph Galloway from Francis Hopkinson? It was Galloway's opinion that, while the struggle for independence might be justifiable, it could not be successful, and the temptation of a larger immediate reward under the British crown than could ever be given by the American Congress in which he had once served. What was it that divided the Rev. Jacob Duché from the Rev. John Witherspoon? It was Duché's fear that the cause for which he had prayed so eloquently in the first Continental Congress was doomed after the capture of Philadelphia, and his unwillingness to go down with that cause instead of enjoying the comfortable fruits of his native wit and eloquence in an easy London chaplaincy. What was it that cut William Franklin off from his professedly prudent and worldly wise old father, Benjamin? It was the luxurious and benumbing charm of the royal governorship of New Jersey.

"Professedly prudent" is the phrase that I have chosen to apply to Benjamin Franklin. For the one thing that is clear, as we turn to look at him and the other men who stood with Washington, is that, whatever their philosophical professions may have been, they were not controlled by prudence. They were really imprudent, and at heart willing to take all risks of poverty and death in a struggle whose cause was just though its issue was dubious. If it be rashness to commit honor and life and property to a great adventure for the general good, then these men were rash to the verge of recklessness. They refused no peril, they withheld no sacrifice, in the following of their ideal.

I hear John Dickinson saying: "It is not our duty to leave wealth to our children, but it is our duty to leave liberty to them. We have counted the cost of this contest, and we find nothing so dreadful as voluntary slavery." I see Samuel Adams, impoverished, living upon a pittance, hardly able to provide a decent coat for his back, rejecting with scorn the offer of a profitable office, wealth, a title even, to win him from his allegiance to the cause of America. I see Robert Morris, the wealthy merchant, opening his purse and pledging his credit to support the Revolution, and later devoting all his fortune and his energy to restore and establish the financial honor of the Republic, with the memorable words, "The United States may command all that I have, except my integrity." I hear the proud John Adams saying to his wife, "I have accepted a seat in the House of Representatives, and thereby have consented to my own ruin, to your ruin, and the ruin of our children"; and I hear her reply, with the tears running down her face, "Well, I am willing in this cause to run all risks with you, and be ruined with you, if you are ruined," I see Benjamin Franklin, in the Congress of 1776, already past his seventieth year, prosperous, famous, by far the most celebrated man in America, accepting without demur the difficult and dangerous mission to France, and whispering to his friend, Dr. Rush, "I am old and good for nothing, but as the store-keepers say of their remnants of cloth, 'I am but a fag-end, and you may have me for what you please.'"

Here is a man who will illustrate and prove, perhaps better than any other of those who stood with Washington, the point at which I am aiming. There was none of the glamour of romance about old Ben

Franklin. He was shrewd, canny, humorous. The chivalric Southerners disliked his philosophy, and the solemn New-Englanders mistrusted his jokes. He made no extravagant claims for his own motives, and some of his ways were not distinctly ideal. He was full of prudential proverbs, and claimed to be a follower of the theory of enlightened self-interest. But there was not a faculty of his wise old head which he did not put at the service of his country, nor was there a pulse of his slow and steady heart which did not beat loyal to the cause of freedom.

He forfeited profitable office and sure preferment under the crown, for hard work, uncertain pay, and certain peril in behalf of the colonies. He followed the inexorable logic, step by step, which led him from the natural rights of his countrymen to their liberty, from their liberty to their independence. He endured with a grim humor the revilings of those whom he called "malevolent critics and bug-writers." He broke with his old and dear associates in England, writing to one of them,

> "You and I were long friends; you are now my enemy and
> I am Yours,
> B. Franklin."

He never flinched or faltered at any sacrifice of personal ease or interest to the demands of his country. His patient, skilful, laborious efforts in France did as much for the final victory of the American cause as any soldier's sword. He yielded his own opinions in regard to the method of making the treaty of peace with England, and thereby imperilled for a time his own prestige. He served as president of Pennsylvania three times, devoting all his salary to public benefactions. His influence in the Constitutional Convention was steadfast on the side of union and harmony, though in many things he differed from the prevailing party. His voice was among those who hailed Washington as the only possible candidate for the Presidency. His last public act was a petition to Congress for the abolition of slavery. At his death the government had not yet settled his accounts in its service, and his country was left apparently his debtor; which, in a sense still larger and deeper, she must remain as long as liberty endures and union triumphs in the Republic.

Is not this, after all, the root of the whole matter? Is not this the thing that is vitally and essentially true of all those great men, clustering about Washington, whose fame we honor and revere with his? They all left the community, the commonwealth, the race, in debt to them. This was their purpose and the ever-favorite object of their hearts. They were deliberate and joyful creditors. Renouncing the maxim of worldly wisdom which bids men "get all you can and keep all you get," they resolved rather to give all they had to advance the common cause, to use every benefit conferred upon them in the service of the general welfare, to bestow upon the world more than they received from it, and to leave a fair and unblotted account of business done with life which should show a clear balance in their favor.

Thus, in brief outline, and in words which seem poor and inadequate, I have ventured to interpret anew the story of Washington and the men who stood with him: not as a stirring ballad of battle and danger, in which the knights ride valiantly, and are renowned for their mighty strokes at the enemy in arms; not as a philosophic epic, in which the development of a great national idea is displayed, and the struggle of opposing policies is traced to its conclusion; but as a drama of the eternal conflict in the soul of man between self-interest in its Protean forms, and loyalty to the right, service to a cause, allegiance to an ideal.

Those great actors who played in it have passed away, but the same drama still holds the stage. The drop-curtain falls between the acts; the scenery shifts; the music alters; but the crisis and its issues are unchanged, and the parts which you and I play are assigned to us by our own choice of "the ever favorite object of our hearts."

Men tell us that the age of ideals is past, and that we are now come to the age of expediency, of polite indifference to moral standards, of careful attention to the bearing of different policies upon our own personal interests. Men tell us that the rights of man are a poetic fiction, that democracy has nothing in it to command our allegiance unless it promotes our individual comfort and prosperity, and that the whole duty of a citizen is to vote with his party and get an office for himself, or for some one who will look after him. Men tell us that to succeed means to get money, because with that all other good things can be secured. Men tell us that the one thing to do is to promote and protect the particular trade, or industry, or corporation in which we have a share: the laws of trade will work out that survival of the fittest which is the only real righteousness, and if we survive that will prove that we are fit. Men tell us that all beyond this is phantasy, dreaming, Sunday-school politics: there is nothing worth living for except to get on in the world; and nothing at all worth dying for, since the age of ideals is past.

It is past indeed for those who proclaim, or whisper, or in their hearts believe, or in their lives obey, this black gospel. And what is to follow? An age of cruel and bitter jealousies between sections and classes; of hatted and strife between the Haves and the Have-nots; of futile contests between parties which have kept their names and confused their principles, so that no man may distinguish them except as the Ins and Outs. An age of greedy privilege and sullen poverty, of blatant luxury and curious envy, of rising palaces and vanishing homes, of stupid frivolity and idiotic publicomania; in which four hundred gilded fribbles give monkey-dinners and Louis XV. revels, while four million ungilded gossips gape at them and read about them in the newspapers. An age when princes of finance buy protection from the representatives of a fierce democracy; when guardians of the savings which insure the lives of the poor, use them as a surplus to pay for the extravagances of the rich; and when men who have climbed above their fellows on golden ladders, tremble at the crack of the blackmailer's whip and come down at the call of an obscene newspaper. An age when the python of political corruption casts its "rings" about the neck of proud cities and sovereign States, and throttles honesty to silence and liberty to death. It is such an age, dark, confused, shameful, that the sceptic and the scorner must face, when they turn their backs upon those ancient shrines where the flames of faith and integrity and devotion are flickering like the deserted altar-fires of a forsaken worship.

But not for us who claim our heritage in blood and spirit from Washington and the men who stood with him,—not for us of other tribes and kindred who

"Have found a fatherland upon this shore,"

and learned the meaning of manhood beneath the shelter of liberty,—not for us, nor for our country, that dark apostasy, that dismal outlook! We see the palladium of the American ideal—goddess of the just eye, the unpolluted heart, the equal hand—standing as the image of Athene stood above the upper streams of Simois:

"It stood, and sun and moonshine rained their light
    On the pure columns of its glen-built hall.
Backward and forward rolled the waves of fight
    Round Troy—but while this stood Troy could not fall."

We see the heroes of the present conflict, the men whose allegiance is not to sections but to the whole people, the fearless champions of fair play. We hear from the chair of Washington a brave and honest voice which cries that our industrial problems must be solved not in the interest of capital, nor of labor, but of the whole people. We believe that the liberties which the heroes of old won with blood and sacrifice are ours to keep with labor and service.

"All that our fathers wrought With true prophetic thought, Must be defended."

No privilege that encroaches upon those liberties is to be endured. No lawless disorder that imperils them is to be sanctioned. No class that disregards or invades them is to be tolerated.

There is a life that is worth living now, as it was worth living in the former days, and that is the honest life, the useful life, the unselfish life, cleansed by devotion to an ideal. There is a battle that is worth fighting now, as it was worth fighting then, and that is the battle for justice and equality. To make our city and our State free in fact as well as in name; to break the rings that strangle real liberty, and to keep them broken; to cleanse, so far as in our power lies, the fountains of our national life from political, commercial, and social corruption; to teach our sons and daughters, by precept and example, the honor of serving such a country as America—that is work worthy of the finest manhood and womanhood. The well born are those who are born to do that work. The well bred are those who are bred to be proud of that work. The well educated are those who see deepest into the meaning and the necessity of that work. Nor shall their labor be for naught, nor the reward of their sacrifice fail them. For high in the firmament of human destiny are set the stars of faith in mankind, and unselfish courage, and loyalty to the ideal; and while they shine, the Americanism of Washington and the men who stood with him shall never, never die.

THE END

WHAT PEACE MEANS

To
My Son in the Faith
My Brother in the Work
Tertius van Dyke

FOREWORD

This little book contains three plain sermons which were preached in New York in the Easter season of 1919, in the Park Avenue Presbyterian Church, of which my son is minister. I had no thought that they would ever be printed. They were, and are, just *daily bread discourses* meant to serve the spiritual needs of a congregation of Christian people, seekers after truth, inquirers about duty, strangers and pilgrims, in the great city and the troubled world.

But if, as friends think, these simple chapters may be of service through the printed page to a larger circle of readers, I willingly and freely let them go.

May the blessing of Jesus follow them on their humble path. May the Spirit of Truth bring them home to some hearts that want them,—to those who desire to escape from evil and do good,—to those who "seek peace and ensue it."

HENRY VAN DYKE.
Park Avenue Church Manse, New York City.

I.

PEACE IN THE SOUL

Peace I leave with you: my peace I give unto you.—ST. JOHN 14:27.

Peace is one of the great words of the Holy Scriptures. It is woven through the Old Testament and the New like a golden thread. It inheres and abides in the character of God,—

> "The central peace subsisting at the heart
> Of endless agitation."

It is the deepest and most universal desire of man, whose prayer in all ages has been, "Grant us Thy Peace, O Lord." It is the reward of the righteous, the blessing of the good, the crown of life's effort, and the glory of eternity.

The prophets foretell the beauty of its coming and the psalmists sing of the joy which it brings. Jesus Christ is its Divine Messiah, its high priest and its holy prince. The evangelists and prophets proclaim and preach it. From beginning to end the Bible is full of the praise of peace.

Yet there never was a book more full of stories of trouble and strife, disaster and sorrow. God Himself is revealed in it not as a calm, untroubled, self-absorbed Deity, occupied in beatific contemplation of His own perfections. He is a God who works and labours, who wars against the evil, who fights for the good. The psalmist speaks of Him as "The Lord of Hosts, strong and mighty in battle." The Revelation of St. John tells us that "There was war in Heaven; Michael and his angels fought against the dragon." Jesus Christ said: "I came not to send peace, but a sword."

It is evident, then, that this idea of "peace," like all good and noble things, has its counterfeit, its false and subtle versary, which steals its name and its garments to deceive and betray the hearts of men. We find this clearly taught in the Bible. Not more earnestly does it praise true peace than it denounces false peace.

There is no peace, saith the Lord, unto the wicked (Isaiah 48:22).

For they have healed the hurt of the daughter of my people slightly, saying, Peace, peace; when there is no peace (Jer. 8:11).

If thou hadst known, even thou, at least in this thy day, the things which belong unto thy peace! but now they are hid from thine eyes (St. Luke 19:42).

For to be carnally minded is death; but to be spiritually minded is life and peace (Romans 8:6).

There never was a time in human history when a right understanding of the nature of true peace, the path which leads to it, the laws which govern it, was more necessary or more important than it is to-day.

The world has just passed through a ghastly experience of war at its worst. Never in history has there been such slaughter, such agony, such waste, such desolation, in a brief space of time, as in the four terrible years of conflict which German militarism forced on the world in the twentieth century. Having seen it, I know what it means.

Now we have "supped full with horrors." We have had more than enough of that bloody banquet The heart of humanity longs for peace, as it has always longed, but now with a new intensity, greater than ever before. Yet the second course of war continues. The dogs fight for the crumbs under the peace-table. Ignorant armies clash by night. Cities are bombarded and sacked. The barbarous Bolsheviki raise the red flag of violence and threaten a war of classes throughout the world.

You can never make a golden age out of leaden men, or a peaceful world out of lovers of strife.

Where shall peace be found? How shall it be attained and safeguarded? Evidently the militarists have assaulted it with their doctrine that might makes right. Evidently the pacifists have betrayed it with their doctrine of passive acceptance of wrong. Somewhere between these two errors there must be a ground of truth on which Christians can stand to defend their faith and maintain their hope of a better future for the world.

Let me begin by speaking of *Peace in the Soul.* That is where religion begins, in the heart of a person. Its flowers and fruits are social. They are for the blessing of the world. But its root is personal. You can never start with a class—conscious or a mass—conscious Christianity. It must begin with just you and God.

Marshal Joffre, that fine Christian soldier, said a memorable thing about the winning of the war: "Our victory will be the fruit of individual sacrifice." So of the coming of peace on earth we may say the same: it will be the fruit of the entrance of peace into individual hearts and lives.

A world at war is the necessary result of human restlessness and enmities. "From whence come wars and fightings among you? Come they not hence, even of your lusts, that war in your members?" Envy, malice, greed, hatred, deceit,—these are the begetters of strife on earth.

A world at peace can come only from the cooperation of peaceful human spirits. Therefore we must commence to learn what peace is, by seeking it in our souls through faith.

Christ promised peace to His disciples at the Communion in that little upper room in Jerusalem, nineteen hundred years ago. Evidently it was not an outward but an inward peace. He told them that they would have a lot of trouble in the world. But He assured them that this could not overcome them if they believed in Him and in His Father God. He warned them of conflict, and assured them of inward peace.

What are the elements of this wondrous gift which Christ gave to His disciples, and which He offers to us?

I. First, the peace of Christ is the peace of being divinely loved. Nothing rests and satisfies the heart like the sense of being loved. Let us take as an illustration the case of a little child, which has grown tired and fretful at its play, and is frightened suddenly by some childish terror. Weeping, it runs to its mother. She takes the child in her arms, folds it to her breast, bends over it, and soothes it with fond words which mean only this: "I love you." Very soon the child sinks to rest, contented and happy, in the sense of being loved. "Herein is love, not that we loved God, but that he loved us, and sent his Son to be the propitiation for our sins." In Jesus Christ God is stretching out His arms to us, drawing us to His bosom, enfolding us in the secret of peace. If we believe in Jesus Christ as the Son of God, He makes us sure of a Divine affection, deep, infinite, inexhaustible, imperishable. "For God so loved the world, that he gave his only begotten Son, that whosoever believeth in him should not perish, but have everlasting life." God, who "spared not his dearly-beloved Son, but delivered him up for us all, how shall he not with him also freely give us all things?" "Nothing shall be able to separate us from the love of God, which is in Christ Jesus our Lord."

II. The Christian peace is the peace of being divinely controlled. The man who accepts Jesus Christ truly, accepts Him as Master and Lord. He believes that Christ has a purpose for him, which will surely be fulfilled? work for him, which will surely be blessed if he only tries to do it. Most of the discords of life come from a conflict of authorities, of plans, of purposes. Suppose that a building were going up, and the architect had one design for it, and the builder had another. What perplexity and confusion there would be! How ill things would fit! What perpetual quarrels and blunders and disappointments! But when the workman accepts the designer's plan and simply does his best to carry that out, harmony, joyful labour, and triumph are the result. If we accept God's plan for us, yield to Him as the daily controller and director of our life, our work, however hard, becomes peaceful and secure. No perils can frighten, no interruptions can dishearten us.

Not many years ago some workmen were digging a tunnel, when a sudden fall of earth blocked the mouth of the opening. Their companions on the outside found out what had happened, and started to dig through the mass of earth to the rescue. It was several hours before they made their way through. When they went in they found the workmen going on with their labour on the tunnel. "We knew," said one of them, "that you'd come to help us, and we thought the best way to make time pass quick was to keep on with the work." That is what a Christian may say to Christ amid the dangers and disasters of life. We know that He will never forsake us, and the best way to be at peace is to be about His business. He says to us: "As the Father sent me, even so send I you."

III. The Christian peace is the peace of being divinely forgiven.

"In every man," said a philosopher, "there is something which, if we knew it, would make us despise him." Let us turn the saying, and change it from a bitter cynicism into a wholesome truth.

In every one of us there is something which, if we realize it, makes us condemn ourselves as sinners, and hunger and thirst after righteousness, and long for forgiveness.

It is this deep consciousness of sin, of evil in our hearts and lives, that makes us restless and unhappy. The plasters and soothing lotions with which the easy-going philosophy of modern times covers it up, do not heal it; they only hide it. There is no cure for it, there is no rest for the sinful soul, except the divine forgiveness. There is no sure pledge of this except in the holy sacrifice and blessed promise of Christ, "Son, daughter, thy sins are forgiven thee, go in peace."

Understand, I do not mean that what we need and want is to have our sins ignored and overlooked. On the contrary, that is just what would fail to bring us true rest. For if God took no account of sins, required no repentance and reparation, He would not be holy, just, and faithful, a God whom we can adore and love and trust.

Nor do I mean that what we need is merely to have the punishment of sins remitted. That would not satisfy the heart. Is the child contented when the father says, "Well, I will not punish you. Go away"? No, what the child wants is to hear the father say, "I forgive you. Come to me." It is to be welcomed back to the father's home, to the father's heart, that the child longs.

Peace means not to have the offense ignored, but to have it pardoned: not to the punishment omitted, but to have separation from God ended and done with. That is the peace of being divinely forgiven,—a peace which recognizes sin, and triumphs over it,—a peace which not merely saves us from death but welcomes us home to the divine love from which we have wandered.

That is the peace which Christ offers to each one of us in His Gospel. We need it in this modern world as much as men and women ever needed it in the old world. No New Era will ever change its meaning or do away with its necessity. Indeed, it seems to me that we need this old-fashioned religion to-day more than ever.

We need it for our own comfort and strength. We need it to deliver us from the vanity and hollowness, the fever and hysteria of the present age. We need it to make us better soldiers and workers for every good cause. Peace is coming to all the earth some day through Christ. And those who shall do most to help Him bring it are the men and women to whom He gives Peace in the Soul.

II.

PEACE ON EARTH THROUGH RIGHTEOUSNESS

And the work of righteousness shall be peace: and the effect of righteousness quietness and confidence forever.—ISAIAH 32:17.

After we have found peace in our own souls through faith in God and in His Son, Jesus Christ our Saviour, if our faith is honest, we must feel the desire and the duty of helping to make peace prevail on earth.

But here we are, in a world of confusion and conflict. Darkness and ignorance strive against light. Evil hates and assaults good. Wrong takes up arms against right. Greed and pride and passion call on violence to defeat justice and enthrone blind force. So has it been since Cain killed Abel, since Christ was crucified on Calvary, and so it is to-day wherever men uphold the false doctrine that "might makes right."

The Bible teaches us that there is no foundation for enduring peace on earth except in righteousness: that it is our duty to suffer for that cause if need be: that we are bound to fight for it if we have the power: and that if God gives us the victory we must use it for the perpetuation of righteous peace.

In these words I sum up what seems to me the Christian doctrine of war and peace,—the truth that in time of war we must stand for the right, and that when peace comes in sight, we must do our best to found it upon justice. These two truths cannot be separated. If we forget the meaning of the Christian duty to which God called us in the late war, all our sacrifice of blood and treasure will have been in vain. If we forget the watchword which called our boys to the colours, our victory will be fruitless. We have fought in this twentieth century against the pagan German doctrine of war as the supreme arbiter between the tribes of mankind. They that took the sword must perish by the sword. But in the hour of victory we must uphold the end for which we have fought and suffered,—the advance of the world towards a peaceful life founded on reason and justice and fair-play for every man.

So there are two heads to this sermon. First, the indelible remembrance of a righteous acceptance of war. Second, the reasonable hope of a righteous foundation of peace.

I. First of all, then, it must never be forgotten that the Allies and America were forced to enter this war as a work of righteousness in order to make the world safe for peace.

Peace means something more than the mere absence of hostilities. It means justice, honour, fair-play, order, security, and the well-protected right of every man and nation to life, liberty, and the pursuit of happiness. It was the German contempt for these Christian ideals, it was the German idolatry of the pagan Odin, naked, cruel, bloody, god of war, it was the German will to power and dream of world-dominion, that made the world unsafe for real peace in 1914.

Never could that safety be secured until that enemy of mankind was overcome. Not only for democracy, but also for human peace, it was necessary, as President Wilson said, that "the German power, a thing without honour, conscience, or capacity for covenanted faith, must be crushed."

I saw, from my post of observation in Holland, the hosts of heathen Germany massing for their attack on the world's peace in the spring of 1914. Long before the pretext of war was provided by the murder of the Austrian Crown-Prince in Serajevo, I saw the troops, the artillery, the

260

mountains of ammunition, assembled at Aix-la-Chapelle and Trier, ready for the invasion of neutral Belgium and Luxembourg, and the foul stroke at France.

Every civilized nation in Europe desired peace and pleaded for it. Little Servia offered to go before the Court of Arbitration at The Hague and be tried for the offense of which she was accused. Russia, Italy, France and England entreated Germany not to make war, but to submit the dispute to judicial settlement, to a righteous decision by a conference of powers. But Germany said no. She had prepared for war, she wanted war, she got war. And now she must abide by the result of her choice.

I have seen also with my own eyes the horrors wrought by Germany in her conduct of the war in Belgium and Northern France. Words fail me to describe them. Childhood has been crucified, womanhood outraged, civilization trampled in the dust. The nations and the men who took arms against these deviltries were the servants of the righteous God and the followers of the merciful Christ.

He told us, "If any man smite thee on the right cheek, turn unto him the left also." But never did He tell us to abandon the bodies and the lives of our women and children to the outrage of beasts in human form. On the contrary, He said to His disciples, in His parting discourse, "He that hath no sword let him sell his garment and buy one."

Does any silly pacifist say that means a spiritual sword? No. You could get that without selling your garment. It means a real sword,—as real as the purse and the scrip which Christ told His followers to carry with them. It means the power of arms dedicated to the service of righteousness without which the world can never be safe for peace.

Here, then, we may stand on the Word of God, on the work of righteousness in making the world safe for peace. Let me tell you of my faith that every one who has given his life for that cause, has entered into eternal rest.

II. Come we now to consider the second part of the text: "the effect of righteousness, quietness and confidence forever."

What shall be the nature of the peace to be concluded after our victory in this righteous war?

Here we have to oppose the demands of the bloodthirsty civilians. They ask that German towns should endure the same sufferings which have been inflicted on the towns of Belgium and Northern France. Let me say frankly that I do not believe you could persuade our officers to order such atrocities, or our soldiers to obey such orders. Read the order which one of the noble warriors of France, General Pétain, issued to his men:

> "To-morrow, in order to better dictate peace, you are going to carry your arms as far as the Rhine. Into that land of Alsace-Lorraine that is so dear to us, you will march as liberators. You will go further; all the way into Germany to occupy lands which are the necessary guarantees for just reparation.
>
> "France has suffered in her ravaged fields and in her ruined villages. The freed provinces have had to submit to intolerable vexations and odious outrages, but you are not to answer these crimes by the commission of violences, which, under the spur of your resentment, may seem to you legitimate.
>
> "You are to remain under discipline and to show respect to persons and property. You will know, after having vanquished your adversary by force of arms, how to impress him further by the dignity of your attitude, and the world will not know which to admire most, your conduct in success or your heroism in fighting."

The destruction of the commonplace Cathedral of Cologne could never recompense the damage done to the glorious Cathedral of Rheims.

Nor could the slaughter of a million German women and children restore the innocent victims of Belgium, France, Servia, and Armenia to life. We do not thirst for blood. We desire justice.

No doubt the ends of justice demand that the principal brigands who are responsible for the atrocities of this war should be tried before an international court If convicted they should be duly punished. But not by mob-law or violence. Nothing could be less desirable than the assassination of William Hohenzollern. It would be absurd and horrible to give a martyr's crown to a criminal. Vengeance belongeth unto God. He alone is wise and great enough to deal adequately with the case. It is for us to keep our righteous indignation free from the poison of personal hatred, and to do no more than is needed to uphold and vindicate the eternal law.

William Hohenzollern, and his fellow-conspirators who are responsible for the beginning and the conduct of the dreadful war from which all the toiling peoples of earth have suffered, must be brought to the bar of justice and sentenced; otherwise the world will have no defense against the anarchists who say that government is a vain thing; and the bloody Bolshevists who proclaim the Empire of the Ignorant,—the Boob-Rah,—as the future rule of the world, will have free scope.

It is evident that a league of free, democratic states, pledged by mutual covenant to uphold the settlement of international differences by reason and justice before the use of violence, offers the only hope of a durable peace among the nations. It is also the only defense against that deadly and destructive war of classes with which Bolshevism threatens the whole world. The spirit of Bolshevism is atheism and enmity; its method is violence and tyranny; its result would be a reign of terror under that empty-headed monster, "the dictatorship of the proletariat." God save us from that! It would be the worst possible outcome of the war in which we have offered and sacrificed so much, and in which God has given us the opportunity to make "a covenant of peace."

How vast, how immeasurable, are the responsibilities which this great victory in righteous war has laid upon the Allies and America. God help us to live up to them. God help us to sow the future not with dragon's teeth, but with seeds of blessed harvest. God paint upon the broken storm-cloud the rainbow of eternal hope. God help us and our friends to make a peace that shall mean good to all mankind. God send upon our victory the light of the cross of Christ our Saviour, where mercy and truth meet together, righteousness and peace kiss each other.

III.

THE POWER OF AN ENDLESS LIFE

Who is made, not after the law of a carnal commandment, but after the power of an endless life.—Hebrews 7:16.

The message and hope of immortality are nowhere more distinctly conveyed to our minds than in connection with that resurrection morn when Jesus appeared to Mary Magdalene. The anniversary of that day will ever be the festival of the human soul. Even those who do not clearly understand or fully accept its meaning in history and religion,—even children and ignorant folk and doubters and unbelievers,—yes, even frivolous people and sullen people, feel that there is something in this festival which meets the need and longing of their hearts. It is a day of joy and gladness, a day of liberation and promise, a day for flowers to bloom and birds to sing, a day of spiritual spring-tide and immortal hope.

Mankind desires and needs such a day. We are overshadowed in all our affections and aspirations, all our efforts, and designs, by the dark mystery of bodily death; the uncertainty and the brevity of earthly existence make us tremble and despair; the futility of our plans dismays us; the insecurity of our dearest treasure in lives linked to ours fills us with dismay.

Is there no escape from Death, the Tyrant, the autocrat, the destroyer, the last enemy? Why love, why look upward, why strive for better things if this imperator of failure, ultimate extinction, rules the universe? No hope beyond the grave means no peace this side of it. A life without hope is a life without God. If Death ends all, then there is no Father in Heaven in whom we can trust. Who shall deliver us from the body of this Death?

Now comes Easter with its immortal promise and assurance, Jesus of Nazareth, who died on Calvary, a martyr of humanity, a sacrifice of Divinity, is alive and appears to His humble followers. The manner of His appearance, to Mary Magdalene, to His disciples, is not the most important thing. The fact is that He did appear. He who was crucified in the cause of righteousness and mercy, lives on and forever. The message of His resurrection is "the power of an endless life."

The proof of this message is in the effect that it produced. It transformed the handful of Jesus' followers from despair to confidence. It gave Christianity its growing influence over the heart of humanity. It is this message of immortality that makes religion vital to the human world to-day, and essential to the foundation of peace on earth.

We must not forget in our personal griefs and longings, in our sorrows for those whom we have lost and our desire to find them again, in our sense of our own mortal frailty and the brief duration of earthly life, the celestial impulse which demands a life triumphant over death.

The strongest of all supports for peace on earth is the faith in immortality. The truth is, the very character of our being here in this world demands continuance beyond death. There is nothing good or great that we think or feel or endeavour, that is not a reaching out to something better. Our finest knowledge is but the consciousness of limitation and the longing that it may be removed. Our best moral effort is but a slow advance towards something better. Our sense of the difference between good and evil, our penitence, our aspiration, all this moral freight with which our souls are laden, is a cargo consigned to an unseen country. Our bill of lading reads, "To the immortal life." If we must sink in mid-ocean, then all is lost, and the voyage of life is a predestined wreck.

266

The wisest, the strongest, the best of mankind, have felt this most deeply. The faith in immortality belongs to the childhood of the race, and the greatest of the sages have always returned to it and taken refuge in it. Socrates and Plato, Cicero and Plutarch, Montesquieu and Franklin, Kant and Emerson, Tennyson and Browning,—how do they all bear witness to the incompleteness of life and reach out to a completion beyond the grave.

"No great Thinker ever lived and taught you
All the wonder that his soul received;
No great Painter ever set on canvas
All the glorious vision he conceived.

"No Musician ever held your spirit
Charmed and bound in his melodious chains;
But, be sure, he heard, and strove to render,
Feeble echoes of celestial strains.

"No real Poet ever wove in numbers
All his dream, but the diviner part,
Hidden from all the world, spake to him only
In the voiceless silence of his heart.

"So with Love: for Love and Art united
Are twin mysteries: different yet the same;
Poor indeed would be the love of any
Who could find its full and perfect name.

"Love may strive; but vain is its endeavour
All its boundless riches to unfold;
Still its tenderest, truest secret lingers
Ever in its deepest depths untold.

"Things of Time have voices: speak and perish.
Art and Love speak; but their words must be
Like sighings of illimitable forests
And waves of an unfathomable sea."

And can it be that death shall put the final seal of irretrievable ruin on all this uncompleted effort? Can it be that the grave shall whelm all this unuttered love in endless silence? Ah, what a wild waste of precious treasure, what a mad destruction of fair designs, what an utter failure, life would be if death must end all!

The very reasonableness of our nature, our sense of order, declare the impotence of Death to create such a wreck. And most of all our deep affections cry out against the conclusion of despair. They will not hear of dissolution. They reach out their hands into the darkness. They demand and they promise an unending fellowship, a deepening communion, a more perfect satisfaction. Do you remember what Thackeray wrote? "If love lives through all life, and survives through all sorrow; and remains steadfast with us through all changes; and in all darkness of spirit burns brightly; and if we die, deplores us forever, and still loves us equally; and exists with the very last gasp and throb of the faithful bosom, whence it passes with the pure soul beyond death, surely it shall be immortal. Though we who remain are separated from it, is it not ours in heaven? If we love still those whom we lose, can we altogether lose those whom we love?"

To deny this instinct is to deny that which lies at the very root of our life. If love perishes with death, then our affections are our worst curses, the world is the cruellest torture-house, and "all things work together for evil to those who love." Do you believe it? Is it possible? Nay, all that is best and noblest and purest within us rejects such a faith in Absolute Evil as the power that has created and rules the world. In the presence of love we feel that we behold that which must belong to a good God and therefore cannot die. Destruction cannot touch it. The grave cannot hold it. Loving and being loved, we dare to stand in the very doorway of the tomb, and assert the power of an endless life.

And it seems to me that this courage never comes to us so fully as when we are brought in closest contact with death, when we are brought face to face with that dread shadow and forced either to deny its power, once and forever, or to give up everything and die with our hopes. I wish that I could make this clear to you as it lies in my own experience. Perhaps in trying to do it I should speak closer to your own heart than in any other way. For surely

"There is no flock, however watched and tended
But one dead lamb is there.
There is no fireside, howsoe'er defended
But has a vacant chair."

A flower grew in your garden. You delighted in its beauty and fragrance. It gave you all it had to give, but it did not love you. It could not. When the time came for it to die, you were sorry. But it did not seem to you strange or unnatural. There was no waste. Its mission was fulfilled. You understood why its petals should fall, its leaf wither, its root and branch decay. And even if a storm came and snapped it, still there was nothing lost that was indispensable, nothing that could not be restored.

A child grew in your household, dearly loved and answering your love. You saw that soul unfold, learning to know the evil from the good, learning to accept duty and to resist selfishness, learning to be brave and true and kind, learning to give you day by day a deeper and a richer sympathy, learning to love God and to pray and to be good. And then perhaps you saw that young heart being perfected under the higher and holier discipline of suffering, bearing pain patiently, facing trouble and danger like a hero, not shrinking even from the presence of death, but trusting all to your love and to God's, and taking just what came from day to day, from hour to hour. And then suddenly the light went out in the shining eyes. The brave heart stopped. The soul was gone. Lost, perished, blotted out forever in the darkness of death? Ah, no; you know better than that. That clear, dawning intelligence, that deepening love, that childlike faith in God, that pure innocence of soul, did not come from the dust. How could they return thither? The music ceases because the instrument is broken. But the player is not dead. He is learning a better music. He is finding a more perfect instrument. It is impossible that he should be holden of death. God wastes nothing so precious.

> "What is excellent
> As God lives is permanent.
> Hearts are dust; hearts' loves remain.
> Hearts' love will meet thee again."

But I am sure that we must go further than this in order to understand the full strength and comfort of the text. The assertion of the impotence of death to end all is based upon something deeper than the prophecy of immortality in the human heart. It has a stronger foundation than the outreachings of human knowledge and moral effort towards a higher state in which completion may be attained. It has a more secure ground to rest upon than the deathless affection with which our love clings to its object The impotence of death is revealed to us in the spiritual perfection of Christ.

Here then, in the "power of an endless life," I find the corner-stone of peace on earth among men of good-will Take this mortal life as a thing of seventy years, more or less, to which death puts a final period, and you have nothing but confusion, chance and futility,—nothing safe, nothing realized, nothing completed. Evil often triumphs. Virtue often is defeated.

> "The good die young,
> And we whose hearts are dry as summer dust
> Burn to the socket."

But take death, as Christ teaches us, not as a full stop, but as only a comma in the story of an endless life, and then the whole aspect of our existence is changed. That which is material, base, evil, drops down. That which is spiritual, noble, good, rises to lead us on.

The conviction of immortality, the forward-looking faith in a life beyond the grave, the spirit of Easter, is essential to peace on earth for three reasons.

I. It is the only faith that lifts man's soul, which is immortal, above his body, which is perishable. It raises him out of the tyranny of the flesh to the service of his ideals. It makes him sure that there are things worth fighting and dying for. The fighting and the dying, for the cause of justice and liberty, are sacrifices on the Divine altar which shall never be forgotten.

II. The faith in immortality carries with it the assurance of a Divine reassessment of earth's inequalities. Those who have suffered unjustly here will be recompensed in the future. Those who have acted wickedly and unjustly here will be punished. Whether that punishment will be final or remedial we do not know. Perhaps it may lead to the extinction of the soul of evil, perhaps to its purifying and deliverance. On these questions I fall back on the word of God: "The wages of sin is death, but the gift of God is eternal life in Christ Jesus our Lord."

III. The faith in immortality brings with it the sense of order, tranquillity, steadiness and courage in the present life. It sets us free from mean and cowardly temptations, makes it easier to resist the wild animal passions of lust and greed and cruelty, brings us into eternal relations and fellowships, makes us partners with the wise and good of all the ages, ennobles our earthly patriotism by giving us a heavenly citizenship. Yea, it knits us in bonds of love with the coming generation. It is better than the fountain of youth. We shall know and see them as they go on their way, long after we have left

271

the path. The faith in immortality sets a touch of the imperishable on every generous impulse and unselfish deed. It inspires to sublime and heroic virtues,—spiritual splendours,—deeds of sacrifice and suffering for which earth has no adequate recompense, but whose reward is great in heaven. Here is the patience of the saints, the glorious courage of patriots, martyrs, and confessors, something more bright and shining than secular morality can bring forth,—a flashing of the inward light which fails not, but grows clearer as death draws near. What noble evidences of this come to us out of the great war.

"Are you in great distress?" asked a nurse of an American soldier whose legs had been shot away on the battle-field. "I am in as great peace," said he, "through Jesus my Lord, as a man can possibly be, out of Paradise."

A secretary of the Y.M.C.A., the night before he was killed, wrote to his father: "I have not been sent here to die: I am to fight: I offer my life for future generations; I shall not die, I shall merely change my direction. He who walks before us is so great that we cannot lose Him from sight."

A simple French boy, grievously wounded, is dying in the ambulance. He is a Protestant The nurse who bends over him is a Catholic sister. She writes down his words as they fall slowly from his lips: "O my God, let Thy will be done and not mine. O my God, Thou knowest that I never wished war, but that I have fought because it was Thy will; I offered my life so that peace might prevail. O my God, I pray for all my dear ones, . . . father, mother, brothers, sisters. Give a hundredfold to those nurses for all they have done for me. I pray for them one and all."

Here, in the midst of carnage and confusion, horror and death, was perfect peace, the triumph of immortality.

What then shall we say of the new teachers and masters, the cynical lords of materialism and misrule, who tell us that they are going to banish this outworn superstition and all others like it from the mind of man? They are going to make a new world in which men shall walk by sight, and not by faith; a world in which universal happiness shall be produced by the forcible division of material goods, and brotherhood promoted by the simple expedient of killing those whom they dislike; a world in which there shall be neither nation, God, nor Church, nor anywhere a thought of any life but this which ends in the grave. It is a mad dream of wild and reckless men. But it threatens evil to all the world. Do you remember what happened when the French Revolution took that course, abolished the Sabbath, defiled the Churches, broke down the altars, and enthroned a harlot as the Goddess of Reason? The Reign of Terror followed. Something like that has happened, recently, in many parts of Europe. And if these new tyrants of ignorance, unbelief, and unmorality have their way, the madness and the darkness will spread until the black cloud charged with death covers the face of the earth for a season with shame and anguish and destruction. A sane world, an orderly world, a peaceful world, can never be founded on materialism. That foundation is a quicksand in which all that is dearest to man goes down in death.

Religion is essential to true peace in the soul and to peace on earth through righteousness. Immortality is essential to true religion. Thanks be to God who hath given us Jesus Christ, who was dead and is alive again and liveth forevermore, to touch and ennoble, to inspire and console, to pacify and uplift our earthly existence with the power of an endless life.

THE SAD SHEPHERD

A Christmas Story

I.

DARKNESS

Out of the Valley of Gardens, where a film of new-fallen snow lay smooth as feathers on the breast of a dove, the ancient Pools of Solomon looked up into the night sky with dark, tranquil eyes, wide-open and passive, reflecting the crisp stars and the small, round moon. The full springs, overflowing on the hill-side, melted their way through the field of white in winding channels; and along their course the grass was green even in the dead of winter.

But the sad shepherd walked far above the friendly valley, in a region where ridges of gray rock welted and scarred the back of the earth, like wounds of half-forgotten strife and battles long ago. The solitude was forbidding and disquieting; the keen air that searched the wanderer had no pity in it; and the myriad glances of the night were curiously cold.

His flock straggle after him. The sheep, weather-beaten and dejected, followed the path with low heads nodding from side to side, as if they had traveled far and found little pasture. The black, lop-eared goats leaped upon the rocks, restless and ravenous, tearing down the tender branches and leaves of the dwarf oaks and wild olives. They reared up against the twisted trunks and crawled and scrambled among the boughs. It was like a company of gray downcast friends and a troop of merry little black devils following the sad shepherd afar off.

He walked looking on the ground, paying small heed to them. Now and again, when the sound of pattering feet and panting breath and the rustling and rending among the copses fell too far behind, he drew out his shepherd's pipe and blew a strain of music, shrill and plaintive, quavering and lamenting through the hollow night. He waited while the troops of gray and black scuffled and bounded and trotted near to him. Then he dropped the pipe into its place again and strode forward, looking on the ground.

The fitful, shivery wind that rasped the hill-top, fluttered the rags of his long mantle of Tyrian blue, torn by thorns and stained by travel. The rich tunic of striped silk beneath it was worn thin, and the girdle about his loins had lost all its ornaments of silver and jewels. His curling hair hung down dishevelled under a turban of fine linen, in which the gilt threads were frayed and tarnished; and his shoes of soft leather were broken by the road. On his brown fingers the places of the vanished rings were still marked in white skin. He carried not the long staff nor the heavy nail-studded rod of the shepherd, but a slender stick of carved cedar battered and scratched by hard usage, and the handle, which must once have been of precious metal, was missing.

He was a strange figure for that lonely place and that humble occupation-a branch of faded beauty from some royal garden tossed by rude winds into the wilderness-a pleasure craft adrift, buffeted and broken, on rough seas.

But he seemed to have passed beyond caring. His young face was frayed and threadbare as his garments. The splendor of the moonlight flooding the wild world meant as little to him as the hardness of the rugged track which he followed. He wrapped his tattered mantle closer around him, and strode ahead, looking on the ground.

As the path dropped from the summit of the ridge toward the Valley of Mills and passed among huge broken rocks, three men sprang at him from the shadows. He lifted his stick, but let it fall again, and a strange ghost of a smile twisted his face as they gripped him and threw him down.

278

"You are rough beggars," he said. "Say what you want, you are welcome to it."

"Your money, dog of a courtier," they muttered fiercely; "give us your golden collar, Herod's hound, quick, or you die!"

"The quicker the better," he answered, closing his eyes.

The bewildered flock of sheep and goats, gathered in a silent ring, stood at gaze while the robbers fumbled over their master

"This is a stray dog," said one, "he has lost his collar, there is not even the price of a mouthful of wine on him. Shall we kill him and leave him for the vultures?" "What have the vultures done for us," said another, "that we should feed them? Let us take his cloak and drive off his flock, and leave him to die in his own time."

With a kick and a curse they left him. He opened his eyes and lay quiet for a moment, with his twisted smile, watching the stars.

"You creep like snails," he said. "I thought you had marked my time tonight. But not even that is given to me for nothing. I must pay for all, it seems."

Far away, slowly scattering and receding, he heard the rustling and bleating of his frightened flock as the robbers, running and shouting, tried to drive them over the hills. Then he stood up and took the shepherd's pipe, a worthless bit of reed, from the breast of his tunic. He blew again that plaintive, piercing air, sounding it out over the ridges and distant thickets. It seemed to have neither beginning nor end; a melancholy, pleading tune that searched forever after something lost.

While he played, the sheep and the goats, slipping away from their captors by roundabout ways, hiding behind the laurel bushes, following the dark gullies, leaping down the broken cliffs, came circling back to him, one after another; and as they came, he interrupted his playing, now and then, to call them by name. When they were nearly all assembled, he went down swiftly toward the lower valley, and they followed him, panting. At the last crook of the path on the steep hillside a straggler came after him along the cliff. He looked up and saw it outlined against the sky. Then he saw it leap, and slip, und fall beyond the path into a deep cleft.

"Little fool," he said, "fortune is kind to you! You have escaped from the big trap of life. What? You are crying for help? You are still in the trap? Then I must go down to you, little fool, for I am a fool too. But why I must do it, I know no more than you know."

He lowered himself quickly and perilously into the cleft, and found the creature with its leg broken and bleeding. It was not a sheep but a young goat. He had no cloak to wrap it in, but he took off his turban and unrolled it, and bound it around the trembling animal. Then he climbed back to the path and strode on at the head of his flock, carrying the little black kid in his arms.

There were houses in the Valley of the Mills; and in some of them lights were burning; and the drone of the mill-stones, where the women were still grinding, came out into the night like the humming of drowsy bees. As the women heard the pattering and bleating of the flock, they wondered who was passing so late. One of them, in a house where there was no mill but many lights, came to the door and looked out laughing, her face and bosom bare.

But the sad shepherd did not stay. His long shadow and the confused mass of lesser shadows behind him drifted down the white moonlight, past the yellow bars of lamplight that gleamed from the doorways. It seemed as if he were bound to go somewhere and would not delay.

Yet with all his haste to be gone, it was plain that he thought little of where he was going. For when he came to the foot of the valley, where the paths divided, he stood between them staring vacantly, without a desire to turn him this way or that. The imperative of choice halted him like a barrier. The balance of his mind hung even because both scales were empty. He could act, he could go, for his strength was untouched; but he could not choose, for his will was broken within him.

The path to the left went up toward the little town of Bethlehem, with huddled roofs and walls in silhouette along the double-crested hill.

It was dark and forbidding as a closed fortress. The sad shepherd looked at it with indifferent eyes; there was nothing there to draw him. The path to the right wound through rock-strewn valleys toward the Dead Sea. But rising out of that crumpled wilderness, a mile or two away, the smooth white ribbon of a chariot-road lay upon the flank of a cone-shaped mountain and curled in loops toward its peak. There the great cone was cut squarely off, and the levelled summit was capped by a palace of marble, with round towers at the corners and flaring beacons along the walls; and the glow of an immense fire, hidden in the central court-yard, painted a false dawn in the eastern sky. All down the clean-cut mountain slopes, on terraces and blind arcades, the lights flashed from lesser pavilions and pleasure-houses.

It was the secret orchard of Herod and his friends, their trysting-place with the spirits of mirth and madness. They called it the Mountain of the Little Paradise. Rich gardens were there; and the cool water from the Pools of Solomon plashed in the fountains; and trees of the knowledge of good and evil fruited blood-red and ivory-white above them; and smooth, curving, glistening shapes, whispering softly of pleasure, lay among the flowers and glided behind the trees. All this was now hidden in the dark. Only the strange bulk of the mountain, a sharp black pyramid girdled and crowned with fire, loomed across the night-a mountain once seen never to be forgotten.

The sad shepherd remembered it well. He looked at it with the eyes of a child who has been in hell. It burned him from afar. Turning neither to the right nor to the left, he walked without a path straight out upon the plain of Bethlehem, still whitened in the hollows and on the sheltered side of its rounded hillocks by the veil of snow.

He faced a wide and empty world. To the west in sleeping Bethlehem, to the east in flaring Herodium, the life of man was infinitely far away from him. Even the stars seemed to withdraw themselves against the blue-black of the sky. They diminished and receded till they were like pin-holes in the vault above him. The moon in mid-heaven shrank into a bit of burnished silver, hard and glittering, immeasurably remote. The ragged, inhospitable ridges of Tekoa lay stretched in mortal slumber along the horizon, and between them he caught a glimpse of the sunken Lake of Death, darkly gleaming in its deep bed. There was no movement, no sound, on the plain where he walked, except the soft-padding feet of his dumb, obsequious flock.

He felt an endless isolation strike cold to his heart, against which he held the limp body of the wounded kid, wondering the while, with a half-contempt for his own foolishness, why he took such trouble to save a tiny scrap of the worthless tissue which is called life.

Even when a man does not know or care where he is going, if he steps onward he will get there. In an hour or more of walking over the plain the sad shepherd came to a sheep-fold of gray stones with a rude tower beside it. The fold was full of sheep, and at the foot of the tower a little fire of thorns was burning, around which four shepherds were crouching, wrapped in their thick woollen cloaks.

As the stranger approached they looked up, and one of them rose quickly to his feet, grasping his knotted club. But when they saw the flock that followed the sad shepherd, they stared at each other and said: "It is one of us, a keeper of sheep. But how comes he here in this raiment? It is what men wear in kings' houses."

"No," said the one who was standing, "it is what they wear when they have been thrown out of them. Look at the rags. He may be a thief and a robber with his stolen flock."

"Salute him when he comes near," said the oldest shepherd. "Are we not four to one? We have nothing to fear from a ragged traveller. Speak him fair. It is the will of God-and it costs nothing."

"Peace be with you, brother," cried the youngest shepherd; "may your mother and father be blessed."

"May your heart be enlarged," the stranger answered, "and may all your families be more blessed than mine, for I have none."

"A homeless man," said the old shepherd, "has either been robbed by his fellows, or punished by God."

"I do not know which it was," answered the stranger; "the end is the same, as you see."

"By your speech you come from Galilee. Where are you going? What are you seeking here?"

"I was going nowhere, my masters; but it was cold on the way there, and my feet turned to your fire."

"Come then, if you are a peaceable man, and warm your feet with us. Heat is a good gift; divide it and it is not less. But you shall have bread and salt too, if you will."

"May your hospitality enrich you. I am your unworthy guest. But my flock?"

"Let your flock shelter by the south wall of the fold: there is good picking there and no wind. Come you and sit with us."

So they all sat down by the fire; and the sad shepherd ate of their bread, but sparingly, like a man to whom hunger brings a need but no joy in the satisfying of it; and the others were silent for a proper time, out of courtesy. Then the oldest shepherd spoke:

"My name is Zadok the son of Eliezer, of Bethlehem. I am the chief shepherd of the flocks of the Temple, which are before you in the fold. These are my sister's sons, Jotham, and Shama, and Nathan: their father Elkanah is dead; and but for these I am a childless man."

"My name," replied the stranger, "is Ammiel the son of Jochanan, of the city of Bethsaida, by the Sea of Galilee, and I am a fatherless man."

"It is better to be childless than fatherless," said Zadok, "yet it is the will of God that children should bury their fathers. When did the blessed Jochanan die?"

"I know not whether he be dead or alive. It is three years since I looked upon his face or had word of him."

"You are an exile then? he has cast you off?"

"It was the other way," said Am-miel, looking on the ground.

At this the shepherd Shama, who had listened with doubt in his face, started up in anger. "Pig of a Galilean," he cried, "despiser of parents! breaker of the law! When I saw you coming I knew you for something vile. Why do you darken the night for us with your presence? You have reviled him who begot you. Away, or we stone you!"

Ammiel did not answer or move.

The twisted smile passed over his bowed face again as he waited to know the shepherds' will with him, even as he had waited for the robbers. But Zadok lifted his hand.

"Not so hasty, Shama-ben-Elkanah. You also break the law by judging a man unheard. The rabbis have told us that there is a tradition of the elders-a rule as holy as the law itself-that a man may deny his father in a certain way without sin. It is a strange rule, and it must be very holy or it would not be so strange. But this is the teaching of the elders: a son may say of anything for which his father asks him-a sheep, or a measure of corn, or a field, or a purse of silver-'it is Corban, a gift that I have vowed unto the Lord;' and so his father shall have no more claim upon him. Have you said 'Corban' to your father, Ammiel-ben-Jochanan? Have you made a vow unto the Lord?"

"I have said 'Corban,'" answered Ammiel, lifting his face, still shadowed by that strange smile, "but it was not the Lord who heard my vow."

"Tell us what you have done," said the old man sternly, "for we will neither judge you, nor shelter you, unless we hear your story."

"There is nothing in it," replied Ammiel indifferently. "It is an old story. But if you are curious you shall hear it. Afterward you shall deal with me as you will."

So the shepherds, wrapped in their warm cloaks, sat listening with grave faces and watchful, unsearchable eyes, while Ammiel in his tattered silk sat by the sinking fire of thorns and told his tale with a voice that had no room for hope or fear-a cool, dead voice that spoke only of things ended.

II.

NIGHTFIRE

"In my father's house I was the second son. My brother was honored and trusted in all things. He was a prudent man and profitable to the household. All that he counselled was done, all that he wished he had. My place was a narrow one. There was neither honor nor joy in it, for it was filled with daily tasks and rebukes. No one cared for me. My mother sometimes wept when I was rebuked. Perhaps she was disappointed in me. But she had no power to make things better. I felt that I was a beast of burden, fed only in order that I might be useful; and the dull life irked me like an ill-fitting harness. There was nothing in it.

"I went to my father and claimed my share of the inheritance. He was rich. He gave it to me. It did not impoverish him and it made me free. I said to him 'Corban,' and shook the dust of Bethsaida from my feet.

"I went out to look for mirth and love and joy and all that is pleasant to the eyes and sweet to the taste. If a god made me, thought I, he made me to live, and the pride of life was strong in my heart and in my flesh. My vow was offered to that well-known god. I served him in Jerusalem, in Alexandria, in Rome, for his altars are everywhere and men worship him openly or in secret.

"My money and youth made me welcome to his followers, and I spent them both freely as if they could never come to an end. I clothed myself in purple and fine linen and fared sumptuously every day. The wine of Cyprus and the dishes of Egypt and Syria were on my table. My dwelling was crowded with merry guests. They came for what I gave them. Their faces were hungry and their soft touch was like the clinging of leeches. To them I was nothing but money and youth; no longer a beast of burden-a beast of pleasure. There was nothing in it.

"From the richest fare my heart went away empty, and after the wildest banquet my soul fell drunk and solitary into sleep.

"Then I thought, Power is better than pleasure. If a man will feast and revel let him do it with the great. They will favor him, and raise him up for the service that he renders them. He will obtain place and authority in the world and gain many friends. So I joined myself to Herod."

When the sad shepherd spoke this name his listeners drew back front him as if it were a defilement to hear it. They spat upon the ground and cursed the Idumean who called himself their king.

"A slave!" Jotham cried, "a bloody tyrant and a slave from Edom! A fox, a vile beast who devours his own children! God burn him in Gehenna."

The old Zadok picked up a stone and threw it into the darkness, saying slowly, "I cast this stone on the grave of the Idumean, the blasphemer, the defiler of the Temple! God send us soon the Deliverer, the Promised One, the true King of Israel!" Ammiel made no sign, but went on with his story.

"Herod used me well,-for his own purpose. He welcomed me to his palace and his table, and gave me a place among his favorites. He was so much my friend that he borrowed my money. There were many of the nobles of Jerusalem with him, Sad-ducees, and proselytes from Rome and Asia, and women from everywhere. The law of Israel was observed in the open court, when the people were watching. But in the secret feasts there was no law but the will of Herod, and many deities were served but no god was worshipped. There the captains and the princes of Rome consorted with the high-priest and his sons by night; and there was much coming and going by hidden ways. Everybody was a borrower or a lender, a buyer or a seller of favors. It was a house of diligent madness. There was nothing in it.

"In the midst of this whirling life a great need of love came upon me and I wished to hold some one in my inmost heart.

"At a certain place in the city, within closed doors, I saw a young slave-girl dancing. She was about fifteen years old, thin and supple; she danced like a reed in the wind; but her eyes were weary as death, and her white body was marked with bruises. She stumbled, and the men laughed at her. She fell, and her mistress beat her, crying out that she would fain be rid of such a heavy-footed slave. I paid the price and took her to my dwelling.

"Her name was Tamar. She was a daughter of Lebanon. I robed her in silk and broidered linen. I nourished her with tender care so that beauty came upon her like the blossoming of an almond tree; she was a garden enclosed, breathing spices. Her eyes were like doves behind her veil, her lips were a thread of scarlet, her neck was a tower of ivory, and her breasts were as two fawns which feed among the lilies. She was whiter than milk, and more rosy than the flower of the peach, and her dancing was like the flight of a bird among the branches. So I loved her.

"She lay in my bosom as a clear stone that one has bought and polished and set in fine gold at the end of a golden chain. Never was she glad at my coming or sorry at my going. Never did she give me anything except what I took from her. There was nothing in it.

"Now whether Herod knew of the jewel that I kept in my dwelling I cannot tell. It was sure that he had his spies in all the city, and himself walked the streets by night in a disguise. On a certain day he sent for me, and had me into his secret chamber, professing great love toward me and more confidence than in any man that lived. So I must go to Rome for him, bearing a sealed letter and a private message to Caesar. All my goods would be left safely in the hands of the king, my friend, who would reward me double. There was a certain place of high authority at Jerusalem which Caesar would gladly bestow on a Jew who had done him a service. This mission would commend me to him. It was a great occasion, suited to my powers. Thus Herod fed me with fair promises, and I ran his errand. There was nothing in it.

"I stood before Caesar and gave him the letter. He read it and laughed, saying that a prince with an incurable hunger is a servant of value to an emperor. Then he asked me if there was nothing sent with the letter. I answered that there was no gift, but a message for his private ear. He drew me aside and I told him that Herod begged earnestly that his dear son, Antipater, might be sent back in haste from Rome to Palestine, for the king had great need of him.

"At this Caesar laughed again. 'To bury him, I suppose,' said he, 'with his brothers, Alexander and Aristobulus! Truly, it is better to be Herod's swine than his son. Tell the old fox he may catch his own prey.' With this he turned from me and I withdrew unrewarded, to make my way back, as best I could with an empty purse, to Palestine. I had seen the Lord of the World. There was nothing in it.

"Selling my rings and bracelets I got passage in a trading ship for Joppa. There I heard that the king was not in Jerusalem, at his Palace of the Upper City, but had gone with his friends to make merry for a month on the Mountain of the Little Paradise. On that hill-top over against us, where the lights are flaring to-night, in the banquet-hall where couches are spread for a hundred guests, I found Herod."

The listening shepherds spat upon the ground again, and Jotham muttered, "May the worms that devour his flesh never die!" But Zadok whispered, "We wait for the Lord's salvation to come out of Zion." And the sad shepherd, looking with fixed eyes at the firelit mountain far away, continued his story:

"The king lay on his ivory couch, and the sweat of his disease was heavy upon him, for he was old, and his flesh was corrupted. But his hair and his beard were dyed and perfumed and there was a wreath of roses on his head. The hall was full of nobles and great men, the sons of the high-priest were there, and the servants poured their wine in cups of

288

gold. There was a sound of soft music; and all the men were watching a girl who danced in the middle of the hall; and the eyes of Herod were fiery, like the eyes of a fox.

"The dancer was Tamar. She glistened like the snow on Lebanon, and the redness of her was ruddier than a pomegranate, and her dancing was like the coiling of white serpents. When the dance was ended her attendants threw a veil of gauze over her and she lay among her cushions, half covered with flowers, at the feet of the king.

"Through the sound of clapping hands and shouting, two slaves led me behind the couch of Herod. His eyes narrowed as they fell upon me. I told him the message of Caesar, making it soft, as if it were a word that suffered him to catch his prey. He stroked his beard softly and his look fell on Tamar. 'I have caught it,' he murmured; 'by all the gods, I have always caught it. And my dear son, Antipater, is coming home of his own will. I have lured him, he is mine.'

"Then a look of madness crossed his face and he sprang up, with frothing lips, and struck at me. 'What is this,' he cried, 'a spy, a servant of my false son, a traitor in my banquet-hall! Who are you?' I knelt before him, protesting that he must know me; that I was his friend, his messenger; that I had left all my goods in his hands; that the girl who had danced for him was mine. At this his face changed again and he fell back on his couch, shaken with horrible laughter. 'Yours!' he cried, 'when was she yours? What is yours? I know you now, poor madman. You are Ammiel, a crazy shepherd from Galilee, who troubled us some time since. Take him away, slaves. He has twenty sheep and twenty goats among my flocks at the foot of the mountain. See to it that he gets them, and drive him away.'

"I fought against the slaves with my bare hands, but they held me. I called to Tamar, begging her to have pity on me, to speak for me, to come with me. She looked up with her eyes like doves behind her veil, but there was no knowledge of me in them. She laughed lazily, as if it were a poor comedy, and flung a broken rose-branch in my face. Then the silver cord was loosened within me, and my heart went out, and I struggled no more. There was nothing in it.

"Afterward I found myself on the road with this flock. I led them past Hebron into the south country, and so by the Vale of Eshcol, and over many hills beyond the Pools of Solomon, until my feet brought me to your fire. Here I rest on the way to nowhere."

He sat silent, and the four shepherds looked at him with amazement.

"It is a bitter tale," said Shama, "and you are a great sinner."

"I should be a fool not to know that," answered the sad shepherd, "but the knowledge does me no good."

"You must repent," said Nathan, the youngest shepherd, in a friendly voice.

"How can a man repent," answered the sad shepherd, "unless he has hope? But I am sorry for everything, and most of all for living."

"Would you not live to kill the fox Herod?" cried Jotham fiercely.

"Why should I let him out of the trap," answered the sad shepherd. "Is he not dying more slowly than I could kill him?"

"You must have faith in God," said Zadok earnestly and gravely.

"He is too far away."

"Then you must have love for your neighbor."

"He is too near. My confidence in man was like a pool by the wayside. It was shallow, but there was water in it, and sometimes a star shone there. Now the feet of many beasts have trampled through it, and the jackals have drunken of it, and there is no more water. It is dry and the mire is caked at the bottom.'

"Is there nothing good in the world?"

"There is pleasure, but I am sick of it. There is power, but I hate it. There is wisdom, but I mistrust it. Life is a game and every player is for his own hand. Mine is played. I have nothing to win or lose."

"You are young, you have many years to live."

"I am old, yet the days before me are too many."

"But you travel the road, you go forward. Do you hope for nothing?"

"I hope for nothing," said the sad shepherd. "Yet if one thing should come to me it might be the beginning of hope. If I saw in man or woman a deed of kindness without a selfish reason, and a proof of love gladly given for its own sake only, then might I turn my face toward that light. Till that comes, how can I have faith in God whom I have never seen? I have seen the world which he has made, and it brings me no faith. There is nothing in it."

"Ammiel-ben-Jochanan," said the old man sternly, "you are a son of Israel, and we have had compassion on you, according to the law. But you are an apostate, an unbeliever, and we can have no more fellowship with you, lest a curse come upon us. The company of the desperate brings misfortune. Go your way and depart from us, for our way is not yours."

So the sad shepherd thanked them for their entertainment, and took the little kid again in his arms, and went into the night, calling his flock. But the youngest shepherd Nathan followed him a few steps and said:

"There is a broken fold at the foot of the hill. It is old and small, but you may find a shelter there for your flock where the wind will not shake you. Go your way with God, brother, and see better days."

Then Ammiel went a little way down the hill and sheltered his flock in a corner of the crumbling walls. He lay among the sheep and the goats with his face upon his folded arms, and whether the time passed slowly or swiftly he did not know, for he slept.

He waked as Nathan came running and stumbling among the scattered stones.

"We have seen a vision," he cried, "a wonderful vision of angels. Did you not hear them? They sang loudly of the Hope of Israel. We are going to Bethlehem to see this thing which is come to pass. Come you and keep watch over our sheep while we are gone."

"Of angels I have seen and heard nothing," said Ammiel, "but I will guard your flocks with mine, since I am in debt to you for bread and fire."

So he brought the kid in his arms, and the weary flock straggling after him, to the south wall of the great fold again, and sat there by the embers at the foot of the tower, while the others were away. The moon rested like a ball on the edge of the western hills and rolled behind them. The stars faded in the east and the fires went out on the Mountain of the Little Paradise. Over the hills of Moab a gray flood of dawn rose slowly, and arrows of red shot far up before the sunrise.

The shepherds returned full of joy and told what they had seen.

"It was even as the angels said unto us," said Shama, "and it must be true. The King of Israel has come. The faithful shall be blessed."

"Herod shall fall," cried Jotham, lifting his clenched fist toward the dark peaked mountain. "Burn, black Idumean, in the bottomless pit, where the fire is not quenched."

Zadok spoke more quietly. "We found the new-born child of whom the angels told us wrapped in swaddling clothes and lying in a manger. The ways of God are wonderful. His salvation comes out of darkness, and we trust in the promised deliverance. But you, Ammiel-ben-Jochanan, except you believe, you shall not see it. Yet since you have kept our flocks faithfully, and because of the joy that has come to us, I give you this piece of silver to help you on your way."

But Nathan came close to the sad shepherd and touched him on the shoulder with a friendly hand, "Go you also to Bethlehem," he said in a low voice, "for it is good to see what we have seen, and we will keep your flock until you return."

"I will go," said Ammiel, looking into his face, "for I think you wish me well. But whether I shall see what you have seen, or whether I shall ever return, I know not. Farewell."

III.

DAWN

The narrow streets of Bethlehem were waking to the first stir of life as the sad shepherd came into the town with the morning, and passed through them like one walking in his sleep.

The court-yard of the great khan and the open rooms around it were crowded with travelers, rousing them from their night's rest and making ready for the day's journey. In front of the stables half hollowed in the rock beside the inn, men were saddling their horses and their beasts of burden, and there was much noise and confusion.

But beyond these, at the end of the line, there was a deeper grotto in the rock, which was used only when the nearer stalls were full. At the entrance of this an ass was tethered, and a man of middle age stood in the doorway.

The sad shepherd saluted him and told his name.

"I am Joseph the carpenter of Nazareth," replied the man. "Have you also seen the angels of whom your brother shepherds came to tell us?"

"I have seen no angels," answered Ammiel, "nor have I any brothers among the shepherds. But I would fain see what they have seen."

"It is our first-born son," said Joseph, "and the Most High has sent him to us. He is a marvellous child: great things are foretold of him. You may go in, but quietly, for the child and his mother Mary are asleep."

So the sad shepherd went in quietly. His long shadow entered before him, for the sunrise was flowing into the door of the grotto. It was made clean and put in order, and a bed of straw was laid in the corner on the ground.

The child was asleep, but the young mother was waking, for she had taken him from the manger into her lap, where her maiden veil of white was spread to receive him. And she was singing very softly as she bent over him in wonder and content.

Ammiel saluted her and kneeled down to look at the child. He saw nothing different from other young children. The mother waited for him to speak of angels, as the other shepherds had done. The sad shepherd did not speak, but only looked. And as he looked his face changed.

"You have suffered pain and danger and sorrow for his sake," he said gently.

"They are past," she answered, "and for his sake I have suffered them gladly."

"He is very little and helpless; you must bear many troubles for his sake."

"To care for him is my joy, and to bear him lightens my burden."

"He does not know you, he can do nothing for you."

"But I know him. I have carried him under my heart, he is my son and my king."

"Why do you love him?"

The mother looked up at the sad shepherd with a great reproach in her soft eyes. Then her look grew pitiful as it rested on his face.

"You are a sorrowful man," she said.

"I am a wicked man," he answered.

She shook her head gently.

"I know nothing of that," she said, "but you must be very sorrowful, since you are born of a woman and yet you ask a mother why she loves her child. I love him for love's sake, because God has given him to me."

So the mother Mary leaned over her little son again and began to croon a song as if she were alone with him.

But Ammiel was still there, watching and thinking and beginning to remember. It came back to him that there was a woman in Galilee who had wept when he was rebuked; whose eyes had followed him when he was unhappy, as if she longed to do something for him; whose voice had broken and dropped silent while she covered her tear-stained face when he went away.

His thoughts flowed swiftly and silently toward her and after her like rapid waves of light. There was a thought of her bending over a little child in her lap, singing softly for pure joy,-and the child was himself. There was a thought of her lifting a little child to the breast that had borne him as a burden and a pain, to nourish him there as a comfort and a treasure,-and the child was himself. There was a thought of her watching and tending and guiding a little child from day to day, from year to year, putting tender arms around him, bending over his first wavering steps, rejoicing in his joys, wiping away the tears from his eyes, as he had never tried to wipe her tears away,-and the child was himself. She had done everything for the child's sake, but what had the child done for her sake? And the child was himself: that was what he had come to,-after the nightfire had burned out, after the darkness had grown thin and melted in the thoughts that pulsed through it like rapid waves of light,-that was what he had come to in the early morning: himself, a child in his mother's arms.

Then he arose and went out of the grotto softly, making the threefold sign of reverence; and the eyes of Mary followed him with kind looks.

Joseph of Nazareth was still waiting outside the door.

"How was it that you did not see the angels?" he asked. "Were you not with the other shepherds?"

"No," answered Ammiel, "I was asleep. But I have seen the mother and the child. Blessed be the house that holds them."

"You are strangely clad for a shepherd," said Joseph. "Where do you come from?"

"From a far country," replied Ammiel; "from a country that you have never visited."

"Where are you going now?" asked Joseph.

"I am going home," answered Ammiel, "to my mother's and my father's house in Galilee."

"Go in peace, friend," said Joseph.

And the sad shepherd took up his battered staff, and went on his way rejoicing.

THE FIRST CHRISTMAS TREE

A STORY OF THE FOREST

So they took the little fir from its place

I.

THE CALL OF THE WOODSMAN

THE day before Christmas, in the year of our Lord 722.

Broad snow-meadows glistening white along the banks of the river Moselle; pallid hill-sides blooming with mystic roses where the glow of the setting sun still lingered upon them; an arch of clearest, faintest azure bending overhead; in the center of the aerial landscape of the massive walls of the cloister of Pfalzel, gray to the east, purple to the west; silence over all,—a gentle, eager, conscious stillness, diffused through the air like perfume, as if earth and sky were hushing themselves to hear the voice of the river faintly murmuring down the valley.

In the cloister, too, there was silence at the sunset hour. All day long there had been a strange and joyful stir among the nuns. A breeze of curiosity and excitement had swept along the corridors and through every quiet cell.

The elder sisters,—the provost, the deaconess, the stewardess, the portress with her huge bunch of keys jingling at her girdle,—had been hurrying to and fro, busied with household cares. In the huge kitchen there was a bustle of hospitable preparation. The little bandy-legged dogs that kept the spits turning before the fires had been trotting steadily for many an hour, until their tongues hung out for want of breath. The big black pots swinging from the cranes had bubbled and gurgled and shaken and sent out puffs of appetizing steam.

St. Martha was in her element. It was a field-day for her virtues.

The younger sisters, the pupils of the convent, had forsaken their Latin books and their embroidery-frames, their manuscripts and their miniatures, and fluttered through the halls in little flocks like merry snow-birds, all in black and white, chattering and whispering together. This was no day for tedious task-work, no day for grammar or arithmetic, no day for picking out illuminated letters in red and gold on stiff parchment, or patiently chasing intricate patterns over thick cloth with the slow needle. It was a holiday. A famous visitor had come to the convent.

It was Winfried of England, whose name in the Roman tongue was Boniface, and whom men called the Apostle of Germany. A great preacher; a wonderful scholar; he had written a Latin grammar himself,—think of it,—and he could hardly sleep without a book under his pillow; but, more than all, a great and daring traveller, a venturesome pilgrim, a high-priest of romance.

He had left his home and his fair estate in Wessex; he would not stay in the rich monastery of Nutescelle, even though they had chosen him as the abbot; he had refused a bishopric at the court of King Karl. Nothing would content him but to go out into the wild woods and preach to the heathen.

Up and down through the forests of Hesse and Thuringia, and along the borders of Saxony, he had wandered for years, with a handful of companions, sleeping under the trees, crossing mountains and marshes, now here, now there, never satisfied with ease and comfort, always in love with hardship and danger.

What a man he was! Fair and slight, but straight as a spear and strong as an oaken staff. His face was still young; the smooth skin was bronzed by wing and sun. His gray eyes, clear and kind, flashed like fire when he spoke of his adventures, and of the evil deeds of the false priests with whom he had contended.

What tales he had told that day! Not of miracles wrought by sacred relics; nor of courts and councils and splendid cathedrals; though he knew much of these things, and had been at Rome and received the Pope's blessing. But to-day he had spoken of long journeyings by sea and land; of perils by fire and flood; of wolves and bears and fierce snowstorms and black nights in the lonely forest; of dark altars of heaven gods, and weird, bloody sacrifices, and narrow escapes from wandering savages.

The little novices had gathered around him, and their faces had grown pale and their eyes bright as they listened with parted lips, entranced in admiration, twining their arms about one another's shoulders and holding closely together, half in fear, half in delight. The older nuns had turned from their tasks and paused, in passing by, to hear the pilgrim's story. Too well they knew the truth of what he spoke. Many a one among them had seen the smoke rising from the ruins of her father's roof. Many a one had a brother far away in the wild country to whom her heart went out night and day, wondering if he were still among the living.

But now the excitements of that wonderful day were over; the hours of the evening meal had come; the inmates of the cloister were assembled in the refectory.

On the dais sat the stately Abbess Addula, daughter of King Dagobert, looking a princess indeed, in her violet tunic, with the hood and cuffs of her long white robe trimmed with fur, and a snowy veil resting like a crown on her snowy hair. At her right hand was the honoured guest, and at her left hand her grandson, the young Prince Gregor, a big, manly boy, just returned from school.

The long, shadowy hall, with its dark-brown raters and beams; the double rows of nuns, with their pure veils and fair faces; the ruddy flow of the slanting sunbeams striking upwards through the tops of the windows and painting a pink glow high up on the walls,—it was all as beautiful as a picture, and as silent. For this was the rule of the cloister, that at the table all should sit in stillness for a little while, and then one should read aloud, while the rest listened.

"It is the turn of my grandson to read to-day," said the abbess to Winfried; "we shall see how much he has learned in the school. Read, Gregor; the place in the book is marked."

The tall lad rose from his seat and turned the pages of the manuscript. It was a copy of Jerome's version of the Scriptures in Latin, and the marked place was in the letter of St. Paul to the Ephesians,—the passage where he describes the preparation of the Christian as the arming of a warrior for glorious battle. The young voice rang out clearly, rolling the sonorous words, without slip or stumbling, to the end of the chapter.

Winfried listened, smiling. "My son," said he, as the reader paused, "that was bravely read. Understandest thou what thou readest?"

"Surely, father," answered the boy; "it was taught me by the masters at Treves; and we have read this epistle clear through, from beginning to end, so that I almost know it by heart."

Then he began again to repeat the passage, turning away from the page as if to show his skill.

But Winfried stopped him with a friendly lifting of the hand.

"No so, my son; that was not my meaning. When we pray, we speak to God; when we read, it is God who speaks to us. I ask whether thou hast heard what He has said to thee, in thine own words, in the common speech. Come, give us again the message of the warrior and his armour and his battle, in the mother-tongue, so that all can understand it."

The boy hesitated, blushed, stammered; then he came around to Winfried's seat, bringing the book. "Take the book, my father," he cried, "and read it for me. I cannot see the meaning plain, though I love the sound of the words. Religion I know, and the doctrines of our faith, and the life of priests and nuns in the cloister, for which my grandmother designs me, though it likes me little. And fighting I know, and the life of warriors and heroes, for I have read of it in Virgil and the ancients, and heard a bit from the soldiers at Treves; and I would fain taste more of it, for it likes me much. But how the two lives fit together, or what need there is of armour for a clerk in holy orders, I can never see. Tell me the meaning, for if there is a man in all the world that knows it, I am sure it is none other than thou."

So Winfried took the book and closed it, clasping the boy's hand with his own.

"Let us first dismiss the others to their vespers," said he, "lest they should be weary."

A sign from the abbess; a chanted benediction; a murmuring of sweet voices and a soft rustling of many feet over the rushes on the floor; the gentle tide of noise flowed out through the doors and ebbed away down the corridors; the three at the head of the table were left alone in the darkening room.

Then Winfried began to translate the parable of the soldier into the realities of life.

At every turn he knew how to flash a new light into the picture out of his own experience. He spoke of the combat with self, and of the wrestling with dark spirits in solitude. He spoke of the demons that men had worshipped for centuries in the wilderness, and whose malice they invoked against the stranger who ventured into the gloomy forest. Gods, they called them, and told strange tales of their dwelling among the impenetrable branches of the oldest trees and in the caverns of the shaggy hills; of their riding on the wind-horses and hurling spears of lightning against their foes. Gods they were not, but foul spirits of the air, rulers of the darkness. Was there not glory and honour in fighting with them, in daring their anger under the shield of faith, in putting them to flight with the sword of truth? What better adventure could a brave man ask than to go forth against them, and wrestle with them, and conquer them?

"Look you, my friends," said Winfried, "how sweet and peaceful is this convent to-night, on the eve of the nativity of the Prince of Peace! It is a garden full of flowers in the heart of winter; a nest among the branches of a great tree shaken by the winds; a still haven on the edge of a tempestuous sea. And this is what religion means for those who are chosen and called to quietude and prayer and meditation.

303

"But out yonder in the wide forest, who knows what storms are raving to-night in the hearts of men, though all the woods are still? who knows what haunts of wrath and cruelty and fear are closed to-night against the advent of the Prince of Peace? And shall I tell you what religion means to those who are called and chosen to dare and to fight, and to conquer the world for Christ? It means to launch out into the deep. It means to go against the strongholds of the adversary. It means to struggle to win an entrance for their Master everywhere. What helmet is strong enough for this strife save the helmet of salvation? What breastplate can guard a man against these fiery darts but the breastplate of righteousness? What shoes can stand the wear of these journeys but the preparation of the gospel of peace?"

"Shoes?" he cried again, and laughed as if a sudden thought had struck him. He thrust out his foot, covered with a heavy cowhide boot, laced high about his leg with thongs of skin.

"See here,—how a fighting man of the cross is shod! I have seen the boots of the Bishop of Tours,—white kid, broidered with silk; a day in the bogs would tear them to shreds. I have seen the sandals that the monks use on the highroads,—yes, and worn them; ten pair of them have I worn out and thrown away in a single journey. Now I shoe my feet with the toughest hides, hard as iron; no rock can cut them, no branches can tear them. Yet more than one pair of these have I outworn, and many more shall I outwear ere my journeys are ended. And I think, if God is gracious to me, that I shall die wearing them. Better so than in a soft bed with silken coverings. The boots of a warrior, a hunter, a woodsman,—these are my preparation of the gospel of peace."

"Come, Gregor," he said, laying his brown hand on the youth's shoulder, "come, wear the forester's boots with me. This is the life to which we are called. Be strong in the Lord, a hunter of the demons, a subduer of the wilderness, a woodsman of the faith. Come!"

The boy's eyes sparkled. He turned to his grandmother. She shook her head vigorously.

"Nay, father," she said, "draw not the lad away from my side with these wild words. I need him to help me with my labours, to cheer my old age."

"Do you need him more than the Master does?" asked Winfried; "and will you take the wood that is fit for a bow to make a distaff?"

"But I fear for the child. Thy life is too hard for him. He will perish with hunger in the woods."

"Once," said Winfried, smiling, "we were camped by the bank of the river Ohru. The table was spread for the morning meal, but my comrades cried that it was empty; the provisions were exhausted; we must go without breakfast, and perhaps starve before we could escape from the wilderness. While they complained, a fish-hawk flew up from the river with flapping wings, and let fall a great pike in the midst of the camp. There was food enough and to spare. Never have I seen the righteous forsaken, nor his seed begging bread."

"But the fierce pagans of the forest," cried the abbess,—"they may pierce the boy with their arrows, or dash out his brains with their axes. He is but a child, too young for the dangers of strife."

"A child in years," replied Winfried, "but a man in spirit. And if the hero must fall early in the battle, he wears the brighter crown, not a leaf withered, not a flower fallen."

The aged princess trembled a little. She drew Gregor close to her side, and laid her hand gently on his brown hair.

"I am not sure that he wants to leave me yet. Besides, there is no horse in the stable to give him, now, and he cannot go as befits the grandson of a king."

Gregor looked straight into her eyes.

"Grandmother," said he, "dear grandmother, if thou wilt not give me a horse to ride with this man of God, I will go with him afoot."

The fields around lay bare to the moon

II.

THE TRAIL THROUGH THE FOREST

TWO years had passed, to a day, almost to an hour, since that Christmas eve in the cloister of Pfalzel. A little company of pilgrims, less than a score a men, were creeping slowly northward through the wide forest that rolled over the hills of central Germany.

At the head of the band marched Winfried, clad in a tunic of fur, with his long black robe girt high about his waist, so that it might not hinder his stride. His hunter's boots were crusted with snow. Drops of ice sparkled like jewels along the thongs that bound his legs. There was no other ornament to his dress except the bishop's cross hanging on his breast, and the broad silver clasp that fastened his cloak about his neck. He carried a strong, tall staff in his hand, fashioned at the top into the form of a cross.

Close beside him, keeping step like a familiar comrade, was the young Prince Gregor. Long marches through the wilderness had stretched his limbs and broadened his back, and made a man of him in stature as well as in spirit. His jacket and cap were of wolfskin, and on his shoulder he carried an axe, with broad, shining blade. He was a mighty woodsman now, and could make a spray of chips fly around him as he hewed his way through the trunk of spruce-tree.

Behind these leaders followed a pair of teamsters, guiding a rude sledge, loaded with food and the equipage of the camp, and drawn by two big, shaggy horses, blowing thick clouds of steam from their frosty nostrils. Tiny icicles hung from the hairs on their lips. Their flanks were smoking. They sank above the fetlocks at every step in the soft snow.

Last of all came the rear guard, armed with bows and javelins. It was no child's play, in those days, to cross Europe afoot.

The weird woodland, sombre and illimitable, covered hill and vale, tableland and mountain-peak. There were wide moors where the wolves hunted in packs as if the devil drove them, and tangled thickets where the lynx and the boar made their lairs. Fierce bears lurked among the rocky passes, and had not yet learned to fear the face of man. The gloomy recesses of the forest gave shelter to inhabitants who were still more cruel and dangerous than beasts of prey,—outlaws and sturdy robbers and mad were-wolves and bands of wandering pillagers.

The pilgrim who would pass from the mouth of the Tiber to the mouth of the Rhine must travel with a little army of retainers, or else trust in God and keep his arrows loose in the quiver.

The travellers were surrounded by an ocean of trees, so vast, so full of endless billows, that it seemed to be pressing on every side to overwhelm them. Gnarled oaks, with branches twisted and knotted as if in rage, rose in groves like tidal waves. Smooth forests of beech-trees, round and gray, swept over the knolls and slopes of land in a mighty ground-swell. But most of all, the multitude of pines and firs, innumerable and monotonous, with straight, stark trunks, and branches woven together in an unbroken Hood of darkest green, crowded through the valleys and over the hills, rising on the highest ridges into ragged crests, like the foaming edge of breakers.

Through this sea of shadows ran a narrow stream of shining whiteness,—an ancient Roman road, covered with snow. It was as if some great ship had ploughed through the green ocean long ago, and left behind it a thick, smooth wake of foam. Along this open track the travellers held their way,—heavily, for the drifts were deep; warily, for the hard winter had driven many packs of wolves down from the moors.

The steps of the pilgrims were noiseless; but the sledges creaked over the dry snow, and the panting of the horses throbbed through the still, cold air. The pale-blue shadows on the western side of the road grew longer. The sun, declining through its shallow arch, dropped behind the tree-tops. Darkness followed swiftly, as if it had been a bird of prey waiting for this sign to swoop down upon the world.

"Father," said Gregor to the leader, "surely this day's march is done. It is time to rest, and eat, and sleep. If we press onward now, we cannot see our steps; and will not that be against the word of the psalmist David, who bids us not to put confidence in the legs of a man?"

Winfried laughed. "Nay, my son Gregor," said he, "thou hast tripped, even now, upon thy text. For David said only, 'I take no pleasure in the legs of a man.' And so say I, for I am not minded to spare thy legs or mine, until we come farther on our way, and do what must be done this night. Draw the belt tighter, my son, and hew me out this tree that is fallen across the road, for our campground is not here."

The youth obeyed; two of the foresters sprang to help him; and while the soft fir-wood yielded to the stroke of the axes, and the snow flew from the bending branches, Winfried turned and spoke to his followers in a cheerful voice, that refreshed them like wine.

"Courage, brothers, and forward yet a little! The moon will light us presently, and the path is plain. Well know I that the journey is weary; and my own heart wearies also for the home in England, where those I love are keeping feast this Christmas eve. But we have work to do before we feast to-night. For this is the Yuletide, and the heathen people of the forest have gathered at the thunder-oak of Geismar to worship their god, Thor. Strange things will be seen there, and deeds which make the soul black. But we are sent to lighten their darkness; and we will teach our kinsmen to keep a Christmas with us such as the woodland has never known. Forward, then, and let us stiffen up our feeble knees!"

A murmur of assent came from the men. Even the horses seemed to take fresh heart. They flattened their backs to draw the heavy loads, and blew the frost from their nostrils as they pushed ahead.

The night grew broader and less oppressive. A gate of brightness was opened secretly somewhere in the sky; higher and higher swelled the clear moon-flood, until it poured over the eastern wall of forest into the road. A drove of wolves howled faintly in the distance, but they were receding, and the sound soon died away. The stars sparkled merrily through the stringent air; the small, round moon shone like silver; little breaths of the dreaming wind wandered whispering across the pointed fir-tops, as the pilgrims toiled bravely onward, following their clue of light through a labyrinth of darkness.

After a while the road began to open out a little. There were spaces of meadow-land, fringed with alders, behind which a boisterous river ran, clashing through spears of ice.

Rude houses of hewn logs appeared in the openings, each one casting a patch of inky blackness upon the snow. Then the travellers passed a larger group of dwellings, all silent and unlighted; and beyond, they saw a great house, with many outbuildings and enclosed courtyards, from which the hounds bayed furiously, and a noise of stamping horses came from the stalls. But there was no other sound of life. The fields around lay bare to the moon. They saw no man, except that once, on a path that skirted the farther edge of a meadow, three dark figures passed by, running very swiftly.

Then the road plunged again into a dense thicket, traversed it, and climbing to the left, emerged suddenly upon a glade, round and level except at the northern side, where a swelling hillock was crowned with a huge oak-tree. It towered above the heath, a giant with contorted arms, beckoning to the host of lesser trees. "Here," cried Winfried, as his eyes flashed and his hand lifted his heavy staff, "here is the Thunder-oak; and here the cross of Christ shall break the hammer of the false god Thor."

The sacred hammer of the god Thor

III.

THE SHADOW OF THE THUNDER-OAK

WITHERED leaves still clung to the branches of the oak: torn and faded banners of the departed summer. The bright crimson of autumn had long since disappeared, bleached away by the storms and the cold. But to-night these tattered remnants of glory were red again: ancient bloodstains against the dark-blue sky. For an immense fire had been kindled in front of the tree. Tongues of ruddy flame, fountains of ruby sparks, ascended through the spreading limbs and flung a fierce illumination upward and around. ward and around. The pale, pure moonlight that bathed the surrounding forests was quenched and eclipsed here. Not a beam of it sifted down-ward through the branches of the oak. It stood like a pillar of cloud between the still light of heaven and the crackling, flashing fire of earth.

But the fire itself was invisible to Winfried and his companions. A great throng of people were gathered around it in a half-circle, their backs to the open glade, their faces towards the oak. Seen against that glowing background, it was but the silhouette of a crowd, vague, black, formless, mysterious.

The travellers paused for a moment at the edge of the thicket, and took counsel together.

"It is the assembly of the tribe," said one of the foresters, "the great night of the council. I heard of it three days ago, as we passed through one of the villages. All who swear by the old gods have been summoned.

They will sacrifice a steed to the god of war, and drink blood, and eat horse-flesh to make them strong. It will be at the peril of our lives if we approach them. At least we must hide the cross, if we would escape death."

"Hide me no cross," cried Winfried, lifting his staff, "for I have come to show it, and to make these blind folk see its power. There is more to be done here to-night than the slaying of a steed, and a greater evil to be stayed than the shameful eating of meat sacrificed to idols. I have seen it in a dream. Here the cross must stand and be our rede."

At his command the sledge was left in the border of the wood, with two of the men to guard it, and the rest of the company moved forward across the open ground. They approached unnoticed, for all the multitude were looking intently towards the fire at the foot of the oak.

Then Winfried's voice rang out, "Hail, ye sons of the forest! A stranger claims the warmth of your fire in the winter night."

Swiftly, and as with a single motion, a thousand eyes were bent upon the speaker. The semicircle opened silently in the middle; Winfried entered with his followers; it closed again behind them.

Then, as they looked round the curving ranks, they saw that the hue of the assemblage was not black, but white,—dazzling, radiant, solemn. White, the robes of the women clustered together at the points of the wide crescent; white, the glittering byrnies of the warriors standing in close ranks; white, the fur mantles of the aged men who held the central place in the circle; white, with the shimmer of silver ornaments and the purity of lamb's-wool, the raiment of a little group of children who stood close by the fire; white, with awe and fear, the faces of all who looked at them; and over all the flickering, dancing radiance of the flames played and glimmered like a faint, vanishing tinge of blood on snow.

The only figure untouched by the glow was the old priest, Hunrad, with his long, spectral robe, flowing hair and beard, and dead-pale face, who stood with his back to the fire and advanced slowly to meet the strangers.

"Who are you? Whence come you, and what seek you here?" His voice was heavy and toneless as a muffled bell.

"You kinsman am I, of the German brotherhood," answered Winfried, "and from England, beyond the sea, have I come to bring you a greeting from that land, and a message from the All-Father, whose servant I am."

"Welcome, then," said Hunrad, "welcome, kinsman, and be silent; for what passes here is too high to wait, and must be done before the moon crosses the middle heaven, unless, indeed, thou hast some sign or token from the gods. Canst thou work miracles?"

The question came sharply, as if a sudden gleam of hope had flashed through the tangle of the old priest's mind. But Winfried's voice sank lower and a cloud of disappointment passed over his face as he replied: "Nay, miracles have I never wrought, though I have heard of many; but the All-Father has given no power to my hands save such as belongs to common man."

"Stand still, then, thou common man," said Hunrad, scornfully, "and behold what the gods have called us hither to do. This night is the death-night of the sun-god, Baldur the Beautiful, beloved of gods and men. This night is the hour of darkness and the power of winter, of sacrifice and mighty fear. This night the great Thor, the god of thunder and war, to whom this oak is sacred, is grieved for the death of Baldur, and angry with this people because they have forsaken his worship. Long is it since an offering has been laid upon his altar, long since the roots of his holy tree have been fed with blood. Therefore its leaves have withered before the time, and its boughs are heavy with death. Therefore the Slavs and the Wends have beaten us in battle. Therefore the harvests have failed, and the wolf-hordes have ravaged the folds, and the strength has departed from the bow, and the wood of the spear has broken, and the wild boar has slain the huntsman. Therefore the plague has fallen on our dwellings, and the dead are more than the living in all our villages. Answer me, ye people, are not these things true?"

314

A hoarse sound of approval ran through the circle. A chant, in which the voices of the men and women blended, like the shrill wind in the pine-trees above the rumbling thunder of a waterfall, rose and fell in rude cadences.

O Thor, the Thunderer,
Mighty and merciless,
Spare us from smiting!
Heave not thy hammer,
Angry, against us;
Plague not thy people.
Take from our treasure
Richest of ransom.
Silver we send thee,
Jewels and javelins,
Goodliest garments,
All our possessions,
Priceless, we proffer.
Sheep will we slaughter,
Steeds will we sacrifice;
Bright blood shall bathe thee,
O tree of Thunder,
Life-floods shall lave thee,
Strong wood of wonder.
Mighty, have mercy,
Smite us no more,
Spare us and save us,
Spare us, Thor! Thor!

With two great shouts the song ended, and a stillness followed so intense that the crackling of the fire was heard distinctly. The old priest stood silent for a moment. His shaggy brows swept down over his eyes like ashes quenching flame. Then he lifted his face and spoke.

"None of these things will please the god. More costly is the offering that shall cleanse your sin, more precious the crimson dew that shall send new life into this holy tree of blood. Thor claims your dearest and your noblest gift."

Hunrad moved nearer to the handful of children who stood watching the red mines in the fire and the swarms of spark-serpents darting upward. They had heeded none of the priest's words, and did not notice now that he approached them, so eager were they to see which fiery snake would go highest among the oak branches. Foremost among them, and most intent on the pretty game, was a boy like a sunbeam, slender and quick, with blithe brown eyes and laughing lips. The priest's hand was laid upon his shoulder. The boy turned and looked up in his face.

"Here," said the old man, with his voice vibrating as when a thick rope is strained by a ship swinging from her moorings, "here is the chosen one, the eldest son of the Chief, the darling of the people. Hearken, Bernhard, wilt thou go to Valhalla, where the heroes dwell with the gods, to bear a message to Thor?"

The boy answered, swift and clear:

"Yes, priest, I will go if my father bids me. Is it far away? Shall I run quickly? Must I take my bow and arrows for the wolves?"

The boy's father, the Chieftain Gundhar, standing among his bearded warriors, drew his breath deep, and leaned so heavily on the handle of his spear that the wood cracked. And his wife, Irma, bending forward from the ranks of women, pushed the golden hair from her forehead with one hand. The other dragged at the silver chain about her neck until the rough links pierced her flesh, and the red drops fell unheeded on the snow of her breast.

A sigh passed through the crowd, like the murmur of the forest before the storm breaks. Yet no one spoke save Hunrad:

"Yes, my Prince, both bow and spear shalt thou have, for the way is long, and thou art a brave huntsman. But in darkness thou must journey for a little space, and with eyes blindfolded. Fearest thou?"

"Naught fear I," said the boy, "neither darkness, nor the great bear, nor the were-wolf. For I am Gundhar's son, and the defender of my folk."

Then the priest led the child in his raiment of lamb's-wool to a broad stone in front of the fire. He gave him his little bow tipped with silver, and his spear with shining head of steel. He bound the child's eyes with a white cloth, and bade him kneel beside the stone with his face to the east. Unconsciously the wide arc of spectators drew inward toward the centre, as the ends of the bow draw together when the cord is stretched. Winfried moved noiselessly until he stood close behind the priest.

The old man stooped to lift a black hammer of stone from the ground,—the sacred hammer of the god Thor. Summoning all the strength of his withered arms, he swung it high in the air. It poised for an instant above the child's fair head—then turned to fall.

One keen cry shrilled out from where the women stood: "Me! take me! not Bernhard!"

The flight of the mother towards her child was swift as the falcon's swoop. But swifter still was the hand of the deliverer.

Winfried's heavy staff thrust mightily against the hammer's handle as it fell. Sideways it glanced from the old man's grasp, and the black stone, striking on the altar's edge, split in twain. A shout of awe and joy rolled along the living circle. The branches of the oak shivered. The flames leaped higher. As the shout died away the people saw the lady Irma, with her arms clasped round her child, and above them, on the altar-stone, Winfried, his face shining like the face of an angel.

Then Winfried told the story of Bethlehem

IV.

THE FELLING OF THE TREE

A SWIFT mountain-flood rolling down its channel; a huge rock tumbling from the hill-side and falling in mid-stream; the baffled waters broken and confused, pausing in their flow, dash high against the rock, foaming and murmuring, with divided impulse, uncertain whether to turn to the right or the left.

Even so Winfried's bold deed fell into the midst of the thoughts and passions of the council. They were at a standstill. Anger and wonder, reverence and joy and confusion surged through the crowd. They knew not which way to move: to resent the intrusion of the stranger as an insult to their gods, or to welcome him as the rescuer of their darling prince.

The old priest crouched by the altar, silent. Conflicting counsels troubled the air. Let the sacrifice go forward; the gods must be appeased. Nay, the boy must not die; bring the chieftain's best horse and slay it in his stead; it will be enough; the holy tree loves the blood of horses. Not so, there is a better counsel yet; seize the stranger whom the gods have led hither as a victim and make his life pay the forfeit of his daring.

The withered leaves on the oak rustled and whispered overhead. The fire flared and sank again. The angry voices clashed against each other and fell like opposing waves. Then the chieftain Gundhar struck the earth with his spear and gave his decision.

"All have spoken, but none are agreed. There is no voice of the council. Keep silence now, and let the stranger speak. His words shall give us judgment, whether he is to live or to die."

Winfried lifted himself high upon the altar, drew a roll of parchment from his bosom, and began to read.

"A letter from the great Bishop of Rome, who sits on a golden throne, to the people of the forest, Hessians and Thuringians, Franks and Saxons. *In nomine Domini, sanctae et individuae trinitatis, amen!*"

A murmur of awe ran through the crowd. "It is the sacred tongue of the Romans: the tongue that is heard and understood by the wise men of every land. There is magic in it. Listen!"

Winfried went on to read the letter, translating it into the speech of the people.

"'We have sent unto you our Brother Boniface, and appointed him your bishop, that he may teach you the only true faith, and baptize you, and lead you back from the ways of error to the path of salvation. Hearken to him in all things like a father. Bow your hearts to his teaching. He comes not for earthly gain, but for the gain of your souls. Depart from evil works. Worship not the false gods, for they are devils. Offer no more bloody sacrifices, nor eat the flesh of horses, but do as our Brother Boniface commands you. Build a house for him that he may dwell among you, and a church where you may offer your prayers to the only living God, the Almighty King of Heaven.'"

It was a splendid message: proud, strong, peaceful, loving. The dignity of the words imposed mightily upon the hearts of the people. They were quieted as men who have listened to a lofty strain of music.

"Tell us, then," said Gundhar, "what is the word that thou bringest to us from the Almighty. What is thy counsel for the tribes of the woodland on this night of sacrifice?"

"This is the word, and this is the counsel," answered Winfried. "Not a drop of blood shall fall to-night, save that which pity has drawn from the breast of your princess, in love for her child. Not a life shall be blotted out in the darkness tonight; but the great shadow of the tree which hides you from the light of heaven shall be swept away. For this is the birth-night of the white Christ, son of the All-Father, and Saviour of mankind. Fairer is He than Baldur the Beautiful, greater than Odin the Wise, kinder than Freya the Good. Since He has come to earth the bloody sacrifices must cease. The dark Thor, on whom you vainly call, is dead. Deep in the shades of Niffelheim he is lost forever. His power in the world is broken. Will you serve a helpless god? See, my brothers, you call this tree his oak. Does he dwell here? Does he protect it?"

A troubled voice of assent rose from the throng. The people stirred uneasily. Women covered their eyes. Hunrad lifted his head and muttered hoarsely, "Thor! take vengeance! Thor!"

Winfried beckoned to Gregor. "Bring the axes, thine and one for me. Now, young woodsman, show thy craft! The king-tree of the forest must fall, and swiftly, or all is lost!"

The two men took their places facing each other, one on each side of the oak. Their cloaks were flung aside, their heads bare. Carefully they felt the ground with their feet, seeking a firm grip of the earth. Firmly they grasped the axe-helves and swung the shining blades.

"Tree-god!" cried Winfried, "art thou angry? Thus we smite thee!"

"Tree-god!" answered Gregor, "art thou mighty? Thus we fight thee!"

Clang! clang! the alternate strokes beat time upon the hard, ringing wood. The axe-heads glittered in their rhythmic flight, like fierce eagles circling about their quarry.

The broad flakes of wood flew from the deepening gashes in the sides of the oak. The huge trunk quivered. There was a shuddering in the branches. Then the great wonder of Winfried's life came to pass.

Out of the stillness of the winter night, a mighty rushing noise sounded overhead.

Was it the ancient gods on their white battle-steeds, with their black hounds of wrath and their arrows of lightning, sweeping through the air to destroy their foes?

A strong, whirling wind passed over the tree-tops. It gripped the oak by its branches and tore it from its roots. Backward it fell, like a ruined tower, groaning and crashing as it split asunder in four great pieces.

Winfried let his axe drop, and bowed his head for a moment in the presence of almighty power.

Then he turned to the people, "Here is the timber," he cried, "already felled and split for your new building. On this spot shall rise a chapel to the true God and his servant St. Peter.

"And here," said he, as his eyes fell on a young fir-tree, standing straight and green, with its top pointing towards the stars, amid the divided ruins of the fallen oak, "here is the living tree, with no stain of blood upon it, that shall be the sign of your new worship. See how it points to the sky. Let us call it the tree of the Christ-child. Take it up and carry it to the chieftain's hall. You shall go no more into the shadows of the forest to keep your feasts with secret rites of shame. You shall keep them at home, with laughter and song and rites of love. The thunder-oak has fallen, and I think the day is coming when there shall not be a home in all Germany where the children are not gathered around the green fir-tree to rejoice in the birth-night of Christ."

So they took the little fir from its place, and carried it in joyous procession to the edge of the glade, and laid it on the sledge. The horses tossed their heads and drew their load bravely, as if the new burden had made it lighter.

When they came to the house of Gundhar, he bade them throw open the doors of the hall and set the tree in the midst of it. They kindled lights among the branches until it seemed to be tangled full of fire-flies. The children encircled it, wondering, and the sweet odour of the balsam filled the house.

Then Winfried stood beside the chair of Gundhar, on the dais at the end of the hall, and told the story of Bethlehem; of the babe in the manger, of the shepherds on the hills, of the host of angels and their midnight song. All the people listened, charmed into stillness.

But the boy Bernhard, on Irma's knee, folded by her soft arm, grew restless as the story lengthened, and began to prattle softly at his mother's ear.

"Mother," whispered the child, "why did you cry out so loud, when the priest was going to send me to Valhalla?"

"Oh, hush, my child," answered the mother, and pressed him closer to her side.

"Mother," whispered the boy again, laying his finger on the stains upon her breast, "see, your dress is red! What are these stains? Did some one hurt you?"

The mother closed his mouth with a kiss. "Dear, be still, and listen!"

The boy obeyed. His eyes were heavy with sleep. But he heard the last words of Winfried as he spoke of the angelic messengers, flying over the hills of Judea and singing as they flew. The child wondered and dreamed and listened. Suddenly his face grew bright. He put his lips close to Irma's cheek again.

"Oh, mother!" he whispered very low, "do not speak. Do you hear them? Those angels have come back again. They are singing now behind the tree."

And some say that it was true; but others say that it was only Gregor and his companions at the lower end of the hall, chanting their Christmas hymn:

> All glory be to God on high,
> And to the earth be peace!
> Good-will, henceforth, from heaven to men
> Begin, and never cease.

THE RED FLOWER

POEMS WRITTEN IN WAR TIME

PREFACE

These are verses that came to me in this dreadful war time amid the cares and labors of a heavy task.

Two of the poems, "A Scrap of Paper" and "Stand Fast," were written in 1914 and bore the signature *Civis Americanus*—the use of my own name at the time being impossible. Two others, "Lights Out" and "Remarks about Kings," were read for me by Robert Underwood Johnson at the meeting of the American Academy in Boston, November, 1915, at which I was unable to be present.

The rest of the verses were printed after I had resigned my diplomatic post and was free to say what I thought and felt, without reserve.

The "Interludes in Holland" are thoughts of the peaceful things that will abide for all the world after we have won this war against war.

SYLVANORA, October 1, 1917.

PREMONITION

THE RED FLOWER

June 1914

In the pleasant time of Pentecost,
　By the little river Kyll,
I followed the angler's winding path
　Or waded the stream at will.
And the friendly fertile German land
　Lay round me green and still.

But all day long on the eastern bank
　Of the river cool and clear,
Where the curving track of the double rails
　Was hardly seen though near,
The endless trains of German troops
　Went rolling down to Trier.

They packed the windows with bullet heads
　And caps of hodden gray;
They laughed and sang and shouted loud
　When the trains were brought to a stay;
They waved their hands and sang again
　As they went on their iron way.

No shadow fell on the smiling land,
    No cloud arose in the sky;
I could hear the river's quiet tune
    When the trains had rattled by;
But my heart sank low with a heavy sense
    Of trouble,—I knew not why.

Then came I into a certain field
    Where the devil's paint-brush spread
'Mid the gray and green of the rolling hills
    A flaring splotch of red,
An evil omen, a bloody sign,
    And a token of many dead.

I saw in a vision the field-gray horde
    Break forth at the devil's hour,
And trample the earth into crimson mud
    In the rage of the Will to Power,—
All this I dreamed in the valley of Kyll,
    At the sign of the blood-red flower.

THE TRIAL AS BY FIRE

A SCRAP OF PAPER

"Will you go to war just for a scrap of paper?"—*Question of the German Chancellor to the British Ambassador, August 3, 1914.*

A mocking question! Britain's answer came
Swift as the light and searching as the flame.

"Yes, for a scrap of paper we will fight
Till our last breath, and God defend the right!

"A scrap of paper where a name is set
Is strong as duty's pledge and honor's debt.

"A scrap of paper holds for man and wife
The sacrament of love, the bound of life.

"A scrap of paper may be Holy Writ
With God's eternal word to hallow it.

"A scrap of paper binds us both to stand
Defenders of a neutral neighbor land.

"By God, by faith, by honor, yes! We fight
To keep our name upon that paper white."

September, 1914

STAND FAST

Stand fast, Great Britain!
Together England, Scotland, Ireland stand
One in the faith that makes a mighty land,
True to the bond you gave and will not break
And fearless in the fight for conscience' sake!
Against Giant Robber clad in steel,
With blood of trampled Belgium on his heel,
Striding through France to strike you down at last,
  Britain, stand fast!

Stand fast, brave land!
The Huns are thundering toward the citadel;
They prate of Culture but their path is Hell;
Their light is darkness, and the bloody sword
They wield and worship is their only Lord.
O land where reason stands secure on right,
O land where freedom is the source of light,
Against the mailed Barbarians' deadly blast,
  Britain, stand fast!

Stand fast, dear land!
Thou island mother of a world-wide race,
Whose children speak thy tongue and love thy face,
Their hearts and hopes are with thee in the strife,
Their hands will break the sword that seeks thy life;
Fight on until the Teuton madness cease;
Fight bravely on, until the word of peace

Is spoken in the English tongue at last,
          Britain, stand fast!

September, 1914.

LIGHTS OUT

(1915)

"Lights out" along the land,
"Lights out" upon the sea.
The night must put her hiding hand
O'er peaceful towns where children sleep,
And peaceful ships that darkly creep
Across the waves, as if they were not free.

The dragons of the air,
The hell-hounds of the deep,
Lurking and prowling everywhere,
Go forth to seek their helpless prey,
Not knowing whom they maim or slay—
Mad harvesters, who care not what they reap.

Out with the tranquil lights,
Out with the lights that burn
For love and law and human rights!
Set back the clock a thousand years:
All they have gained now disappears,
And the dark ages suddenly return.

Kaiser who loosed wild death
And terror in the night
God grant you draw no quiet breath,
Until the madness you began
Is ended, and long-suffering man,
Set free from war lords, cries, "Let there be Light."

October, 1915.

Read at the meeting of the American Academy, Boston,
November, 1915.

REMARKS ABOUT KINGS

God said, "I am tired of kings."—EMERSON.

God said, "I am tired of kings,"—
But that was a long time ago!
And meantime man said, "No,
I like their looks in their robes and rings."
So he crowned a few more,
And they went on playing the game as before
Fighting and spoiling things.

Man said, "I am tired of kings!
Sons of the robber-chiefs of yore,
They make me pay for their lust and their war;
I am the puppet, they pull the strings;
The blood of my heart is the wine they drink.
I will govern myself for while I think,
And see what that brings!"

Then God, who made the first remark,
Smiled in the dark.

Read at the meeting of the American Academy, Boston.
November, 1915.

WAR-MUSIC

Break off! Dance no more!
Danger is at the door.
Music is in arms.
To signal war's alarms,

Hark, a sudden trumpet calling
Over the hill
Why are you calling, trumpet, calling?
What is your will?

Men, men, men!
Men who are ready to fight
For their country's life, and the right.
Of a liberty-loving land to be
Free, free, free!
Free from a tyrant's chain,
Free from dishonor's stain,
Free to guard and maintain
All that her fathers fought for,
All that her sons have wrought for,
Resolute, brave, and free!

Call again, trumpet, call again,
Call up the men!

335

Do you hear the storm of cheers
Mingled with the women's tears
And the tramp, tramp, tramp of marching feet?
Do you hear the throbbing drum
As the hosts of battle come
Keeping time, time, time to its beat?
O Music give a song
To make their spirit strong
For the fury of the tempest they must meet.

The hoarse roar
Of the monster guns;
And the sharp bark
Of the lesser guns;
The whine of the shells,
The rifles' clatter
Where the bullets patter,
The rattle, rattle, rattle
Of the mitrailleuse in battle,
And the yells
Of the men who charge through hells
Where the poison gas descends.
And the bursting shrapnel rends
Limb from limb
In the dim
Chaos and clamor of the strife
Where no man thinks of his life
But only of fighting through,
Blindly fighting through, through!

'Tis done
At last!
The victory won,
The dissonance of warfare past!

O Music mourn the dead
Whose loyal blood was shed,
And sound the taps for every hero slain;
Then lend into the song
That made their spirit strong,
And tell the world they did not die in vain.

Thank God we can see, in the glory of morn,
The invincible flag that our fathers defended;
And our hearts can repeat what the heroes have sworn,
That war shall not end till the war-lust is ended,
Then the bloodthirsty sword shall no longer be lord
Of the nations oppressed by the conqueror's horde,
But the banners of freedom shall peacefully wave
O'er the world of the free and the lands of the brave.

May, 1916

MIGHT AND RIGHT

If Might made Right, life were a wild-beasts' cage;
If Right made Might, this were the golden age;
But now, until we win the long campaign
Right must gain Might to conquer and to reign.

July 1, 1915.

THE PRICE OF PEACE

Peace without Justice is a low estate,—
A coward cringing to an iron Fate!
But Peace through Justice is the great ideal,—
We'll pay the price of war to make it real.

December 28, 1916.

STORM MUSIC

O Music hast thou only heard
The laughing river, the singing bird,
The murmuring wind in the poplar-trees,—
Nothing but Nature's melodies?
   Nay, thou hearest all her tones,
      As a Queen must hear!
      Sounds of wrath and fear,
      Mutterings, shouts, and moans,
   Mildness, tumult, and despair,—
   All she has that shakes the air
   With voices fierce and wild!
Thou art a Queen and not a dreaming child,—
Put on thy crown and let us hear thee reign
Triumphant in a world of storm and strain!

   Echo the long-drawn sighs
Of the mounting wind in the pines;
And the sobs of the mounting waves that rise
   In the dark of the troubled deep
To break on the beach in fiery lines.
   Echo the far-off roll of thunder,

                    Rumbling loud
          And ever louder, under
          The blue-black curtain of cloud,
          Where the lightning serpents gleam,
                    Echo the moaning
          Of the forest in its sleep
          Like a giant groaning
In the torment of a dream.

          Now an interval of quiet
          For a moment holds the air
          In the breathless hush
          Of a silent prayer.

          Then the sudden rush
          Of the rain, and the riot
          Of the shrieking, tearing gale
          Breaks loose in the night,
          With a fusillade of hail!
          Hear the forest fight,
With its tossing arms that crack and clash
          In the thunder's cannonade,
          While the lightning's forkèd flash
Brings the old hero-trees to the ground with a crash!
Hear the breakers' deepening roar,
          Driven like a herd of cattle
          In the wild stampede of battle,
Trampling, trampling, trampling, to overwhelm the shore.

          Is it the end of all?
          Will the land crumble and fall?
          Nay, for a voice replies

Out of the hidden skies,
"Thus far, O sea, shalt thou go,
So long, O wind, shalt thou blow:
Return to your bounds and cease,
And let the earth have peace!"

O Music, lead the way—
    The stormy night is past,
Lift up our heads to greet the day,
    And the joy of things that last.

The dissonance and pain
    That mortals must endure
Are changed in thine immortal strain
    To something great and pure.

True love will conquer strife,
    And strength from conflict flows,
For discord is the thorn of life
    And harmony the rose.

May, 1916.

FRANCE AND BELGIUM

THE BELLS OF MALINES

AUGUST 17, 1914

The gabled roofs of old Malines
Are russet red and gray and green,
And o'er them in the sunset hour
Looms, dark and huge, St. Rombold's tower.
High in that rugged nest concealed,
The sweetest bells that ever pealed,
The deepest bells that ever rung,
The lightest bells that ever sung,
Are waiting for the master's hand
To fling their music o'er the land.

And shall they ring to-night, Malines?
In nineteen hundred and fourteen,
The frightful year, the year of woe,
When fire and blood and rapine flow
Across the land from lost Liége,
Storm-driven by the German rage?
The other carillons have ceased;
Fallen is Hasselt, fallen Diesl,
From Ghent and Bruges no voices come,
Antwerp is silent, Brussels dumb!

But in thy belfry, O Malines,
The master of the bells unseen
Has climbed to where the keyboard stands,—
To-night his heart is in his hands!
Once more, before invasion's hell
Breaks round the tower he loves so well,
Once more he strikes the well-worn keys,
And sends aërial harmonies
Far-floating through the twilight dim
In patriot song and holy hymn.

O listen, burghers of Malines!
Soldier and workman, pale béguine.
And mother with a trembling flock
Of children clinging to thy frock,—
Look up and listen, listen all!
What tunes are these that gently fall
Around you like a benison?
"The Flemish Lion," "Brabançonne,"
"O brave Liége," and all the airs
That Belgium in her bosom bears.

Ring up, ye silvery octaves high,
Whose notes like circling swallows fly;
And ring, each old sonorous bell,—
"Jesu," "Maria," "Michaël!"
Weave in and out, and high and low,
The magic music that you know,
And let it float and flutter down
To cheer the heart of the troubled town.
Ring out, "Salvator," lord of all,—
"Roland" in Ghent may hear thee call!

O brave bell-music of Malines,
In this dark hour how much you mean!
The dreadful night of blood and tears
Sweeps down on Belgium, but she hears
Deep in her heart the melody
Of songs she learned when she was free.
She will not falter, faint, nor fail,
But fight until her rights prevail
And all her ancient belfries ring
"The Flemish Lion," "God Save the King!"

THE NAME OF FRANCE

Give us a name to fill the mind
With the shining thoughts that lead mankind,
The glory of learning, the joy of art,—
A name that tells of a splendid part.
In long, long toil and the strenuous fight
Of the human race to win its way
From the feudal darkness into the day
Of Freedom, Brotherhood, Equal Right,—
A name like a star, a name of light.
I give you *France*!

Give us a name to stir the blood
With a warmer glow and a swifter flood,
At the touch of a courage that knows not fear,—
A name like the sound of a trumpet, clear.
And silver-sweet, and iron-strong,
That calls three million men to their feet,
Ready to march, and steady to meet
The foes who threaten that name with wrong,—

343

A name that rings like a battle-song.
I give you *France*!

Give us a name to move the heart
With the strength that noble griefs impart,
A name that speaks of the blood outpoured
To save mankind from the sway of the sword,—
A name that calls on the world to share
In the burden of sacrificial strife
When the cause at stake is the world's free life
And the rule of the people everywhere,—
A name like a vow, a name like a prayer.
I give you *France*!

The Hague, September, 1916.

JEANNE D'ARC RETURNS

1914 1916

What hast thou done, O womanhood of France,
   Mother and daughter, sister, sweetheart, wife,
   What hast thou done, amid this fateful strife,
To prove the pride of thine inheritance.
In this fair land of freedom and romance?
   I hear thy voice with tears and courage rife,—
   Smiling against the swords that seek thy life—
Make answer in a noble utterance:
"I give France all I have, and all she asks.
   Would it were more! Ah, let her ask and take;

344

My hands to nurse her wounded, do her tasks,—
    My feet to run her errands through the dark,—
My heart to bleed in triumph for her sake,—
    And all my soul to follow thee, Jeanne d'Arc!"

April 16, 1916.

INTERLUDES IN HOLLAND

THE HEAVENLY HILLS OF HOLLAND

The heavenly hills of Holland,—
　　How wondrously they rise
Above the smooth green pastures
　　Into the azure skies!
With blue and purple hollows,
　　With peaks of dazzling snow,
Along the far horizon
　　The clouds are marching slow,

No mortal fool has trodden
　　The summits of that range,
Nor walked those mystic valleys
　　Whose colors ever change;
Yet we possess their beauty,
　　And visit them in dreams,
While the ruddy gold of sunset
　　From cliff and canyon gleams.

In days of cloudless weather
　　They melt into the light;
When fog and mist surround us
　　They're hidden from our sight;
But when returns a season

Clear shining after rain,
While the northwest wind is blowing,
   We see the hills again.

The old Dutch painters loved them,
   Their pictures show them clear,—
Old Hobbema and Ruysduel,
   Van Goyen and Vermeer,
Above the level landscape,
   Rich polders, long-armed mills,
Canals and ancient cities,—
   Float Holland's heavenly hills.

The Hague, November, 1916.

THE PROUD LADY

When Stävoren town was in its prime
   And queened the Zuyder Zee,
Its ships went out to every clime
   With costly merchantry.

A lady dwelt in that rich town,
   The fairest in all the land;
She walked abroad in a velvet gown,
   With many rings on her hand.

Her hair was bright as the beaten gold,
   Her lips as coral red,
Her roving eyes were blue and bold,
   And her heart with pride was fed.

For she was proud of her father's ships,
    As she watched them gayly pass;
And pride looked out of her eyes and lips
    When she saw herself in the glass.

"Now come," she said to the captains ten,
    Who were ready to put to sea,
"Ye are all my men and my father's men,
    And what will ye do for me?"

"Go north and south, go east and west,
    And get me gifts," she said.
"And he who bringeth me home the best,
    With that man will I wed."

So they all fared forth, and sought with care
    In many a famous mart,
For satins and silks and jewels rare,
    To win that lady's heart.

She looked at them all with never a thought
    And careless put them by;
"I am not fain of the things ye brought,
    Enough of these have I."

The last that came was the head of the fleet,
    His name was Jan Borel;
He bent his knee at the lady's feet,—
    In truth he loved her well.

"I've brought thee home the best i' the world,
    A shipful of Danzig corn!"

She stared at him long; her red lips curled,
  Her blue eyes filled with scorn.

"Now out on thee, thou feckless kerl,
  A loon thou art," she said.
"Am I a starving beggar girl?
  Shall I ever lack for bread?"

"Go empty all thy sacks of grain
  Into the nearest sea,
And never show thy face again
  To make a mock of me."

Young Jan Borel, he answered naught,
  But in the harbor cast
The sacks of golden corn he brought,
  And groaned when fell the last.

Then Jan Borel, he hoisted sail,
  And out to sea he bore;
He passed the Helder in a gale
  And came again no more.

But the grains of corn went drifting down
  Like devil-scattered seed,
To sow the harbor of the town
  With a wicked growth of weed.

The roots were thick and the silt and sand
  Were gathered day by day,
Till not a furlong out from land
  A shoal had barred the way.

Then Stävoren town saw evil years,
    No ships could out or in.
The boats lay rolling at the piers,
    And the mouldy grain in the bin.

The grass-grown streets were all forlorn,
    The town in ruin stood,
The lady's velvet gown was torn,
    Her rings were sold for food.

Her father had perished long ago,
    But the lady held her pride.
She walked with a scornful step and slow,
    Till at last in her rags she died.

Yet still on the crumbling piers of the town,
    When the midnight moon shines free,
A woman walks in a velvet gown
    And scatters corn in the sea.

FLOOD-TIDE OF FLOWERS

IN HOLLAND

The laggard winter ebbed so slow
With freezing rain and melting snow,
It seemed as if the earth would stay
Forever where the tide was low,
In sodden green and watery gray.

But now from depths beyond our sight,
The tide is turning in the night,

And floods of color long concealed
Come silent rising toward the light,
Through garden bare and empty field.

And first, along the sheltered nooks,
The crocus runs in little brooks
Of joyance, till by light made bold
They show the gladness of their looks
In shining pools of white and gold.

The tiny scilla, sapphire blue,
Is gently sweeping in, to strew
The earth with heaven; and sudden rills
Of sunlit yellow, sweeping through,
Spread into lakes of daffodils.

The hyacinths, with fragrant heads,
Have overflowed their sandy beds,
And fill the earth with faint perfume,
The breath that Spring around her sheds.
And now the tulips break in bloom!

A sea, a rainbow-tinted sea,
A splendor and a mystery,
Floods o'er the fields of faded gray:
The roads are full of folks in glee,
For lo,—to-day is Easter Day!

April, 1916.

ENTER AMERICA

AMERICA'S PROSPERITY

They tell me thou art rich, my country: gold
  In glittering flood has poured into thy chest;
  Thy flocks and herds increase, thy barns are pressed
With harvest, and thy stores can hardly hold
Their merchandise; unending trains are rolled
  Along thy network rails of East and West;
  Thy factories and forges never rest;
Thou art enriched in all things bought and sold!

But dost *thou* prosper? Better news I crave.
  O dearest country, is it well with thee
      Indeed, and is thy soul in health?
A nobler people, hearts more wisely brave,
  And thoughts that lift men up and make them free.—
      These are prosperity and vital wealth!

The Hague, October 1, 1916.

THE GLORY OF SHIPS

The glory of ships is an old, old song,
  since the days when the sea-rovers ran
In their open boats through the roaring surf,

and the spread of the world began;
The glory of ships is a light on the sea,
   and a star in the story of man.

When Homer sang of the galleys of Greece
   that conquered the Trojan shore,
And Solomon lauded the barks of Tyre that
   brought great wealth to his door,
'Twas little they knew, those ancient men,
   what would come of the sail and the oar.

The Greek ships rescued the West from the East,
   when they harried the Persians home;
And the Roman ships were the wings of strength
   that bore up the empire, Rome;
And the ships or Spain found a wide new world
   far over the fields of foam.

Then the tribes of courage at last saw clear
   that the ocean was not a bound,
But a broad highway, and a challenge to seek
   for treasure as yet unfound;
So the fearless ships fared forth to the search,
   in joy that the globe was round.

Their hulls were heightened, their sails spread out.
   they grew with the growth of their quest;
They opened the secret doors of the East,
   and the golden gates of the West;
And many a city of high renown
   was proud of a ship on its crest.

The fleets of England and Holland and France
    were at strife with each other and Spain;
And battle and storm sent a myriad ships
    to sleep in the depths of the main;
But the seafaring spirit could never be drowned,
    and it filled up the fleets again.

They greatened and grew, with the aid of steam,
    to a wonderful, vast array,
That carries the thoughts and the traffic of men
    into every harbor and bay;
And now in the world-wide work of the ships
    'tis England that leads the way.

O well for the leading that follows the law
    of a common right on the sea!
But ill for the leader who tries to hold
    what belongs to mankind in fee!
The way of the ships is an open way,
    and the ocean must ever be free!

Remember, O first of the maritime folk,
    how the rise of your greatness began.
It will live if you safeguard the round-the-world road
    from the shame of a selfish ban;
For the glory of ships is a light on the sea,
    and a star in the story of man!

September 12, 1916.

MARE LIBERUM

I

You dare to say with perjured lips,
"We fight to make the ocean free"?
You, whose black trail of butchered ships
Bestrews the bed of every sea
Where German submarines have wrought
Their horrors! Have you never thought,—
What you call freedom, men call piracy!

II

Unnumbered ghosts that haunt the wave,
Where you have murdered, cry you down;
And seamen whom you would not save,
Weave now in weed grown depths a crown
Of shame for your imperious head,—
A dark memorial of the dead,—
Women and children whom you sent to drown.

III

Nay, not till thieves are set to guard
The gold, and corsairs called to keep
O'er peaceful commerce watch and ward
And wolves do herd the helpless sheep,
Shall men and women look to thee,
Thou ruthless Old Man of the Sea,
To safeguard law and freedom on the deep!

IV

In nobler breeds we put our trust;
The nations in whose sacred lore
The "Ought" stands out above the "Must,"
And honor rules in peace and war.
With these we hold in soul and heart,
With these we choose our lot and part,
Till Liberty is safe on sea and shore.

London Times, February 12, 1917.

"LIBERTY ENLIGHTENING THE WORLD"

Thou warden of the western gate, above Manhattan Bay,
The fogs of doubt that hid thy face are driven clean away:
Thine eyes at last look far and clear, thou liftest high thy hand
To spread the light of liberty world-wide for every land.

No more thou dreamest of a peace reserved alone for thee,
While friends are fighting for thy cause beyond the guardian sea;
The battle that they wage is thine; thou fallest if they fall;
The swollen flood of Prussian pride will sweep unchecked o'er all.

O cruel is the conquer-lust in Hohenzollern brains;
The paths they plot to gain their goal are dark with shameful stains:
No faith they keep, no law revere, no god but naked Might;—
They are the foemen of mankind. Up, Liberty; and smite!

Britain, and France, and Italy, and Russia newly born,
Have waited for thee in the night. Oh, come as comes the morn!

Serene and strong and full of faith, America, arise,
With steady hope and mighty help to join thy brave Allies.

O dearest country of my heart, home of the high desire,
Make clean thy soul for sacrifice on Freedom's altar-fire;
For thou must suffer, thou must fight, until the war-lords cease,
And all the peoples lift their heads in liberty and peace.

London Times, April 12, 1917.

THE OXFORD THRUSHES

FEBRUARY, 1917

I never thought again to hear
The Oxford thrushes singing clear,
Amid the February rain,
Their sweet, indomitable strain.

A wintry vapor lightly spreads
Among the trees, and round the beds
Where daffodil and jonquil sleep,
Only the snowdrop wakes to weep.

It is not springtime yet. Alas,
What dark, tempestuous days must pass,
Till England's trial by battle cease,
And summer comes again with peace.

The lofty halls, the tranquil towers,
Where Learning in untroubled hours

Held her high court, serene in fame,
Are lovely still, yet not the same.

The novices in fluttering gown
No longer fill the ancient town,
But fighting men in khaki drest—
And in the Schools the wounded rest.

Ah, far away, 'neath stranger skies
Full many a son of Oxford lies,
And whispers from his warrior grave,
"I died to keep the faith you gave."

The mother mourns, but does not fail,
Her courage and her love prevail
O'er sorrow, and her spirit hears
The promise of triumphant years.

Then sing, ye thrushes, in the rain
Your sweet, indomitable strain.
Ye bring a word from God on high
And voices in our hearts reply.

HOMEWARD BOUND

Home, for my heart still calls me;
    Home, through the danger zone;
Home, whatever befalls me,
    I will sail again to my own!

Wolves of the sea are hiding
    Closely along the way,

Under the water biding
   Their moment to rend and slay.

Black is the eagle that brands them,
   Black are their hearts as the night,
Black is the hate that sends them
   To murder but not to fight.

Flower of the German Culture,
   Boast of the Kaiser's Marine,
Choose for your emblem the vulture,
   Cowardly, cruel, obscene!

Forth from her sheltered haven
   Our peaceful ship glides slow,
Noiseless in flight as a raven,
   Gray as a hoodie crow.

She doubles and turns in her bearing,
   Like a twisting plover she goes;
The way of her westward faring
   Only the captain knows.

In a lonely bay concealing
   She lingers for days, and slips
At dusk from her covert, stealing
   Thro' channels feared by the ships.

Brave are the men, and steady,
   Who guide her over the deep,—
British mariners, ready
   To face the sea-wolf's leap.

Lord of the winds and waters,
    Bring our ship to her mark,
Safe from this game of hide-and-seek
    With murderers in the dark!

On the S.S. *Baltic*, May, 1917.

THE SPIRIT OF CHRISTMAS

A DREAM-STORY

THE CHRISTMAS ANGEL

It was the hour of rest in the Country Beyond the Stars. All the silver bells that swing with the turning of the great ring of light which lies around that land were softly chiming; and the sound of their commotion went down like dew upon the golden ways of the city, and the long alleys of blossoming trees, and the meadows of asphodel, and the curving shores of the River of Life.

At the hearing of that chime, all the angels who had been working turned to play, and all who had been playing gave themselves joyfully to work. Those who had been singing, and making melody on different instruments, fell silent and began to listen. Those who had been walking alone in meditation met together in companies to talk. And those who had been far away on errands to the Earth and other planets came homeward like a flight of swallows to the high cliff when the day is over.

It was not that they needed to be restored from weariness, for the inhabitants of that country never say, "I am tired." But there, as here, the law of change is the secret of happiness, and the joy that never ends is woven of mingled strands of labour and repose, society and solitude, music and silence. Sleep comes to them not as it does to us, with a darkening of the vision and a folding of the wings of the spirit, but with an opening of the eyes to deeper and fuller light, and with an effortless outgoing of the soul upon broader currents of life, as the sun-loving bird poises and circles upward, without a wing-beat, on the upholding air.

It was in one of the quiet corners of the green valley called Peacefield, where the little brook of Brighthopes runs smoothly down to join the River of Life, that I saw a company of angels, returned from various labours on Earth, sitting in friendly converse on the hill-side, where cyclamens and arbutus and violets and fringed orchids and pale lady's-tresses, and all the sweet-smelling flowers which are separated in the lower world by the seasons, were thrown together in a harmony of fragrance. There were three of the company who seemed to be leaders, distinguished not only by more radiant and powerful looks, but by a tone of authority in their speech and by the willing attention with which the others listened to them, as they talked of their earthly tasks, of the tangles and troubles, the wars and miseries that they had seen among men, and of the best way to get rid of them and bring sorrow to an end.

"The Earth is full of oppression and unrighteousness," said the tallest and most powerful of the angels. His voice was deep and strong, and by his shining armour and the long two-handed sword hanging over his shoulder I knew that he was the archangel Michael, the mightiest one among the warriors of the King, and the executor of the divine judgments upon the unjust. "The Earth is tormented with injustice," he cried, "and the great misery that I have seen among men is that the evil hand is often stronger than the good hand and can beat it down.

"The arm of the cruel is heavier than the arm of the kind. The unjust get the better of the just and tread on them. I have seen tyrant kings crush their helpless folk. I have seen the fields of the innocent trampled into bloody ruin by the feet of conquering armies. I have seen the wicked nation overcome the peoples that loved liberty, and take away their treasure by force of arms. I have seen poverty mocked by arrogant wealth, and purity deflowered by brute violence, and gentleness and fair-dealing bruised in the winepress of iniquity and pride.

"There is no cure for this evil, but by the giving of greater force to the good hand. The righteous cause must be strengthened with might to resist the wicked, to defend the helpless, to punish all cruelty and unfairness, to uphold the right everywhere, and to enforce justice with unconquerable arms. Oh, that the host of Heaven might be called, arrayed, and sent to mingle in the wars of men, to make the good victorious, to destroy all evil, and to make the will of the King prevail!

"We would shake down the thrones of tyrants, and loose the bands of the oppressed. We would hold the cruel and violent with the bit of fear, and drive the greedy and fierce-minded men with the whip of terror. We would stand guard, with weapons drawn, about the innocent, the gentle, the kind, and keep the peace of God with the sword of the angels!"

As he spoke, his hands were lifted to the hilt of his long blade, and he raised it above him, straight and shining, throwing sparkles of light around it, like the spray from the sharp prow of a moving ship. Bright flames of heavenly ardour leaped in the eyes of the listening angels; a martial air passed over their faces as if they longed for the call to war.

But no silver trumpet blared from the battlements of the City of God; no crimson flag was unfurled on those high, secret walls; no thrilling drum-beat echoed over the smooth meadow. Only the sound of the brook of Brighthopes was heard tinkling and murmuring among the roots of the grasses and flowers; and far off a cadence of song drifted down from the inner courts of the Palace of the King.

Then another angel began to speak, and made answer to Michael. He, too, was tall and wore the look of power. But it was power of the mind rather than of the hand. His face was clear and glistening, and his eyes were lit with a steady flame which neither leaped nor fell. Of flame also were his garments, which clung about him as the fire enwraps a torch burning where there is no wind; and his great wings, spiring to a point far above his head, were like a living lamp before the altar of the Most High. By this sign I knew that it was the archangel Uriel, the spirit of the Sun, clearest in vision, deepest in wisdom of all the spirits that surround the throne.

"I hold not the same thought," said he, "as the great archangel Michael; nor, though I desire the same end which he desires, would I seek it by the same way. For I know how often power has been given to the good, and how often it has been turned aside and used for evil. I know that the host of Heaven, and the very stars in their courses, have fought on the side of a favoured nation; yet pride has followed triumph and oppression has been the first-born child of victory. I know that the deliverers of the people have become tyrants over those whom they have set free, and the fighters for liberty have been changed into the soldiers of fortune. Power corrupts itself, and might cannot save.

"Does not the Prince Michael remember how the angel of the Lord led the armies of Israel, and gave them the battle against every foe, except the enemy within the camp? And how they robbed and crushed the peoples against whom they had fought for freedom? And how the wickedness of the tribes of Canaan survived their conquest and overcame their conquerors, so that the children of Israel learned to worship the idols of their enemies, Moloch, and Baal, and Ashtoreth?

"Power corrupts itself, and might cannot save. Was not Persia the destroyer of Babylon, and did not the tyranny of Persia cry aloud for destruction? Did not Rome break the yoke of the East, and does not the yoke of Rome lie heavy on the shoulders of the world? Listen!"

There was silence for a moment on the slopes of Peacefield, and then over the encircling hills a cool wind brought the sound of chains clanking in prisons and galleys, the sighing of millions of slaves, the weeping of wretched women and children, the blows of hammers nailing men to their crosses. Then the sound passed by with the wind, and Uriel spoke again:

"Power corrupts itself, and might cannot save. The Earth is full of ignorant strife, and for this evil there is no cure but by the giving of greater knowledge. It is because men do not understand evil that they yield themselves to its power. Wickedness is folly in action, and injustice is the error of the blind. It is because men are ignorant that they destroy one another, and at last themselves.

366

"If there were more light in the world there would be no sorrow. If the great King who knows all things would enlighten the world with wisdom—wisdom to understand his law and his ways, to read the secrets of the earth and the stars, to discern the workings of the heart of man and the things that make for joy and peace—if he would but send us, his messengers, as a flame of fire to shine upon those who sit in darkness, how gladly would we go to bring in the new day!

"We would speak the word of warning and counsel to the erring, and tell knowledge to the perplexed. We would guide the ignorant in the paths of prudence, and the young would sit at our feet and hear us gladly in the school of life. Then folly would fade away as the morning vapour, and the sun of wisdom would shine on all men, and the peace of God would come with the counsel of the angels."

A murmur of pleasure followed the words of Uriel, and eager looks flashed around the circle of the messengers of light as they heard the praise of wisdom fitly spoken. But there was one among them on whose face a shadow of doubt rested, and though he smiled, it was as if he remembered something that the others had forgotten. He turned to an angel near him.

"Who was it," said he, "to whom you were sent with counsel long ago? Was it not Balaam the son of Beor, as he was riding to meet the King of Moab? And did not even the dumb beast profit more by your instruction than the man who rode him? And who was it," he continued, turning to Uriel, "that was called the wisest of all men, having searched out and understood the many inventions that are found under the sun? Was not Solomon, prince of fools and philosophers, unable by much learning to escape weariness of the flesh and despair of the spirit? Knowledge also is vanity and vexation. This I know well, because I have dwelt among men and held converse with them since the day when I was sent to instruct the first man in Eden."

Then I looked more closely at him who was speaking and recognised the beauty of the archangel Raphael, as it was pictured long ago:

"A seraph winged; six wings he wore to shade
His lineaments divine; the pair that clad
Each shoulder broad came mantling o'er his breast,
With regal ornament; the middle pair
Girt like a starry zone his waist, and round
Skirted his loins and thighs with downy gold
And colours dipped in Heav'n; the third his feet
Shadowed from either heel with feathered mail,
Sky-tinctured grain. Like Maia's son he stood
And shook his plumes, that Heavenly fragrance filled
The circuit wide."

"Too well I know," he spoke on, while the smile on his face deepened into a look of pity and tenderness and desire, "too well I know that power corrupts itself and that knowledge cannot save. There is no cure for the evil that is in the world but by the giving of more love to men. The laws that are ordained for earth are strange and unequal, and the ways where men must walk are full of pitfalls and dangers. Pestilence creeps along the ground and flows in the rivers; whirlwind and tempest shake the habitations of men and drive their ships to destruction; fire breaks forth from the mountains and the foundations of the world tremble. Frail is the flesh of man, and many are his pains and troubles. His children can never find peace until they learn to love one another and to help one another.

"Wickedness is begotten by disease and misery. Violence comes from poverty and hunger. The cruelty of oppression is when the strong tread the weak under their feet; the bitterness of pride is when the wise and learned despise the simple; the crown of folly is when the rich think they are gods, and the poor think that God is not.

"Hatred and envy and contempt are the curse of life. And for these there is no remedy save love—the will to give and to bless—the will of the King himself, who gives to all and is loving unto every man. But how shall the hearts of men be won to this will? How shall it enter into them and possess them? Even the gods that men fashion for themselves are cruel and proud and false and unjust. How shall the miracle be wrought in human nature to reveal the meaning of humanity? How shall men be made like God?"

At this question a deep hush fell around the circle, and every listener was still, even as the rustling leaves hang motionless when the light breeze falls away in the hour of sunset. Then through the silence, like the song of a far-away thrush from its hermitage in the forest, a voice came ringing: "I know it, I know it, I know it."

Clear and sweet—clear as a ray of light, sweeter than the smallest silver bell that rang the hour of rest—was that slender voice floating on the odorous and translucent air. Nearer and nearer it came, echoing down the valley, "I know it, I know it, I know it!"

Then from between the rounded hills, among which the brook of Brighthopes is born, appeared a young angel, a little child, with flying hair of gold, and green wreaths twined about his shoulders, and fluttering hands that played upon the air and seemed to lift him so lightly that he had no need of wings. As thistle-down, blown by the wind, dances across the water, so he came along the little stream, singing clear above the murmur of the brook.

All the angels rose and turned to look at him with wondering eyes. Multitudes of others came flying swiftly to the place from which the strange, new song was sounding. Rank within rank, like a garden of living flowers, they stood along the sloping banks of the brook while the child-angel floated into the midst of them, singing:

"I know it, I know it, I know it! Man shall be made like God because the Son of God shall become a man."

At this all the angels looked at one another with amazement, and gathered more closely about the child-angel, as those who hear wonderful news.

"How can this be?" they asked. "How is it possible that the Son of God should be a man?"

"I do not know," said the young angel. "I only know that it is to be."

"But if he becomes a man," said Raphael, "he will be at the mercy of men; the cruel and the wicked will have power upon him; he will suffer."

"I know it," answered the young angel, "and by suffering he will understand the meaning of all sorrow and pain; and he will be able to comfort every one who cries; and his own tears will be for the healing of sad hearts; and those who are healed by him will learn for his sake to be kind to each other."

"But if the Son of God is a true man," said Uriel, "he must first be a child, simple, and lowly, and helpless. It may be that he will never gain the learning of the schools. The masters of earthly wisdom will despise him and speak scorn of him."

"I know it," said the young angel, "but in meekness will he answer them; and to those who become as little children he will give the heavenly wisdom that comes, without seeking, to the pure and gentle of heart."

"But if he becomes a man," said Michael, "evil men will hate and persecute him: they may even take his life, if they are stronger than he."

"I know it," answered the young angel, "they will nail him to a cross. But when he is lifted up, he will draw all men unto him, for he will still be the Son of God, and no heart that is open to love can help loving him, since his love for men is so great that he is willing to die for them."

"But how do you know these things?" cried the other angels. "Who are you?"

"I am the Christmas angel," he said. "At first I was sent as the dream of a little child, a holy child, blessed and wonderful, to dwell in the heart of a pure virgin, Mary of Nazareth. There I was hidden till the word came to call me back to the throne of the King, and tell me my name, and give me my new message. For this is Christmas day on Earth, and to-day the Son of God is born of a woman. So I must fly quickly, before the sun rises, to bring the good news to those happy men who have been chosen to receive them."

As he said this, the young angel rose, with arms outspread, from the green meadow of Peacefield and, passing over the bounds of Heaven, dropped swiftly as a shooting-star toward the night shadow of the Earth. The other angels followed him—a throng of dazzling forms, beautiful as a rain of jewels falling from the dark-blue sky. But the child-angel went more swiftly than the others, because of the certainty of gladness in his heart.

And as the others followed him they wondered who had been favoured and chosen to receive the glad tidings.

"It must be the Emperor of the World and his counsellors," they thought. But the flight passed over Rome.

"It may be the philosophers and the masters of learning," they thought. But the flight passed over Athens.

"Can it be the High Priest of the Jews, and the elders and the scribes?" they thought. But the flight passed over Jerusalem.

It floated out over the hill country of Bethlehem; the throng of silent angels holding close together, as if perplexed and doubtful; the child-angel darting on far in advance, as one who knew the way through the darkness.

The villages were all still: the very houses seemed asleep; but in one place there was a low sound of talking in a stable, near to an inn—a sound as of a mother soothing her baby to rest.

All over the pastures on the hillsides a light film of snow had fallen, delicate as the veil of a bride adorned for the marriage; and as the child-angel passed over them, alone in the swiftness of his flight, the pure fields sparkled round him, giving back his radiance.

And there were in that country shepherds abiding in the fields, keeping watch over their flocks by night. And lo! the angel of the Lord came upon them, and the glory of the Lord shone round about them, and they were sore afraid. And the angel said unto them: "Fear not; for behold I bring you glad tidings of great joy which shall be to all nations. For unto you is born this day, in the city of David, a Saviour, which is Christ the Lord. And this shall be a sign unto you; ye shall find the babe wrapped in swaddling clothes, lying in a manger."

And suddenly there was with the angel a multitude of the heavenly host, praising God and saying: "Glory to God in the highest, and on earth peace, good-will toward men." And the shepherds said one to another: "Let us now go, even to Bethlehem, and see this thing which is come to pass."

So I said within myself that I also would go with the shepherds, even to Bethlehem. And I heard a great and sweet voice, as of a bell, which said, "Come!" And when the bell had sounded twelve times, I awoke; and it was Christmas morn; and I knew that I had been in a dream.

Yet it seemed to me that the things which I had heard were true.

A LITTLE ESSAY

CHRISTMAS-GIVING AND CHRISTMAS-LIVING

I

The custom of exchanging presents on a certain day in the year is very much older than Christmas, and means very much less. It has obtained in almost all ages of the world, and among many different nations. It is a fine thing or a foolish thing, as the case may be; an encouragement to friendliness, or a tribute to fashion; an expression of good nature, or a bid for favour; an outgoing of generosity, or a disguise of greed; a cheerful old custom, or a futile old farce, according to the spirit which animates it and the form which it takes.

But when this ancient and variously interpreted tradition of a day of gifts was transferred to the Christmas season, it was brought into vital contact with an idea which must transform it, and with an example which must lift it up to a higher plane. The example is the life of Jesus. The idea is unselfish interest in the happiness of others.

The great gift of Jesus to the world was himself. He lived with and for men. He kept back nothing. In every particular and personal gift that he made to certain people there was something of himself that made it precious.

For example, at the wedding in Cana of Galilee, it was his thought for the feelings of the giver of the feast, and his wish that every guest should find due entertainment, that lent the flavour of a heavenly hospitality to the wine which he provided.

When he gave bread and fish to the hungry multitude who had followed him out among the hills by the Lake of Gennesaret, the people were refreshed and strengthened by the sense of the personal care of Jesus for their welfare, as much as by the food which he bestowed upon them. It was another illustration of the sweetness of "a dinner of herbs, where love is."

The gifts of healing which he conferred upon many different kinds of sufferers were, in every case, evidences that Jesus was willing to give something of himself, his thought, his sympathy, his vital power, to the men and women among whom he lived. Once, when a paralytic was brought to Jesus on a bed, he surprised everybody, and offended many, by giving the poor wretch the pardon of his sins, before he gave new life to his body. That was just because Jesus thought before he gave; because he desired to satisfy the deepest need; because in fact he gave something of himself in every gift. All true Christmas-giving ought to be after this pattern.

Not that it must all be solemn and serious. For the most part it deals with little wants, little joys, little tokens of friendly feeling. But the feeling must be more than the token; else the gift does not really belong to Christmas.

It takes time and effort and unselfish expenditure of strength to make gifts in this way. But it is the only way that fits the season.

The finest Christmas gift is not the one that costs the most money, but the one that carries the most love.

II

But how seldom Christmas comes—only once a year; and how soon it is over—a night and a day! If that is the whole of it, it seems not much more durable than the little toys that one buys of a fakir on the street-

374

corner. They run for an hour, and then the spring breaks, and the legs come off, and nothing remains but a contribution to the dust heap.

But surely that need not and ought not to be the whole of Christmas—only a single day of generosity, ransomed from the dull servitude of a selfish year,—only a single night of merry-making, celebrated in the slave-quarters of a selfish race! If every gift is the token of a personal thought, a friendly feeling, an unselfish interest in the joy of others, then the thought, the feeling, the interest, may remain after the gift is made.

The little present, or the rare and long-wished-for gift (it matters not whether the vessel be of gold, or silver, or iron, or wood, or clay, or just a small bit of birch bark folded into a cup), may carry a message something like this:

"I am thinking of you to-day, because it is Christmas, and I wish you happiness. And to-morrow, because it will be the day after Christmas, I shall still wish you happiness; and so on, clear through the year. I may not be able to tell you about it every day, because I may be far away; or because both of us may be very busy; or perhaps because I cannot even afford to pay the postage on so many letters, or find the time to write them. But that makes no difference. The thought and the wish will be here just the same. In my work and in the business of life, I mean to try not to be unfair to you or injure you in any way. In my pleasure, if we can be together, I would like to share the fun with you. Whatever joy or success comes to you will make me glad. Without pretense, and in plain words, good-will to you is what I mean, in the Spirit of Christmas."

It is not necessary to put a message like this into high-flown language, to swear absolute devotion and deathless consecration. In love and friendship, small, steady payments on a gold basis are better than immense promissory notes. Nor, indeed, is it always necessary to put the message into words at all, nor even to convey it by a tangible token. To feel it and to act it out—that is the main thing.

There are a great many people in the world whom we know more or less, but to whom for various reasons we cannot very well send a Christmas gift. But there is hardly one, in all the circles of our acquaintance, with whom we may not exchange the touch of Christmas life.

In the outer circles, cheerful greetings, courtesy, consideration; in the inner circles, sympathetic interest, hearty congratulations, honest encouragement; in the inmost circle, comradeship, helpfulness, tenderness,—

> *"Beautiful friendship tried by sun and wind*
> *Durable from the daily dust of life."*

After all, Christmas-living is the best kind of Christmas-giving.

A SHORT CHRISTMAS SERMON

KEEPING CHRISTMAS

ROMANS, xiv, 6: *He that regardeth the day, regardeth it unto the Lord.*

It is a good thing to observe Christmas day. The mere marking of times and seasons, when men agree to stop work and make merry together, is a wise and wholesome custom. It helps one to feel the supremacy of the common life over the individual life. It reminds a man to set his own little watch, now and then, by the great clock of humanity which runs on sun time.

But there is a better thing than the observance of Christmas day, and that is, keeping Christmas.

Are you willing to forget what you have done for other people, and to remember what other people have done for you; to ignore what the world owes you, and to think what you owe the world; to put your rights in the background, and your duties in the middle distance, and your chances to do a little more than your duty in the foreground; to see that your fellow-men are just as real as you are, and try to look behind their faces to their hearts, hungry for joy; to own that probably the only good reason for your existence is not what you are going to get out of life, but what you are going to give to life; to close your book of complaints against the management of the universe, and look around you for a place where you can sow a few seeds of happiness—are you willing to do these things even for a day? Then you can keep Christmas.

Are you willing to stoop down and consider the needs and the desires of little children; to remember the weakness and loneliness of people who are growing old; to stop asking how much your friends love you, and ask yourself whether you love them enough; to bear in mind the things that other people have to bear on their hearts; to try to understand what those who live in the same house with you really want, without waiting for them to tell you; to trim your lamp so that it will give more light and less smoke, and to carry it in front so that your shadow will fall behind you; to make a grave for your ugly thoughts, and a garden for your kindly feelings, with the gate open—are you willing to do these things even for a day? Then you can keep Christmas.

Are you willing to believe that love is the strongest thing in the world—stronger than hate, stronger than evil, stronger than death—and that the blessed life which began in Bethlehem nineteen hundred years ago is the image and brightness of the Eternal Love? Then you can keep Christmas.

And if you keep it for a day, why not always?

But you can never keep it alone.

TWO CHRISTMAS PRAYERS

A CHRISTMAS PRAYER FOR THE HOME

Father of all men, look upon our family,
Kneeling together before Thee,
And grant us a true Christmas.

With loving heart we bless Thee:
    For the gift of Thy dear Son Jesus Christ,
    For the peace He brings to human homes,
    For the good-will He teaches to sinful men,
    For the glory of Thy goodness shining in His face.

With joyful voice we praise Thee:
    For His lowly birth and His rest in the manger,
    For the pure tenderness of His mother Mary,
    For the fatherly care that protected Him,
    For the Providence that saved the Holy Child
     To be the Saviour of the world.

With deep desire we beseech Thee:
    Help us to keep His birthday truly,
    Help us to offer, in His name, our Christmas prayer.

From the sickness of sin and the darkness of doubt,
From selfish pleasures and sullen pains,

From the frost of pride and the fever of envy,
        God save us every one, through the blessing of Jesus.

In the health of purity and the calm of mutual trust,
In the sharing of joy and the bearing of trouble,
In the steady glow of love and the clear light of hope,
        God keep us every one, by the blessing of Jesus.

In praying and praising, in giving and receiving,
In eating and drinking, in singing and making merry,
In parents' gladness and in children's mirth,
In dear memories of those who have departed,

In good comradeship with those who are here,
In kind wishes for those who are far away,
In patient waiting, sweet contentment, generous cheer,
        God bless us every one, with the blessing of Jesus.

By remembering our kinship with all men,
By well-wishing, friendly speaking and kindly doing,
By cheering the downcast and adding sunshine to daylight,
By welcoming strangers (poor shepherds or wise men),
By keeping the music of the angels' song in this home,
        God help us every one to share the blessing of Jesus:

In whose name we keep Christmas:
And in whose words we pray together:

380

Our Father which art in heaven, hallowed be Thy name.

Thy kingdom come. Thy will be done in earth, as it is in heaven.

Give us this day our daily bread. And forgive us our debts, as we forgive our debtors.

And lead us not into temptation, but deliver us from evil:

For Thine is the kingdom, and the power, and the glory, forever. Amen.

A CHRISTMAS PRAYER FOR LONELY FOLKS

Lord God of the solitary,
Look upon me in my loneliness.
Since I may not keep this Christmas in the home,
Send it into my heart.

Let not my sins cloud me in,
But shine through them with forgiveness in the face of the child Jesus.
Put me in loving remembrance of the lowly lodging in the stable of Bethlehem,
The sorrows of the blessed Mary, the poverty and exile of the Prince of Peace.

For His sake, give me a cheerful courage to endure my lot,
And an inward comfort to sweeten it.

Purge my heart from hard and bitter thoughts.
Let no shadow of forgetting come between me and friends far away:
Bless them in their Christmas mirth:
Hedge me in with faithfulness,
That I may not grow unworthy to meet them again.

Give me good work to do,
That I may forget myself and find peace in doing it for Thee.

Though I am poor, send me to carry some gift to those who are poorer,

Some cheer to those who are more lonely.
Grant me the joy to do a kindness to one of Thy little ones:
Light my Christmas candle at the gladness of an innocent and grateful
      heart.

Strange is the path where Thou leadest me:
Let me not doubt Thy wisdom, nor lose Thy hand.
Make me sure that Eternal Love is revealed in Jesus, Thy dear Son,
To save us from sin and solitude and death.
Teach me that I am not alone,
But that many hearts, all round the world,
Join with me through the silence, while I pray in His name:

Our Father which art in heaven, hallowed be Thy name.
Thy kingdom come. Thy will be done in earth, as it is in heaven.
Give us this day our daily bread. And forgive us our debts, as we forgive our
      debtors.
And lead us not into temptation, but deliver us from evil:
For Thine is the kingdom, and the power, and the glory, forever. Amen.